HELLBOY
JUNIOR™

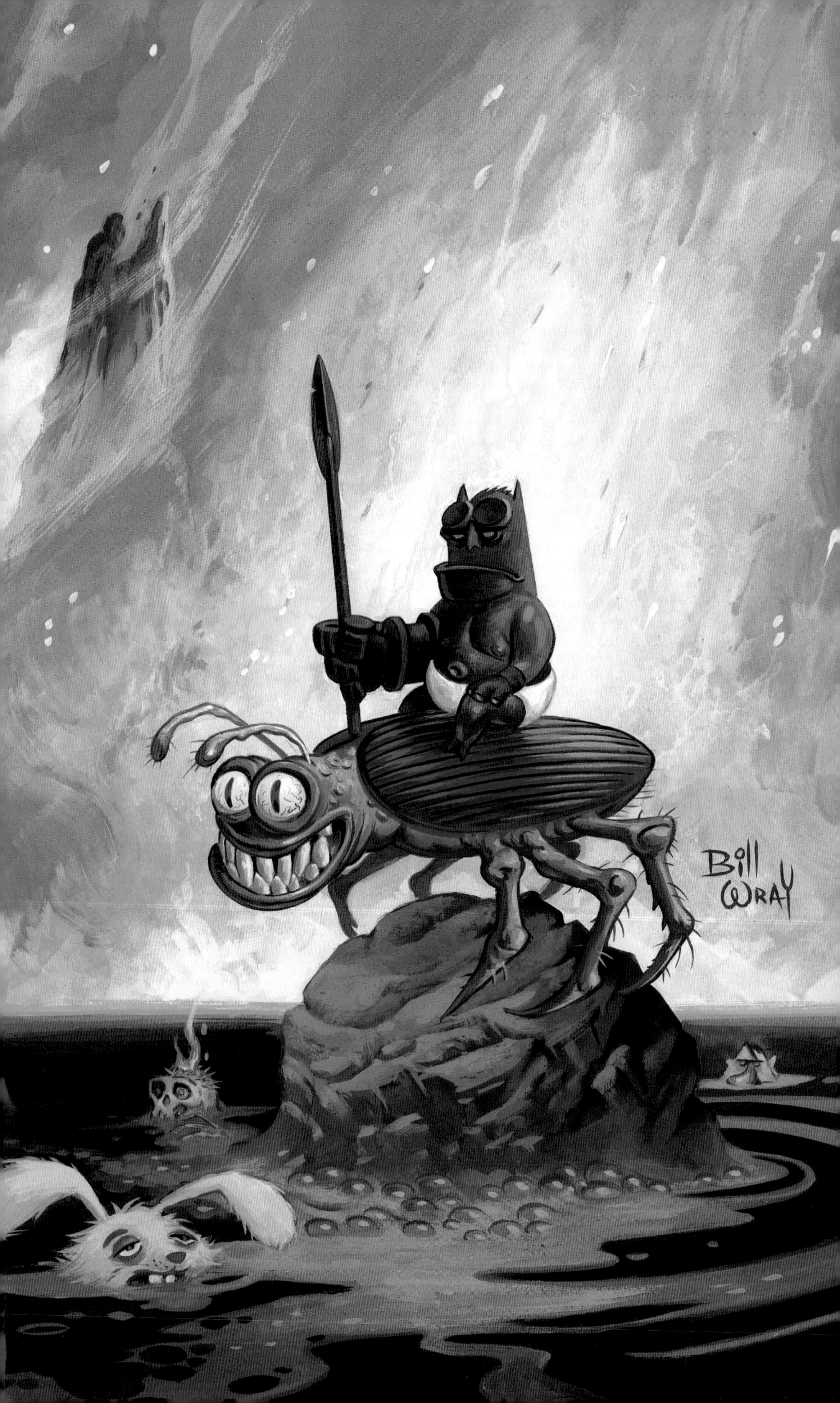
Bill Wray

HELLBOY JUNIOR™

featuring

Mike Mignola, Bill Wray, Stephen DeStefano,

Dave Cooper, Hilary Barta, Pat McEown,

Glenn Barr, Kevin Nowlan, Dave Stewart,

and **John Costanza**

editor
Scott Allie
with **Matt Dryer**

designer
Amy Arendts

publisher
Mike Richardson

DARK HORSE BOOKS™

I'd like to dedicate this book to the guy who made
it possible, my hero, Mike Mignola.

Thanks must go to the artists, Stephen DeStefano, Dave Cooper,
Hilary Barta, Pat McEwon; and to my editor, Scott Allie,
who, despite having a different definition of humor
than myself, put up with my filth.

Love you all,
Bill Wray

Special thanks also to Trevor Zajac.

Dark Horse Books
A division of Dark Horse Comics, Inc.
10956 SE Main Street
Milwaukie OR 97222

First edition
January 2004
ISBN: 1-56971-988-8

3 5 7 9 10 8 6 4 2
Printed in China

Hellboy Junior's Retarded Adventure

By Steve Niles

If you picked up this collection you probably already know about Mike Mignola and his brilliant creation Hellboy, the supernatural crime fighter, hero, adventurer. Hellboy is Mignola's jewel, his crowning achievement, often praised by critics and awarded every honor known in comics. Mignola and his creation bring the art of comics to a new level.

But we're not here to talk about Mike and Hellboy. We're here to talk about Bill Wray and his bastard offspring *Hellboy Junior*.

Part parody, part Harvey Comics tribute, *Hellboy Junior* is everything that *Hellboy* isn't. It's rude, crude, disgusting, *and funny as Hell*. Writer/artist Bill Wray is exactly the same. (Except for that part about Harvey. There's nothing Harvey Comics about Bill despite his love of wearing a giant diaper while he draws, but that is both a lifestyle choice and a necessity for Bill, so lay off!) Joining Bill and Mike are Stephen DeStefano, Dave Cooper, Pat McEown, and Hilary Barta—some of the funniest cartoonists working today, and these oddball collaborations with Bill stand out as some of their best and weirdest work.

What *Hellboy Junior* represents is the unlikely marriage of two creative minds: Mignola's dry wit and imagination, and Wray's fervent, raunchy talent for absurdity. It's an improbable pairing, but one that results in some of the funniest and most original comics ever to haunt the shelves.

So, while some might call *Hellboy Junior* offensive, I say it's of-*fun*-sive. Sit back, read this collection, and laugh until milk shoots out your nose.

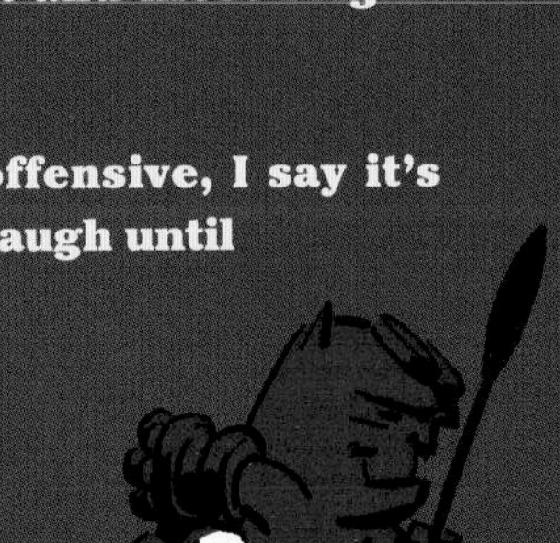

xoxo

Steve Niles
Los Angeles
2003

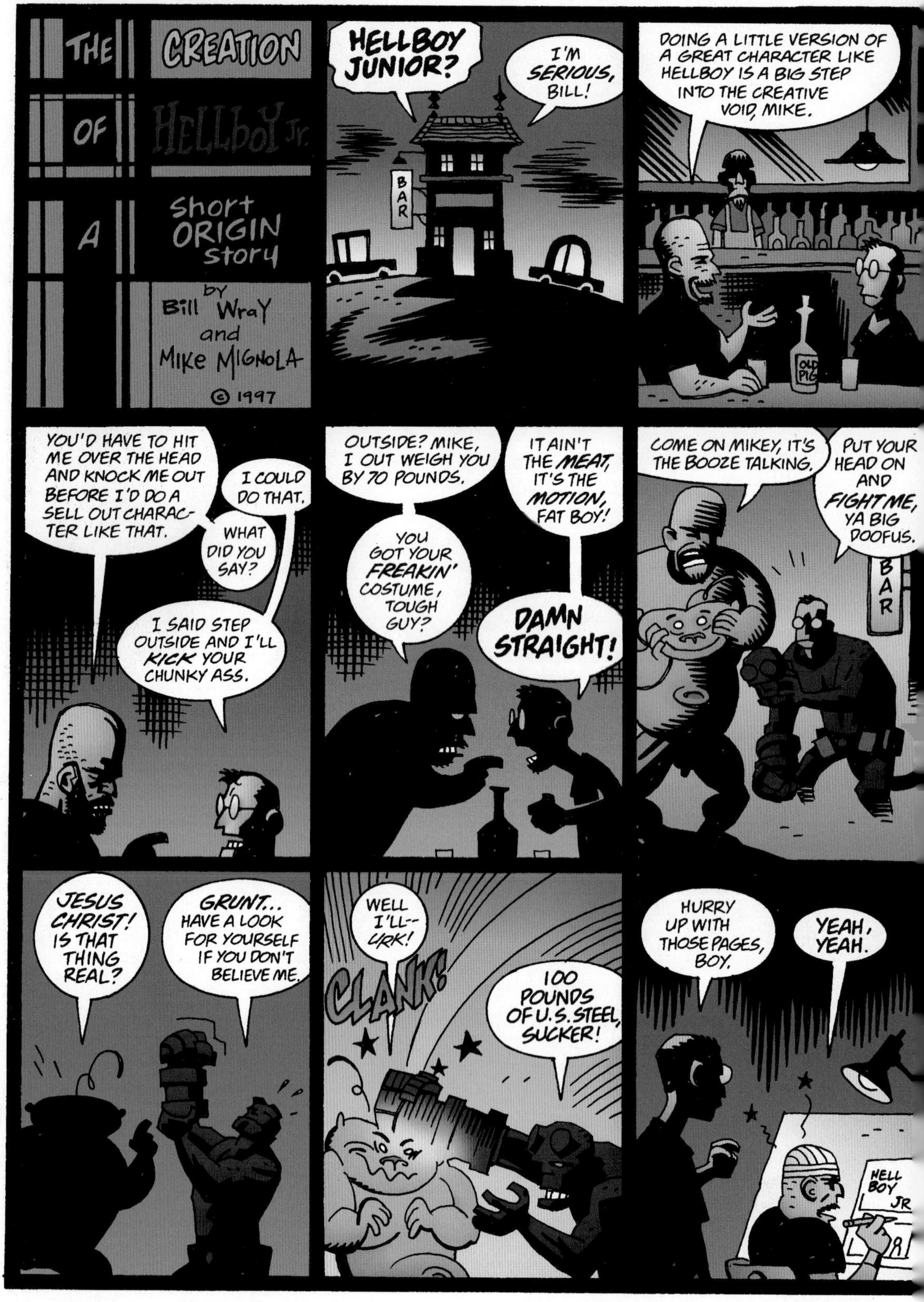

THE CREATION OF HELLBOY JR.
A Short ORIGIN story
by Bill Wray and Mike Mignola
© 1997
HELLBOY JUNIOR?
I'M SERIOUS, BILL!
BAR
DOING A LITTLE VERSION OF A GREAT CHARACTER LIKE HELLBOY IS A BIG STEP INTO THE CREATIVE VOID, MIKE.
OLD PIG
YOU'D HAVE TO HIT ME OVER THE HEAD AND KNOCK ME OUT BEFORE I'D DO A SELL OUT CHARACTER LIKE THAT.
I COULD DO THAT.
WHAT DID YOU SAY?
I SAID STEP OUTSIDE AND I'LL KICK YOUR CHUNKY ASS.
OUTSIDE? MIKE, I OUT WEIGH YOU BY 70 POUNDS.
IT AIN'T THE MEAT, IT'S THE MOTION, FAT BOY!
YOU GOT YOUR FREAKIN' COSTUME, TOUGH GUY?
DAMN STRAIGHT!
COME ON MIKEY, IT'S THE BOOZE TALKING.
PUT YOUR HEAD ON AND FIGHT ME, YA BIG DOOFUS.
BAR
JESUS CHRIST! IS THAT THING REAL?
GRUNT... HAVE A LOOK FOR YOURSELF IF YOU DON'T BELIEVE ME.
WELL I'LL-- URK!
CLANK!
100 POUNDS OF U.S. STEEL, SUCKER!
HURRY UP WITH THOSE PAGES, BOY.
YEAH, YEAH.
HELL BOY JR

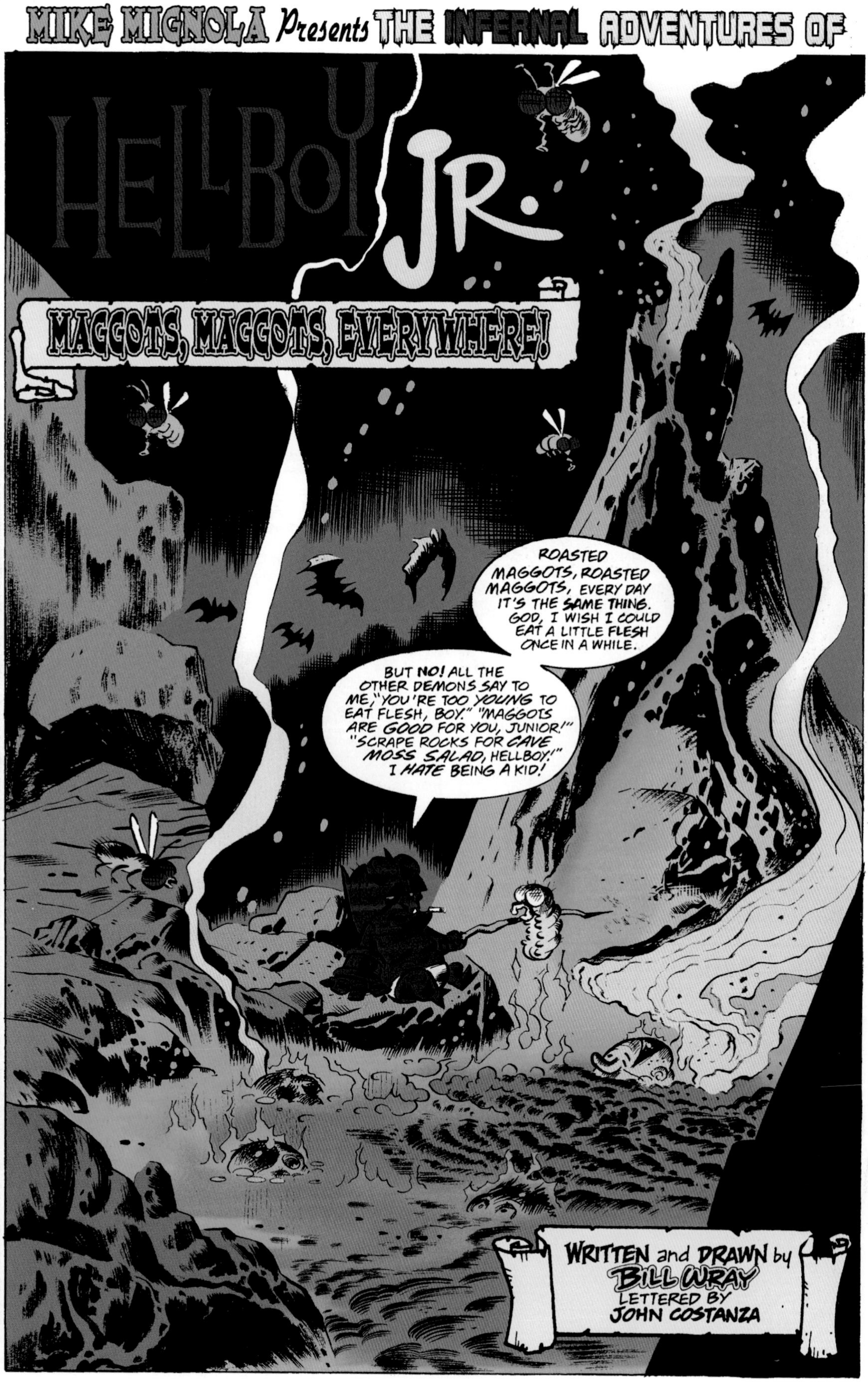
MIKE MIGNOLA Presents THE INFERNAL ADVENTURES OF
HELLBOY JR.
MAGGOTS, MAGGOTS, EVERYWHERE!
ROASTED MAGGOTS, ROASTED MAGGOTS, EVERY DAY IT'S THE SAME THING. GOD, I WISH I COULD EAT A LITTLE FLESH ONCE IN A WHILE.
BUT NO! ALL THE OTHER DEMONS SAY TO ME, "YOU'RE TOO YOUNG TO EAT FLESH, BOY." "MAGGOTS ARE GOOD FOR YOU, JUNIOR!" "SCRAPE ROCKS FOR CAVE MOSS SALAD, HELLBOY!" I HATE BEING A KID!
WRITTEN and DRAWN by BILL WRAY LETTERED BY JOHN COSTANZA

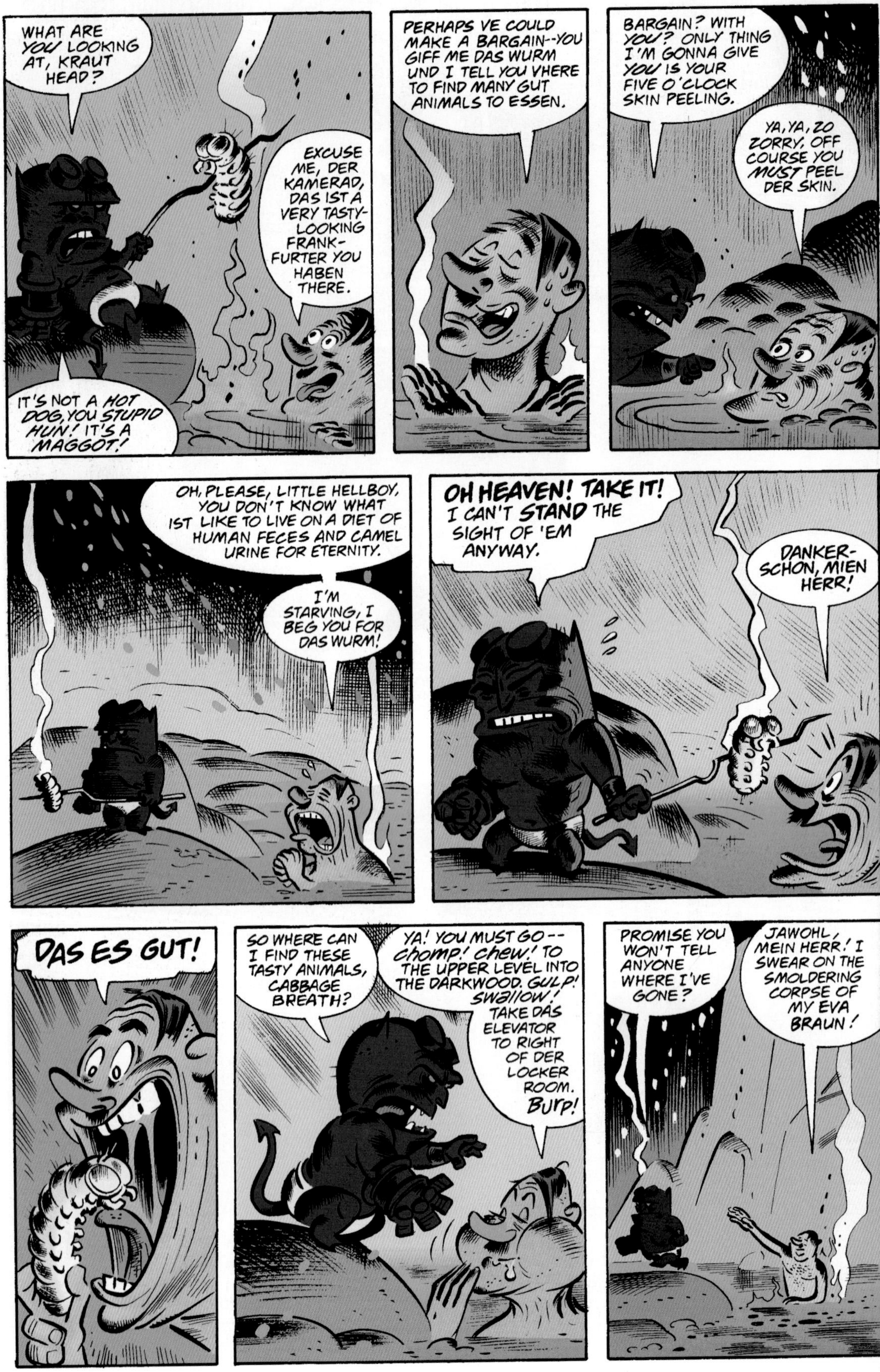
WHAT ARE YOU LOOKING AT, KRAUT HEAD?
EXCUSE ME, DER KAMERAD, DAS IST A VERY TASTY-LOOKING FRANK-FURTER YOU HABEN THERE.
IT'S NOT A HOT DOG, YOU STUPID HUN! IT'S A MAGGOT!
PERHAPS VE COULD MAKE A BARGAIN--YOU GIFF ME DAS WURM UND I TELL YOU VHERE TO FIND MANY GUT ANIMALS TO ESSEN.
BARGAIN? WITH YOU? ONLY THING I'M GONNA GIVE YOU IS YOUR FIVE O'CLOCK SKIN PEELING.
YA, YA, ZO ZORRY, OFF COURSE YOU MUST PEEL DER SKIN.
OH, PLEASE, LITTLE HELLBOY, YOU DON'T KNOW WHAT IST LIKE TO LIVE ON A DIET OF HUMAN FECES AND CAMEL URINE FOR ETERNITY.
I'M STARVING, I BEG YOU FOR DAS WURM!
OH HEAVEN! TAKE IT! I CAN'T STAND THE SIGHT OF 'EM ANYWAY.
DANKER-SCHON, MIEN HERR!
DAS ES GUT!
SO WHERE CAN I FIND THESE TASTY ANIMALS, CABBAGE BREATH?
YA! YOU MUST GO-- chomp! chew! TO THE UPPER LEVEL INTO THE DARKWOOD. GULP! swallow! TAKE DAS ELEVATOR TO RIGHT OF DER LOCKER ROOM. Burp!
PROMISE YOU WON'T TELL ANYONE WHERE I'VE GONE?
JAWOHL, MEIN HERR! I SWEAR ON THE SMOLDERING CORPSE OF MY EVA BRAUN!

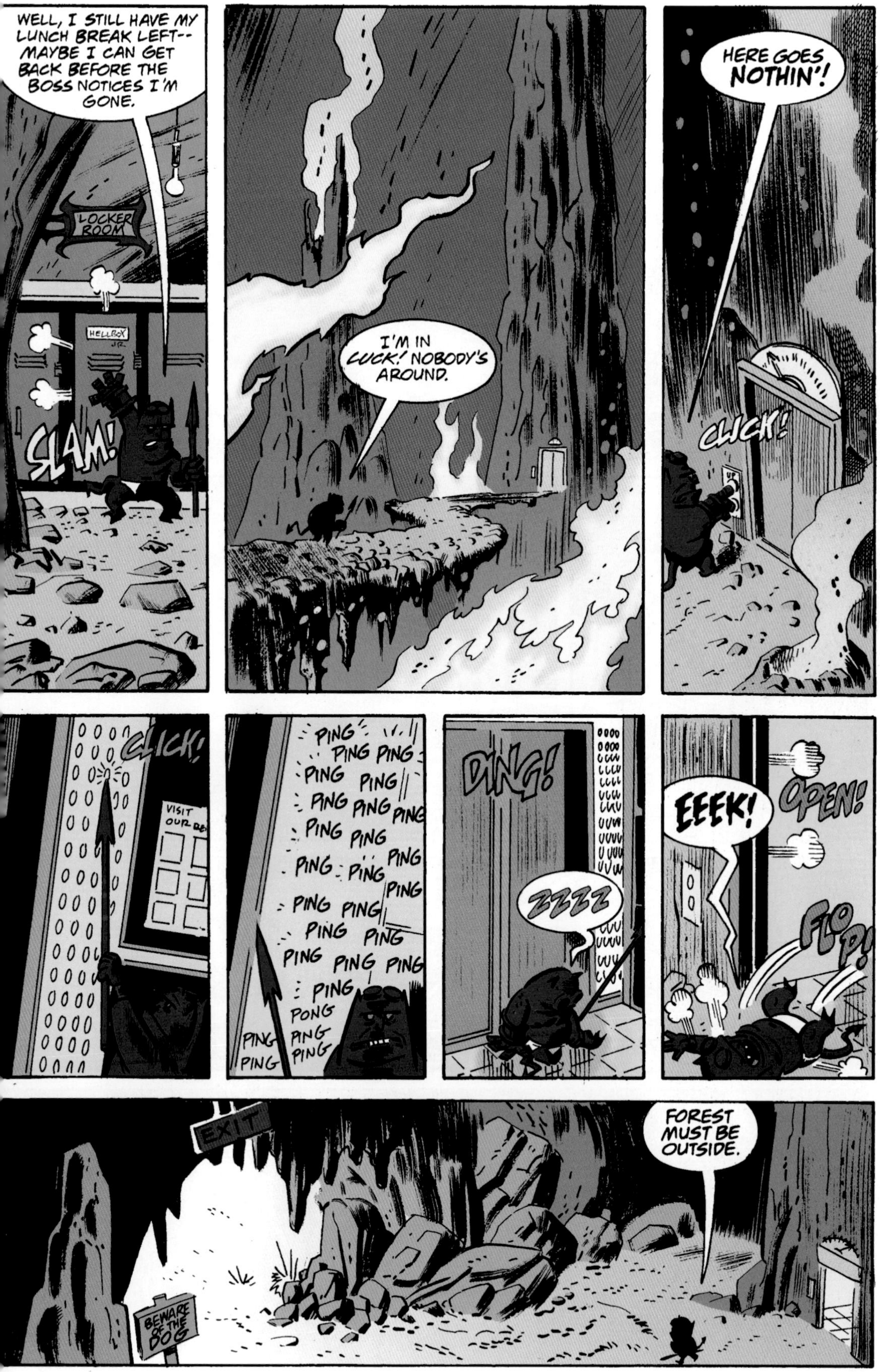
WELL, I STILL HAVE MY LUNCH BREAK LEFT-- MAYBE I CAN GET BACK BEFORE THE BOSS NOTICES I'M GONE.
LOCKER ROOM
HELLBOY JR.
SLAM!
I'M IN LUCK! NOBODY'S AROUND.
HERE GOES NOTHIN'!
CLICK!
UP
CLICK!
VISIT OUR
PING PING PING PING PING PING PING PING PING PING PING PING PING PING PING PING PING PING PING PING PING PING PING PONG PING PING PING PING
DING!
ZZZZ
EEEK!
OPEN!
FLOP!
EXIT
BEWARE OF THE DOG
FOREST MUST BE OUTSIDE.

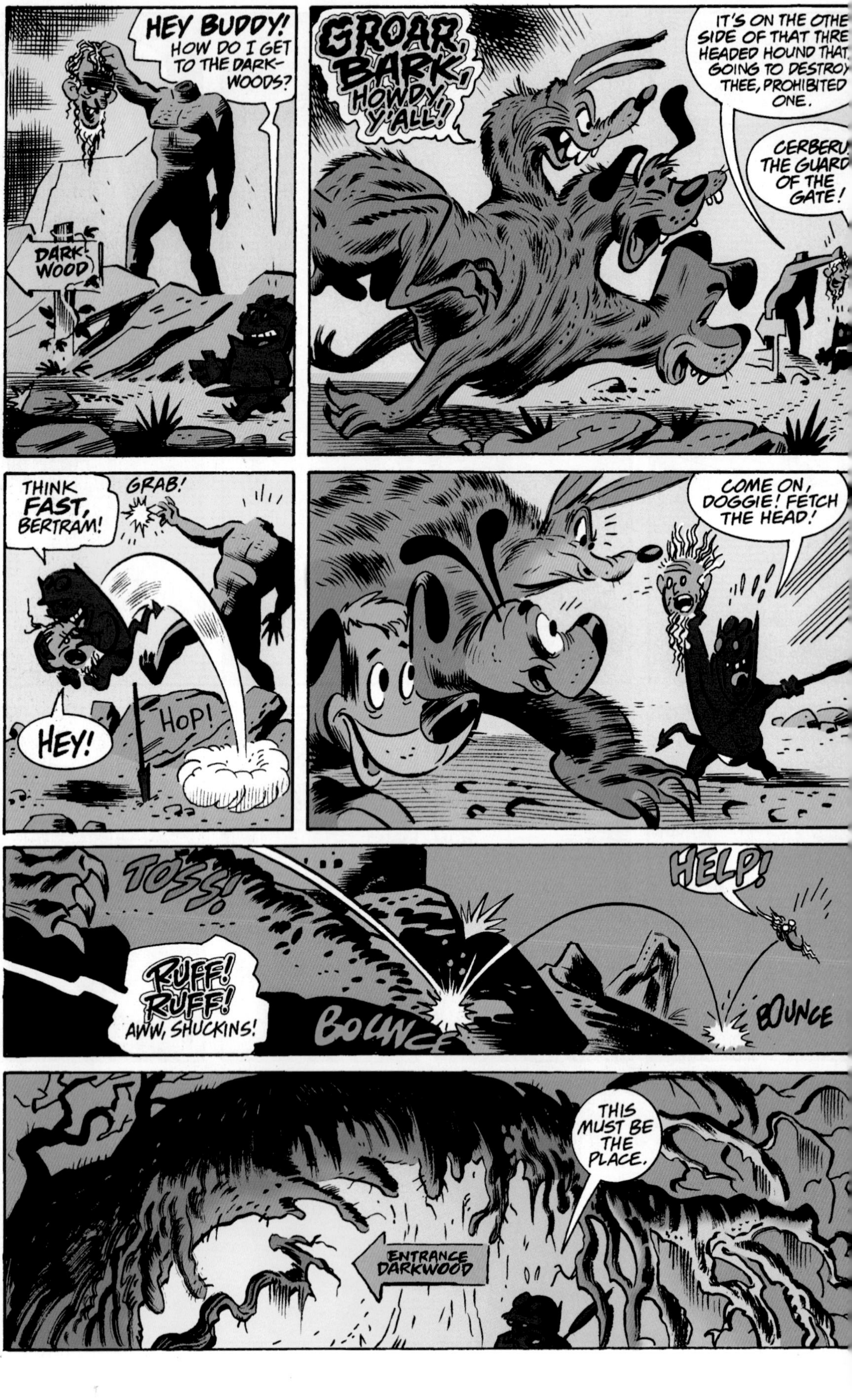
HEY BUDDY! HOW DO I GET TO THE DARK-WOODS?
DARK WOOD
GROAR, BARK, HOWDY, Y'ALL!
IT'S ON THE OTHE SIDE OF THAT THRE HEADED HOUND THAT GOING TO DESTROY THEE, PROHIBITED ONE.
CERBERU THE GUARD OF THE GATE!
THINK FAST, BERTRAM!
GRAB!
HEY!
HOP!
COME ON, DOGGIE! FETCH THE HEAD!
TOSS!
HELP!
RUFF! RUFF! AWW, SHUCKINS!
BOUNCE
BOUNCE
THIS MUST BE THE PLACE.
ENTRANCE DARKWOOD

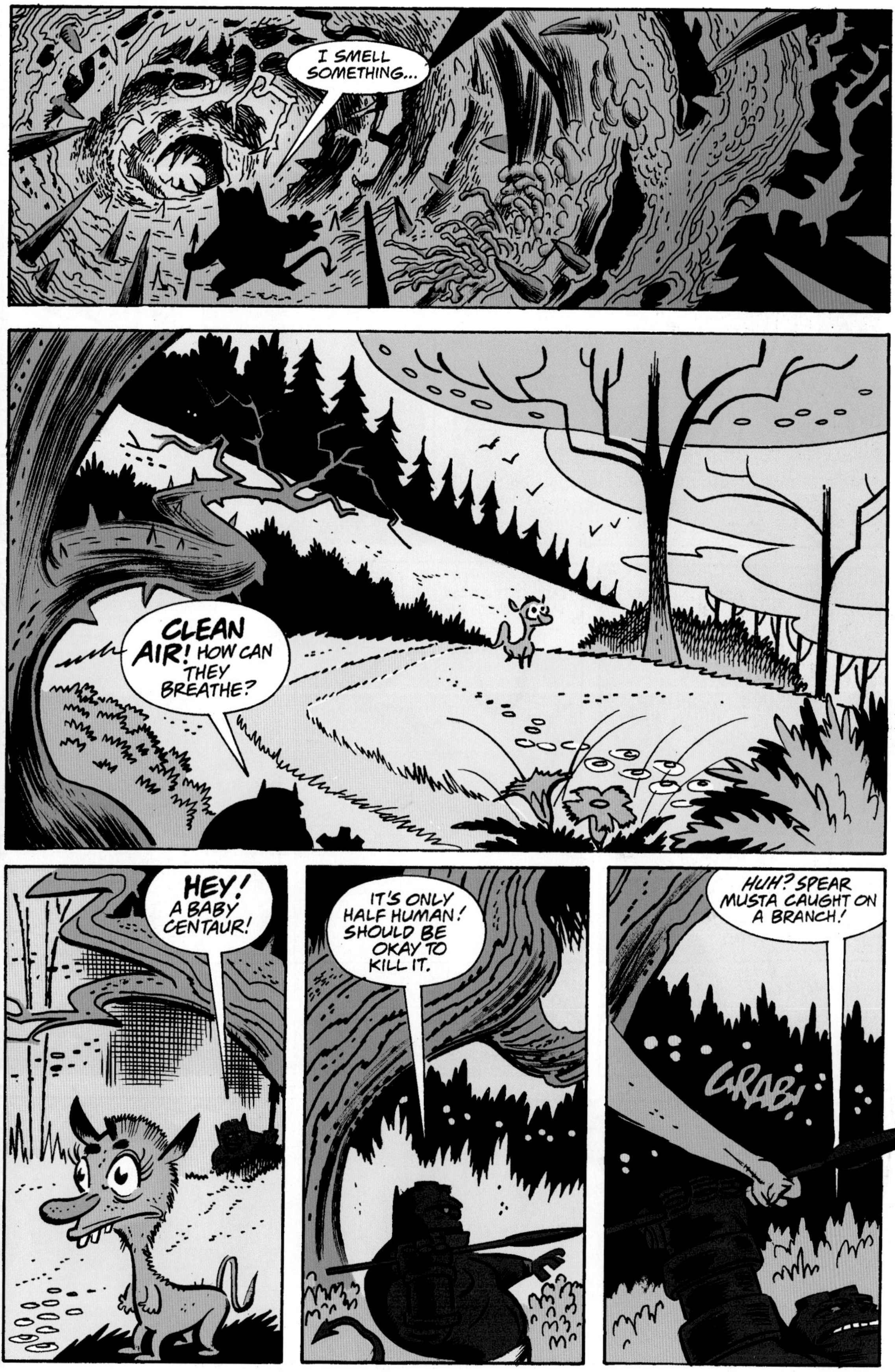
I SMELL SOMETHING...
CLEAN AIR! HOW CAN THEY BREATHE?
HEY! A BABY CENTAUR!
IT'S ONLY HALF HUMAN! SHOULD BE OKAY TO KILL IT.
HUH? SPEAR MUSTA CAUGHT ON A BRANCH!
GRAB!

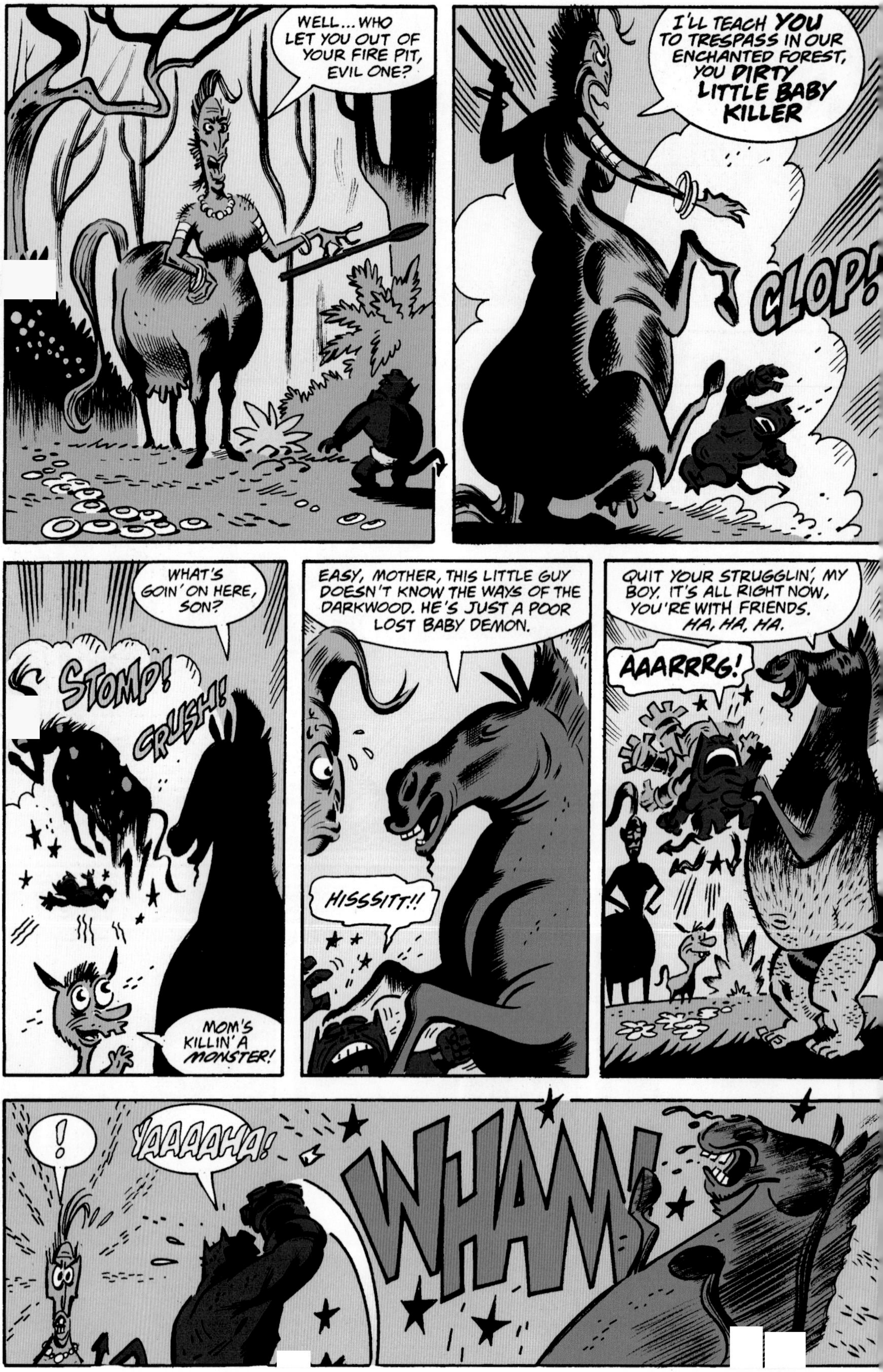

WELL... WHO LET YOU OUT OF YOUR FIRE PIT, EVIL ONE?
I'LL TEACH YOU TO TRESPASS IN OUR ENCHANTED FOREST, YOU DIRTY LITTLE BABY KILLER
CLOP!
WHAT'S GOIN' ON HERE, SON?
STOMP!
CRUSH!
MOM'S KILLIN' A MONSTER!
EASY, MOTHER, THIS LITTLE GUY DOESN'T KNOW THE WAYS OF THE DARKWOOD. HE'S JUST A POOR LOST BABY DEMON.
HISSSITT!!
QUIT YOUR STRUGGLIN', MY BOY, IT'S ALL RIGHT NOW, YOU'RE WITH FRIENDS. HA, HA, HA.
AAARRRG!
!
YAAAAHA!
WHAM!

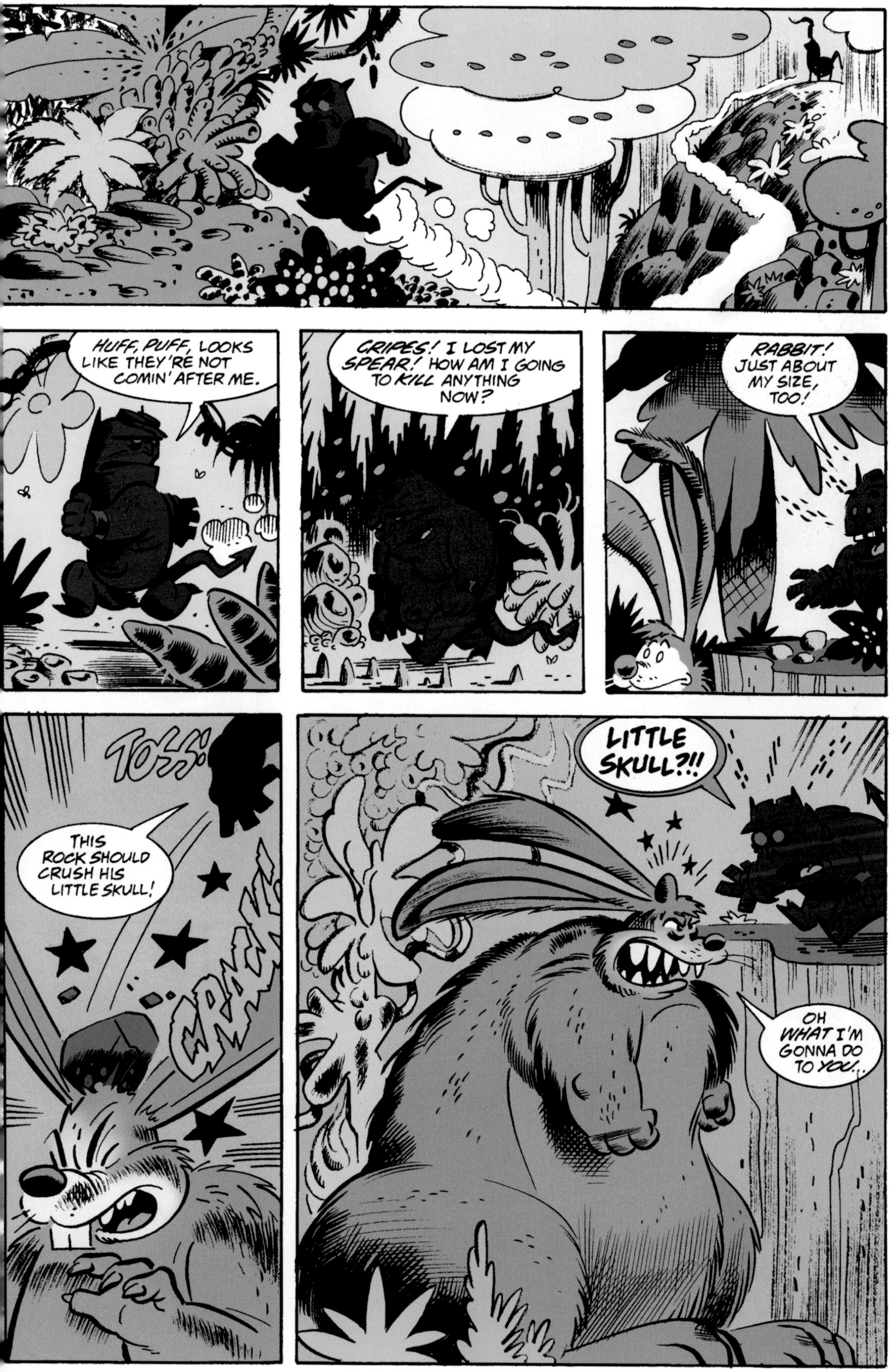
HUFF, PUFF, LOOKS LIKE THEY'RE NOT COMIN' AFTER ME.
CRIPES! I LOST MY SPEAR! HOW AM I GOING TO KILL ANYTHING NOW?
RABBIT! JUST ABOUT MY SIZE, TOO!
TOSS!
THIS ROCK SHOULD CRUSH HIS LITTLE SKULL!
CRACK!
LITTLE SKULL?!!
OH WHAT I'M GONNA DO TO YOU...

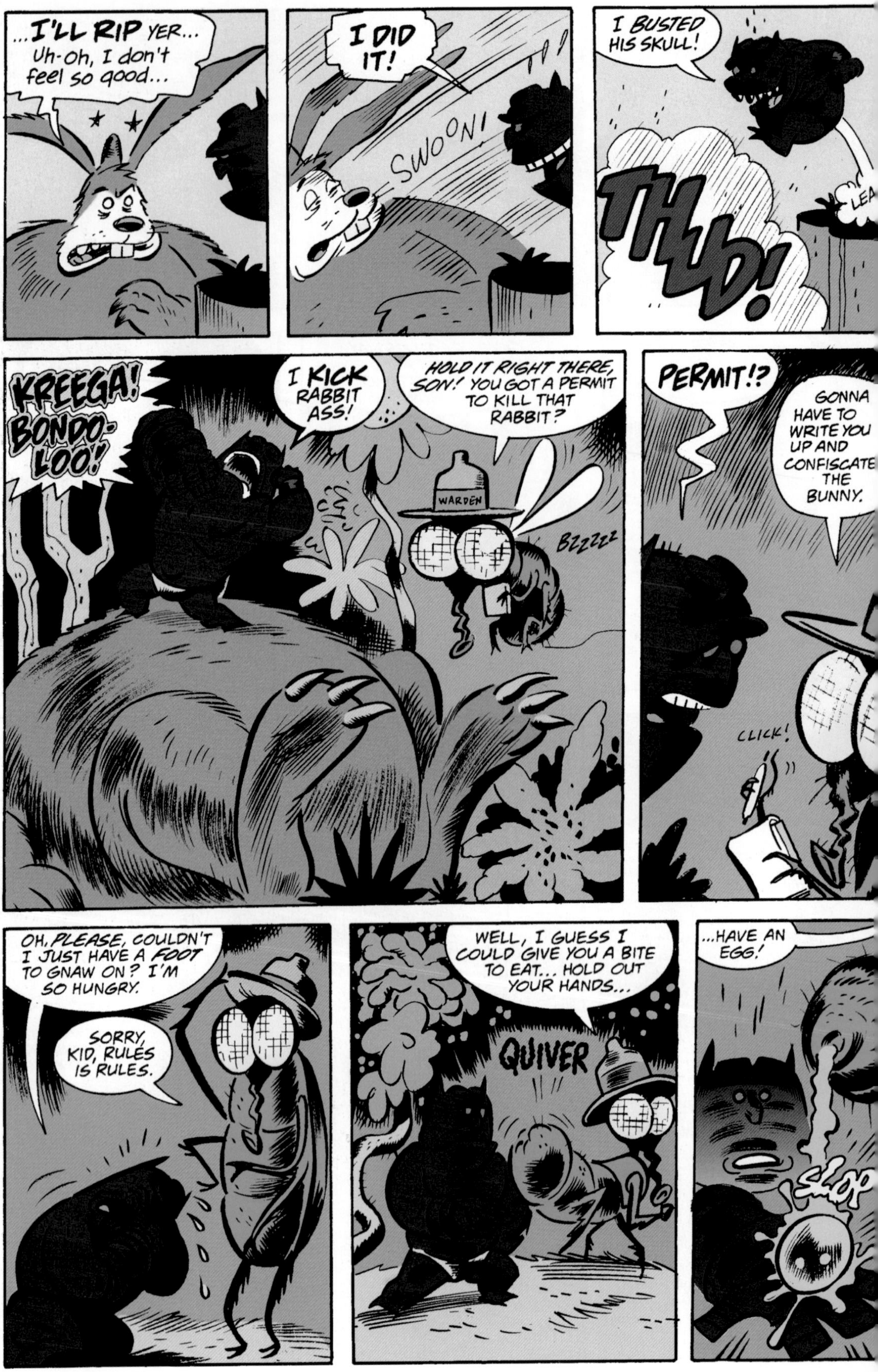
...I'LL RIP YER... Uh-oh, I don't feel so good...
I DID IT!
SWOOON!
I BUSTED HIS SKULL!
THUD!
KREEGA! BONDO-LOO!
I KICK RABBIT ASS!
HOLD IT RIGHT THERE, SON! YOU GOT A PERMIT TO KILL THAT RABBIT?
WARDEN
BZZZZZ
PERMIT!?
GONNA HAVE TO WRITE YOU UP AND CONFISCATE THE BUNNY.
CLICK!
OH, PLEASE, COULDN'T I JUST HAVE A FOOT TO GNAW ON? I'M SO HUNGRY.
SORRY, KID, RULES IS RULES.
WELL, I GUESS I COULD GIVE YOU A BITE TO EAT... HOLD OUT YOUR HANDS...
QUIVER
...HAVE AN EGG!
SLOP

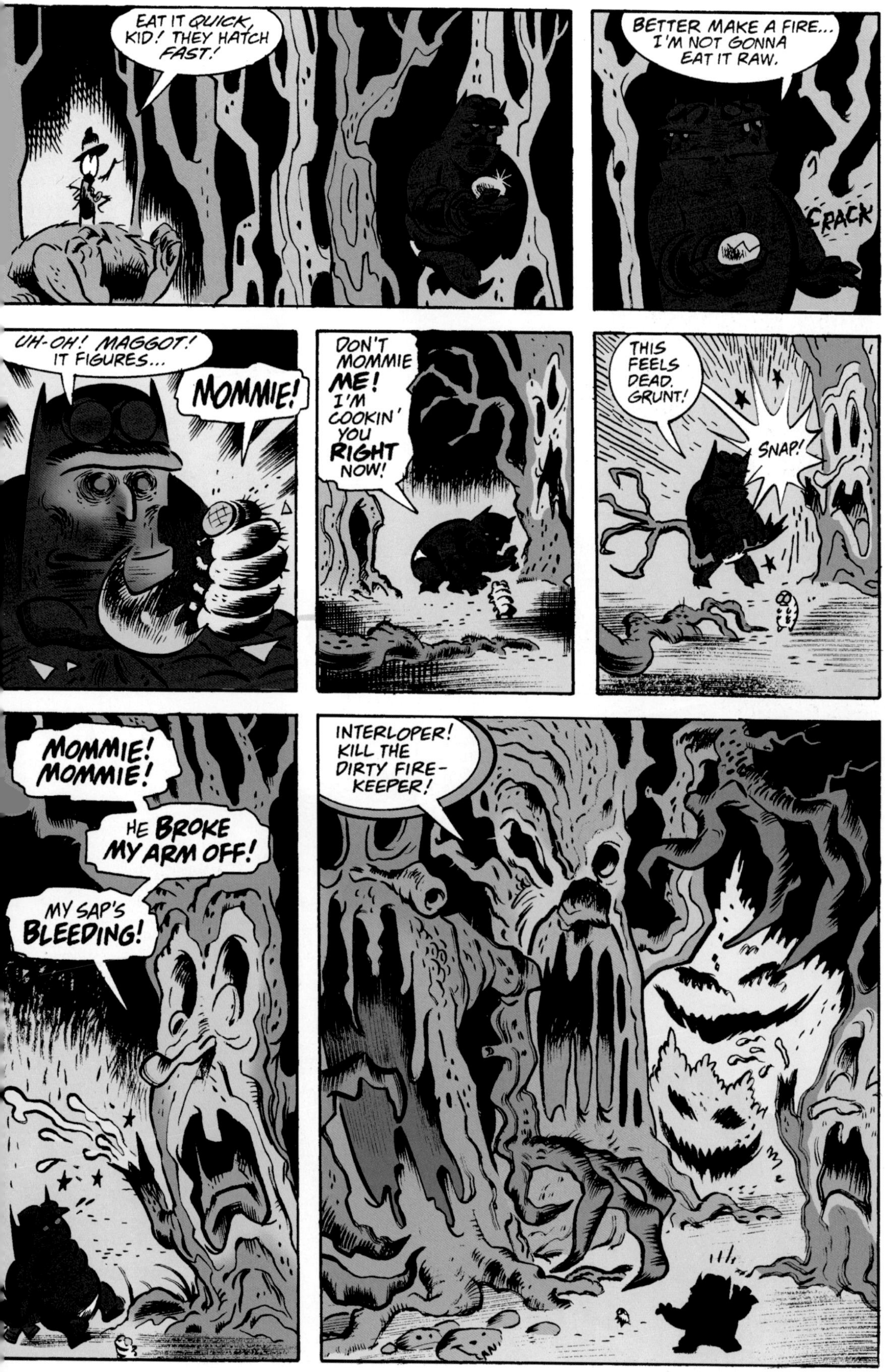
EAT IT QUICK, KID! THEY HATCH FAST!
BETTER MAKE A FIRE... I'M NOT GONNA EAT IT RAW.
CRACK
UH-OH! MAGGOT! IT FIGURES...
MOMMIE!
DON'T MOMMIE ME! I'M COOKIN' YOU RIGHT NOW!
THIS FEELS DEAD, GRUNT!
SNAP!
MOMMIE! MOMMIE!
HE BROKE MY ARM OFF!
MY SAP'S BLEEDING!
INTERLOPER! KILL THE DIRTY FIRE-KEEPER!

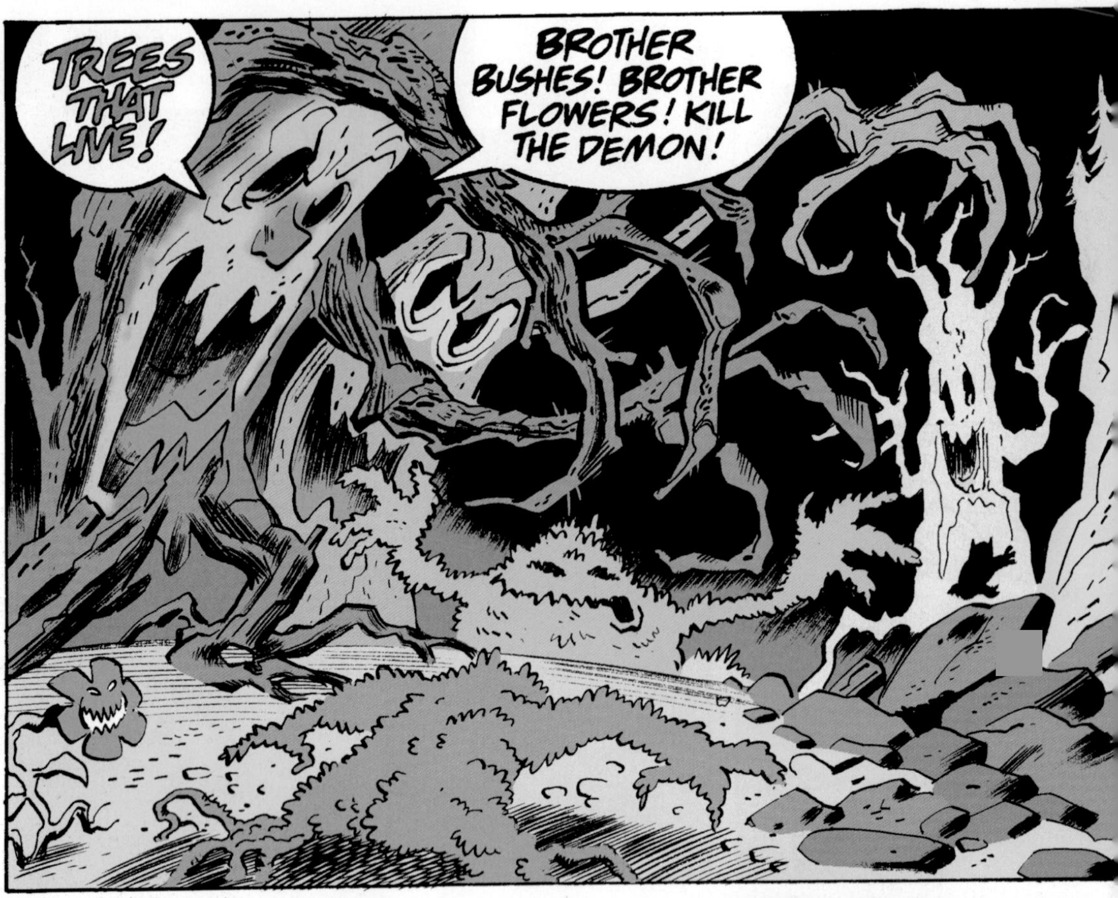
TREES THAT LIVE!
BROTHER BUSHES! BROTHER FLOWERS! KILL THE DEMON!

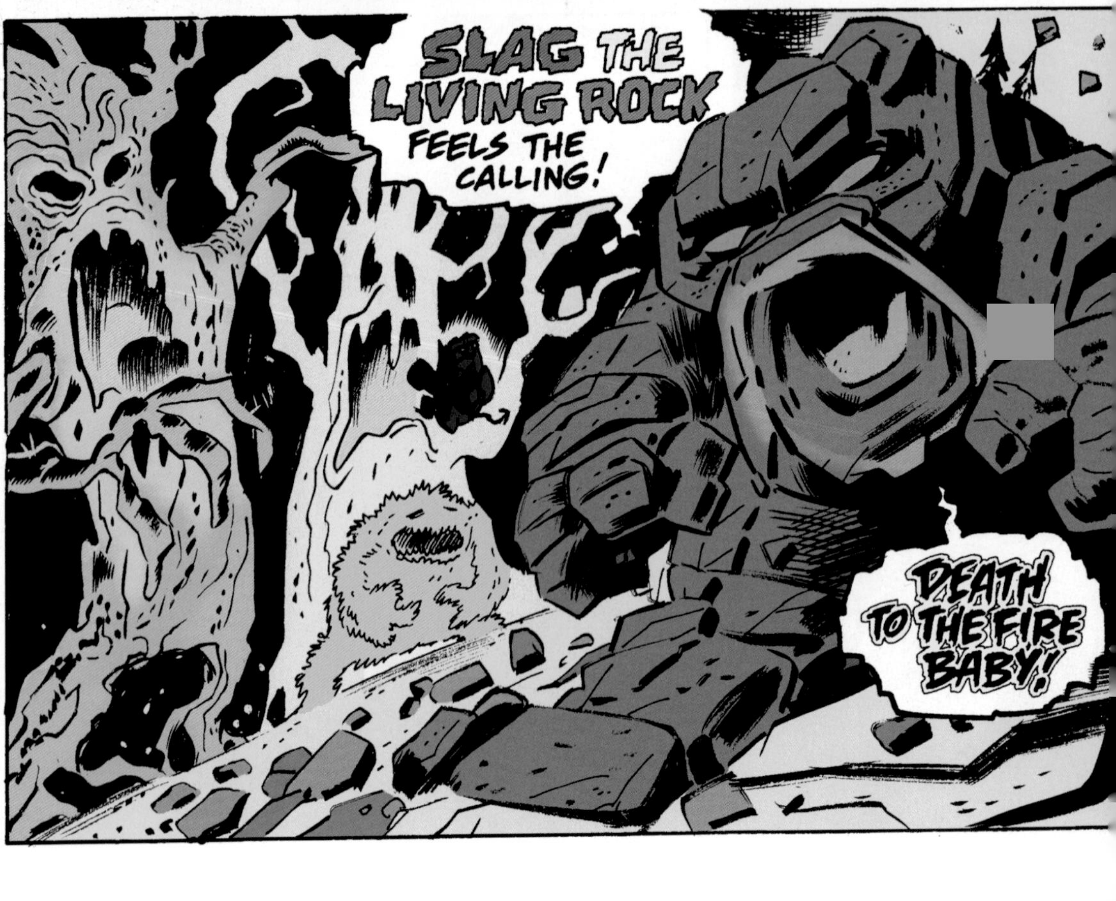
SLAG THE LIVING ROCK FEELS THE CALLING!
DEATH TO THE FIRE BABY!

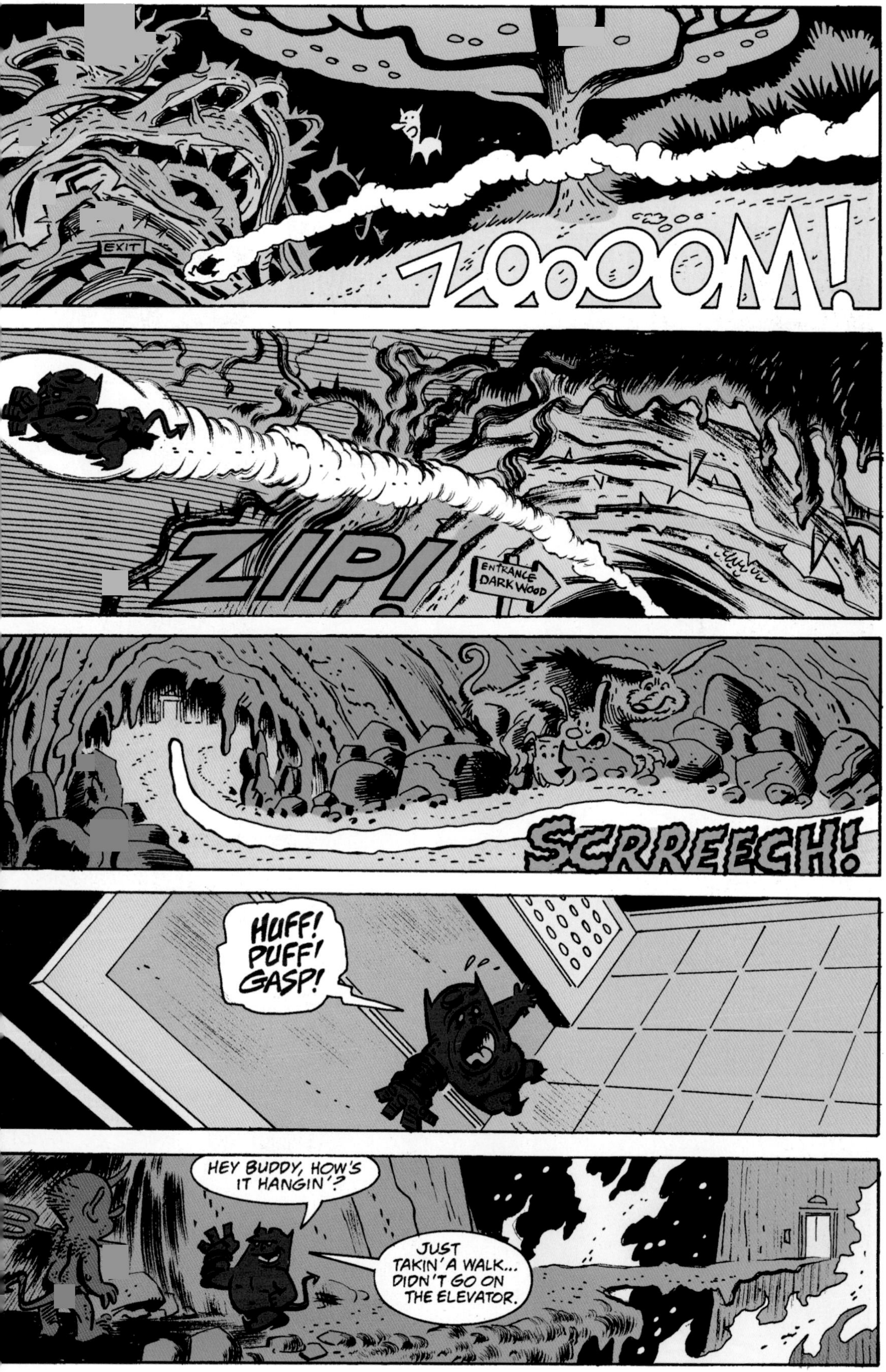
EXIT
ZOOOOM!
ZIP!
ENTRANCE DARKWOOD
SCRREECH!
HUFF! PUFF! GASP!
HEY BUDDY, HOW'S IT HANGIN'?
JUST TAKIN' A WALK... DIDN'T GO ON THE ELEVATOR.

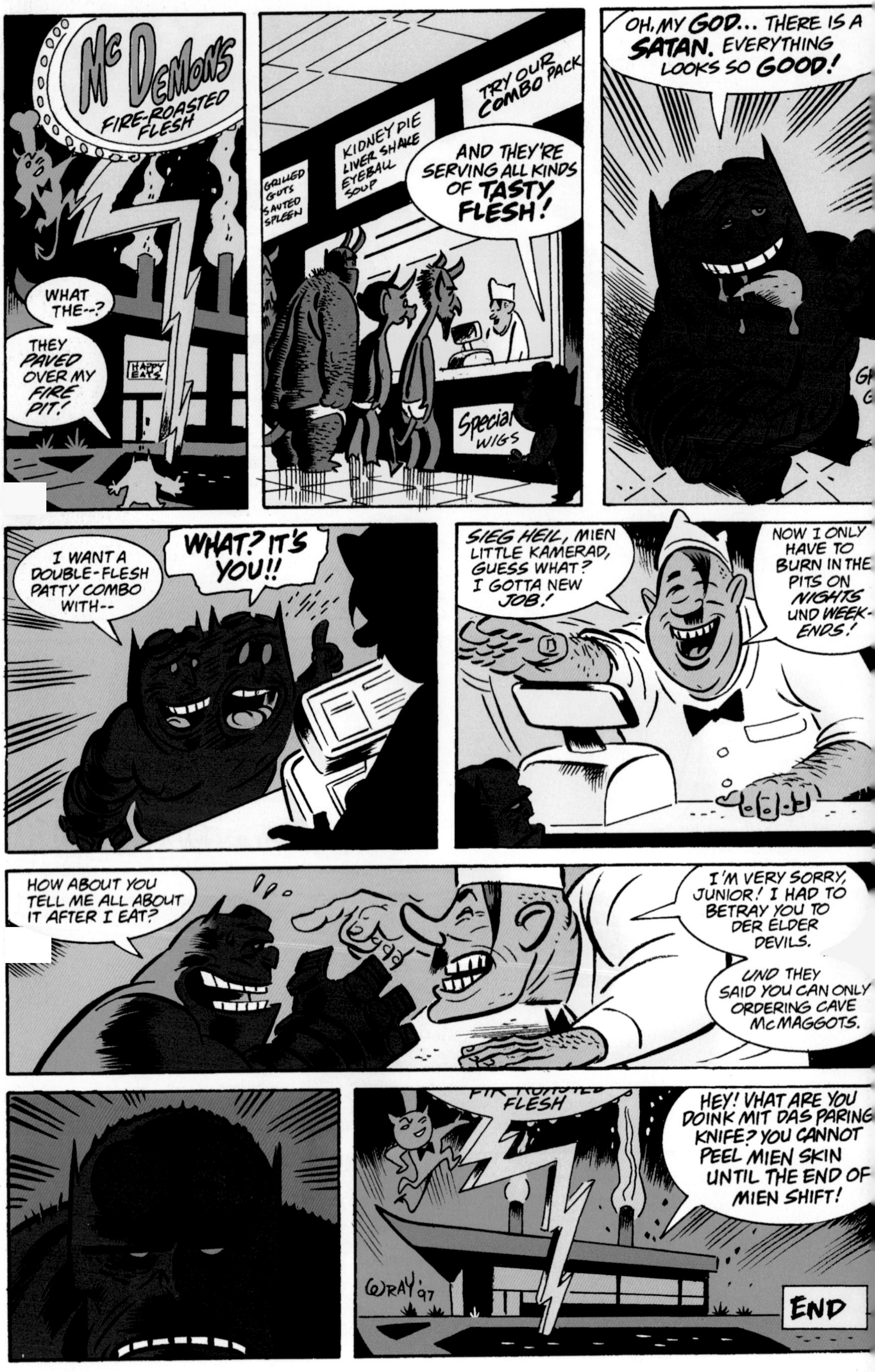

McDEMONS
FIRE-ROASTED FLESH
WHAT THE--?
THEY PAVED OVER MY FIRE PIT!
HAPPY EATS
TRY OUR COMBO PACK
KIDNEY PIE
LIVER SHAKE
EYEBALL SOUP
GRILLED GUTS
SAUTED SPLEEN
AND THEY'RE SERVING ALL KINDS OF TASTY FLESH!
Special WIGS
OH, MY GOD... THERE IS A SATAN. EVERYTHING LOOKS SO GOOD!
I WANT A DOUBLE-FLESH PATTY COMBO WITH--
WHAT? IT'S YOU!!
SIEG HEIL, MIEN LITTLE KAMERAD, GUESS WHAT? I GOTTA NEW JOB!
NOW I ONLY HAVE TO BURN IN THE PITS ON NIGHTS UND WEEK-ENDS!
HOW ABOUT YOU TELL ME ALL ABOUT IT AFTER I EAT?
I'M VERY SORRY, JUNIOR! I HAD TO BETRAY YOU TO DER ELDER DEVILS.
UND THEY SAID YOU CAN ONLY ORDERING CAVE McMAGGOTS.
FLESH
HEY! VHAT ARE YOU DOINK MIT DAS PARING KNIFE? YOU CANNOT PEEL MIEN SKIN UNTIL THE END OF MIEN SHIFT!
©RAY '97
END

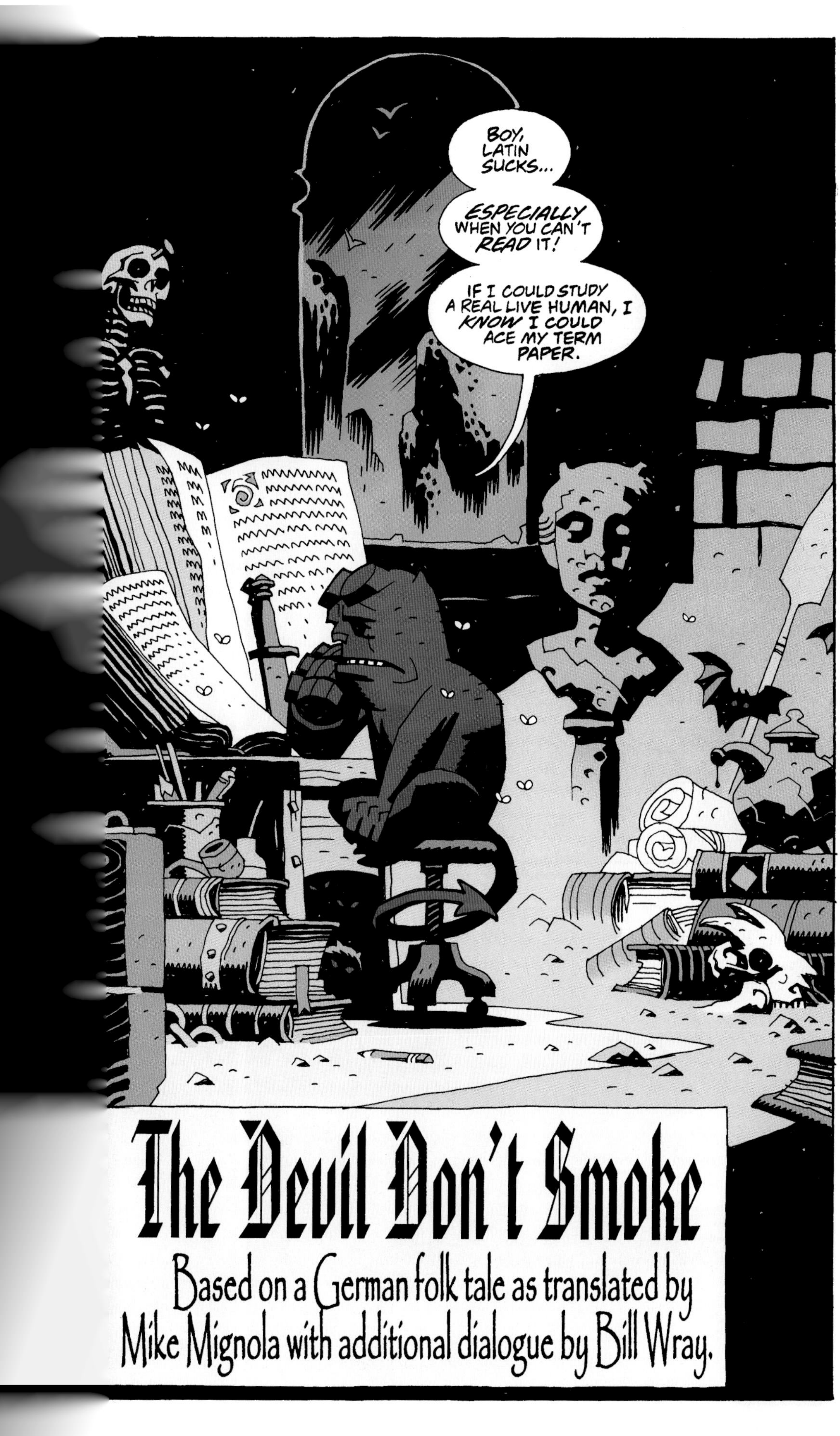
BOY, LATIN SUCKS...
ESPECIALLY WHEN YOU CAN'T READ IT!
IF I COULD STUDY A REAL LIVE HUMAN, I KNOW I COULD ACE MY TERM PAPER.

The Devil Don't Smoke

Based on a German folk tale as translated by Mike Mignola with additional dialogue by Bill Wray.

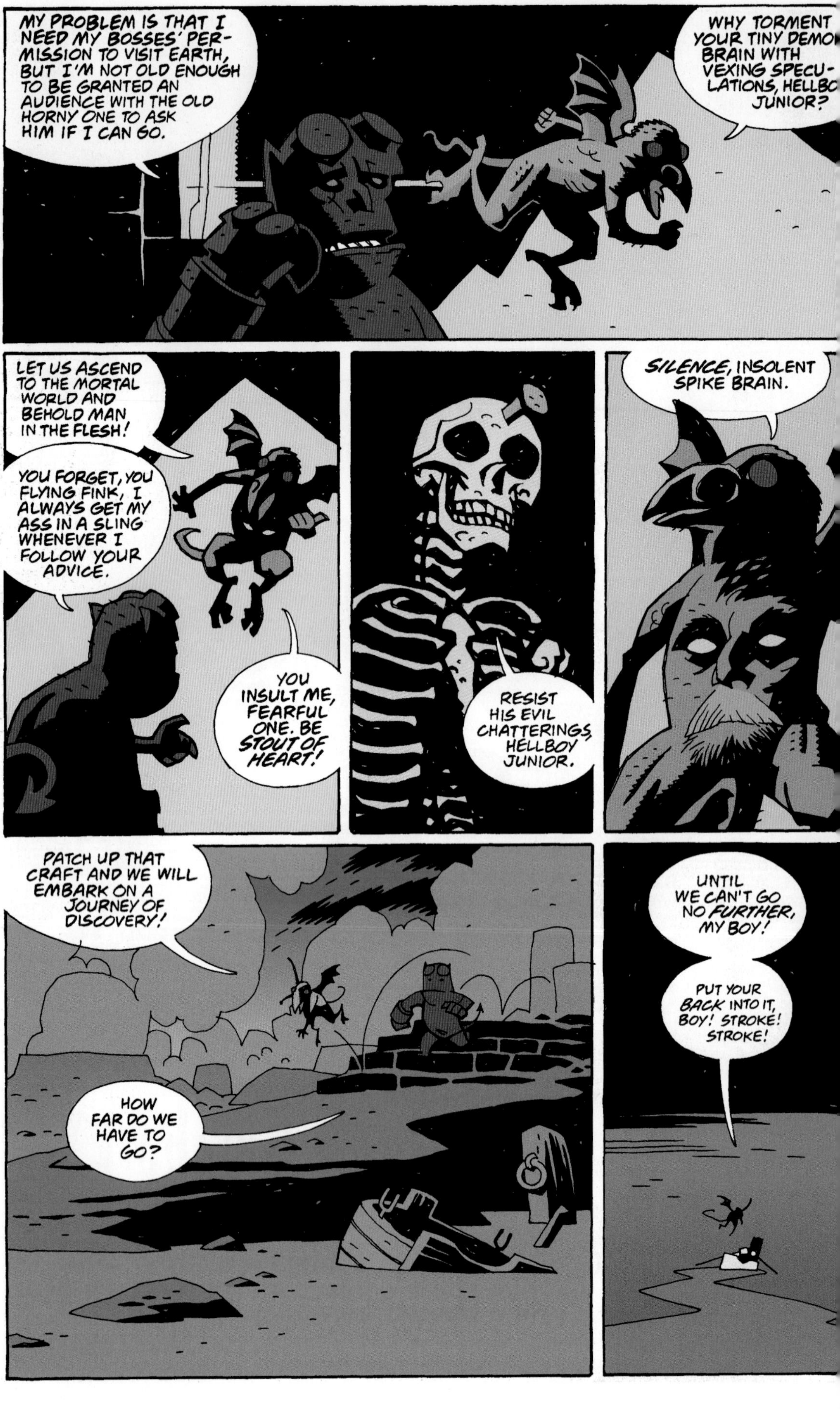
MY PROBLEM IS THAT I NEED MY BOSSES' PERMISSION TO VISIT EARTH, BUT I'M NOT OLD ENOUGH TO BE GRANTED AN AUDIENCE WITH THE OLD HORNY ONE TO ASK HIM IF I CAN GO.
WHY TORMENT YOUR TINY DEMO BRAIN WITH VEXING SPECULATIONS, HELLBO JUNIOR?
LET US ASCEND TO THE MORTAL WORLD AND BEHOLD MAN IN THE FLESH!
YOU FORGET, YOU FLYING FINK, I ALWAYS GET MY ASS IN A SLING WHENEVER I FOLLOW YOUR ADVICE.
YOU INSULT ME, FEARFUL ONE. BE STOUT OF HEART!
RESIST HIS EVIL CHATTERINGS, HELLBOY JUNIOR.
SILENCE, INSOLENT SPIKE BRAIN.
PATCH UP THAT CRAFT AND WE WILL EMBARK ON A JOURNEY OF DISCOVERY!
HOW FAR DO WE HAVE TO GO?
UNTIL WE CAN'T GO NO FURTHER, MY BOY!
PUT YOUR BACK INTO IT, BOY! STROKE! STROKE!

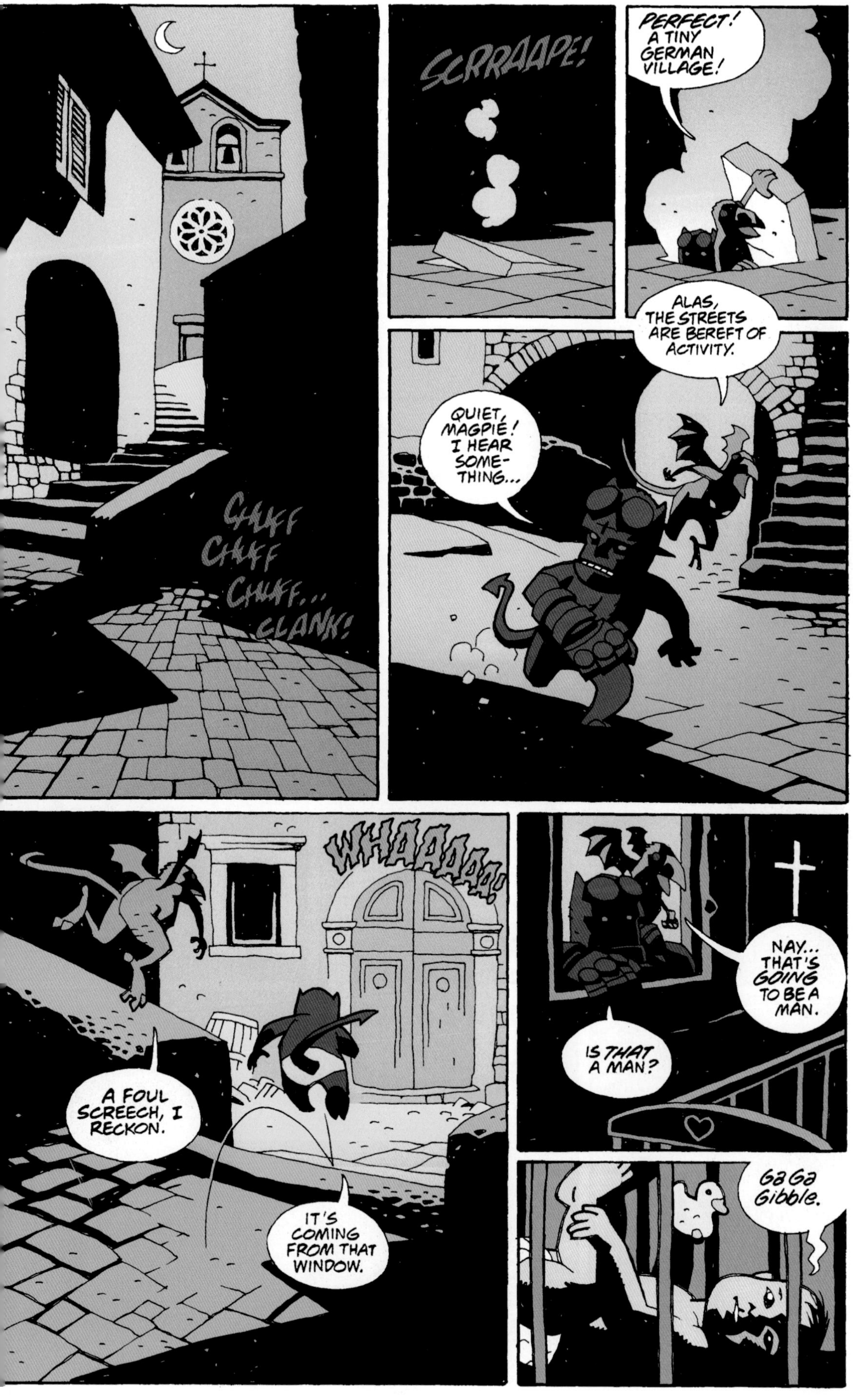
CHUFF
CHUFF
CHUFF...
CLANK!
SCRRAAPE!
PERFECT! A TINY GERMAN VILLAGE!
ALAS, THE STREETS ARE BEREFT OF ACTIVITY.
QUIET, MAGPIE! I HEAR SOME-THING...
WHAAAAA!
A FOUL SCREECH, I RECKON.
IT'S COMING FROM THAT WINDOW.
IS THAT A MAN?
NAY... THAT'S GOING TO BE A MAN.
Ga Ga Gibble.

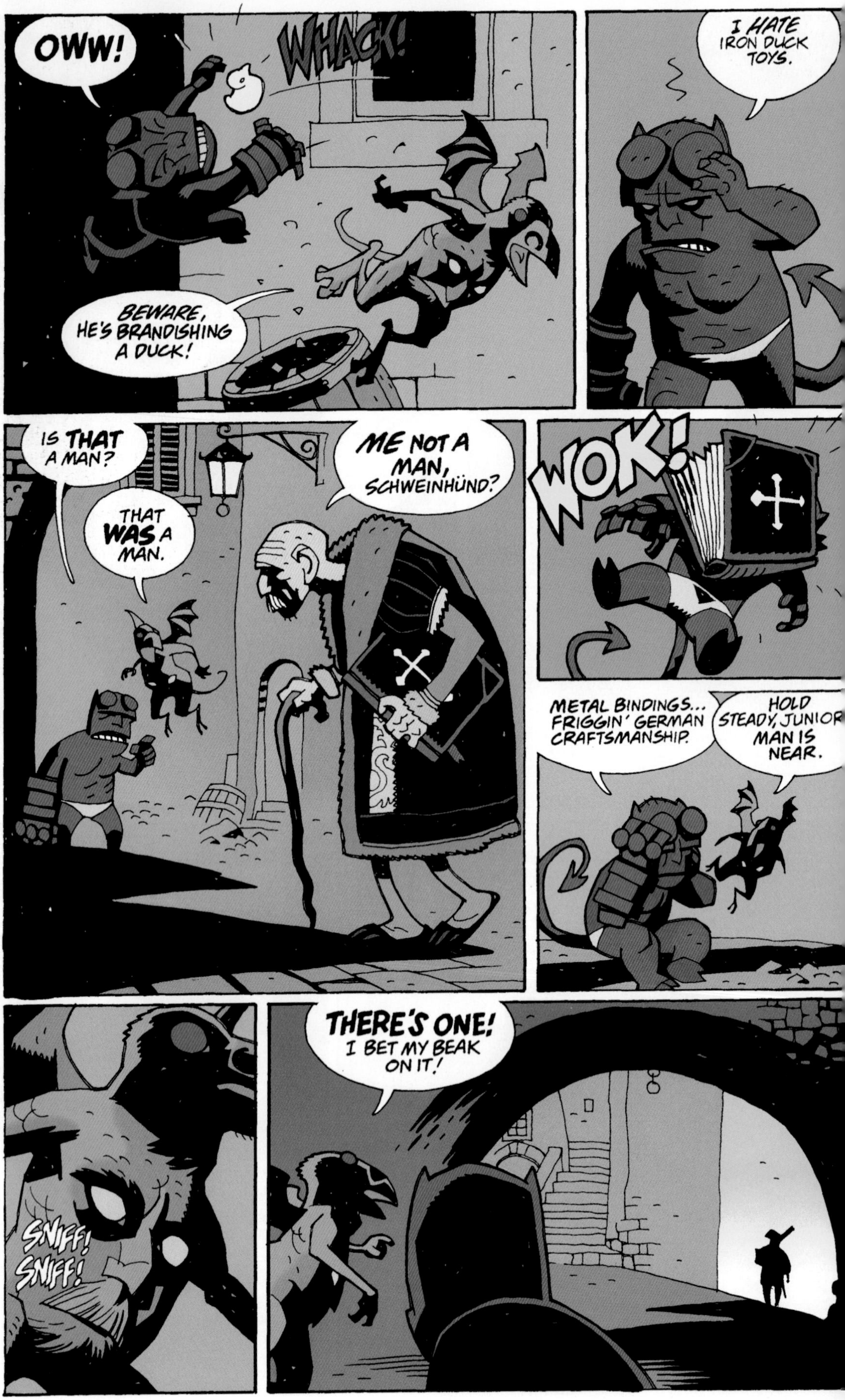
OWW!
WHACK!
BEWARE, HE'S BRANDISHING A DUCK!
I HATE IRON DUCK TOYS.
IS THAT A MAN?
THAT WAS A MAN.
ME NOT A MAN, SCHWEINHÜND?
WOK!
METAL BINDINGS... FRIGGIN' GERMAN CRAFTSMANSHIP.
HOLD STEADY, JUNIOR MAN IS NEAR.
SNIFF! SNIFF!
THERE'S ONE! I BET MY BEAK ON IT!

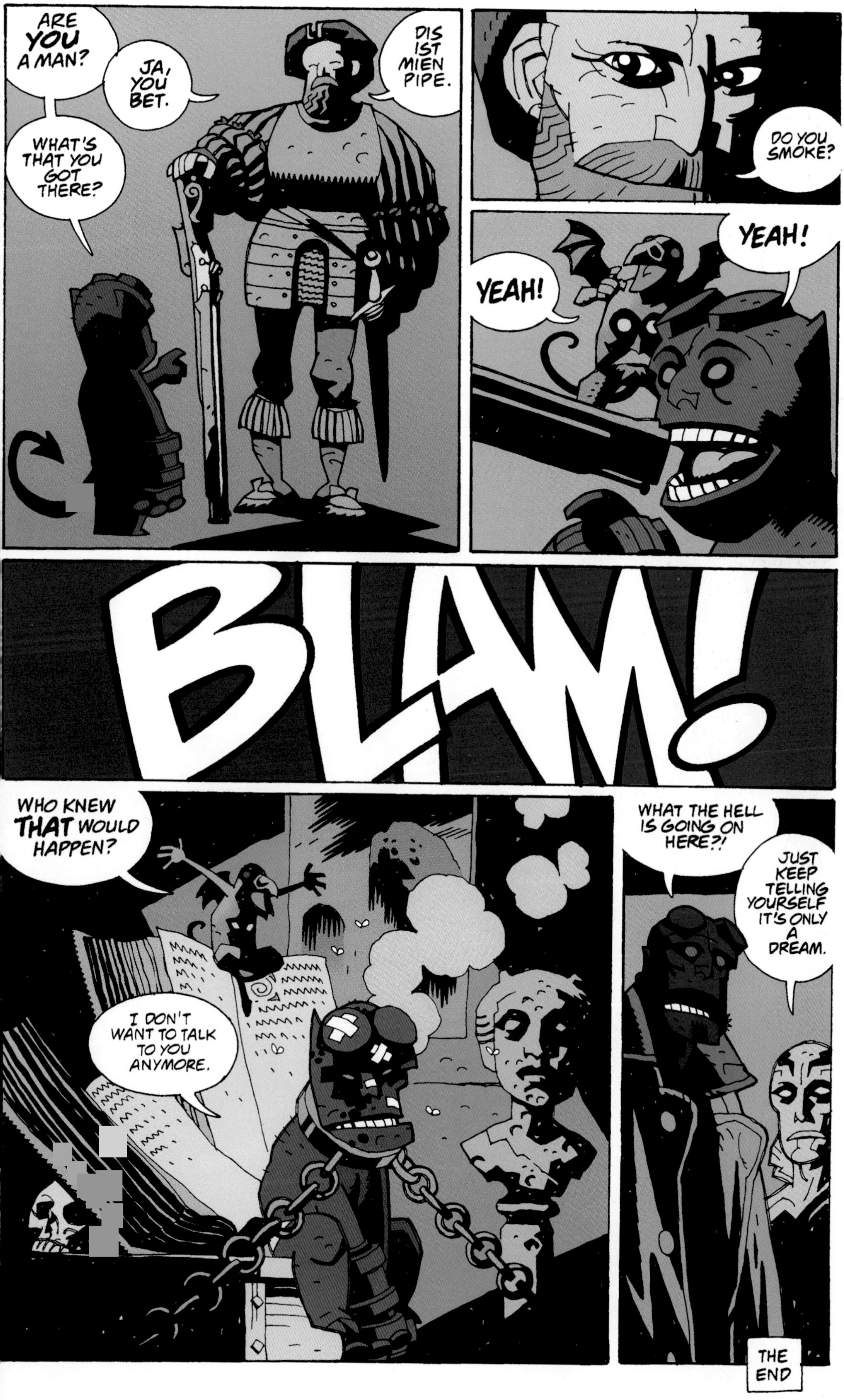

ARE YOU A MAN?
JA, YOU BET.
WHAT'S THAT YOU GOT THERE?
DIS IST MIEN PIPE.
DO YOU SMOKE?
YEAH!
YEAH!
BLAM!
WHO KNEW THAT WOULD HAPPEN?
I DON'T WANT TO TALK TO YOU ANYMORE.
WHAT THE HELL IS GOING ON HERE?!
JUST KEEP TELLING YOURSELF IT'S ONLY A DREAM.
THE END

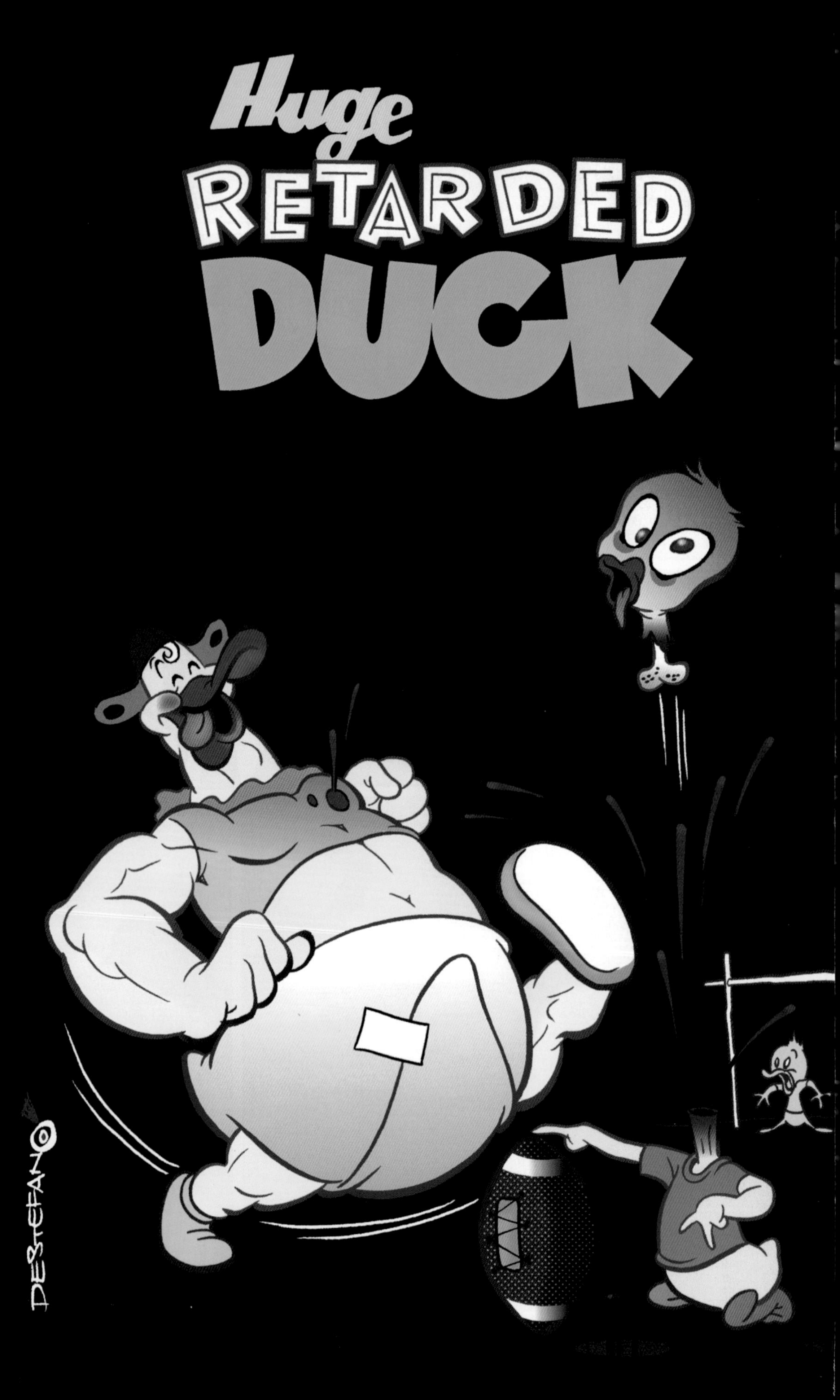
Huge
RETARDED
DUCK
DESTEFANO

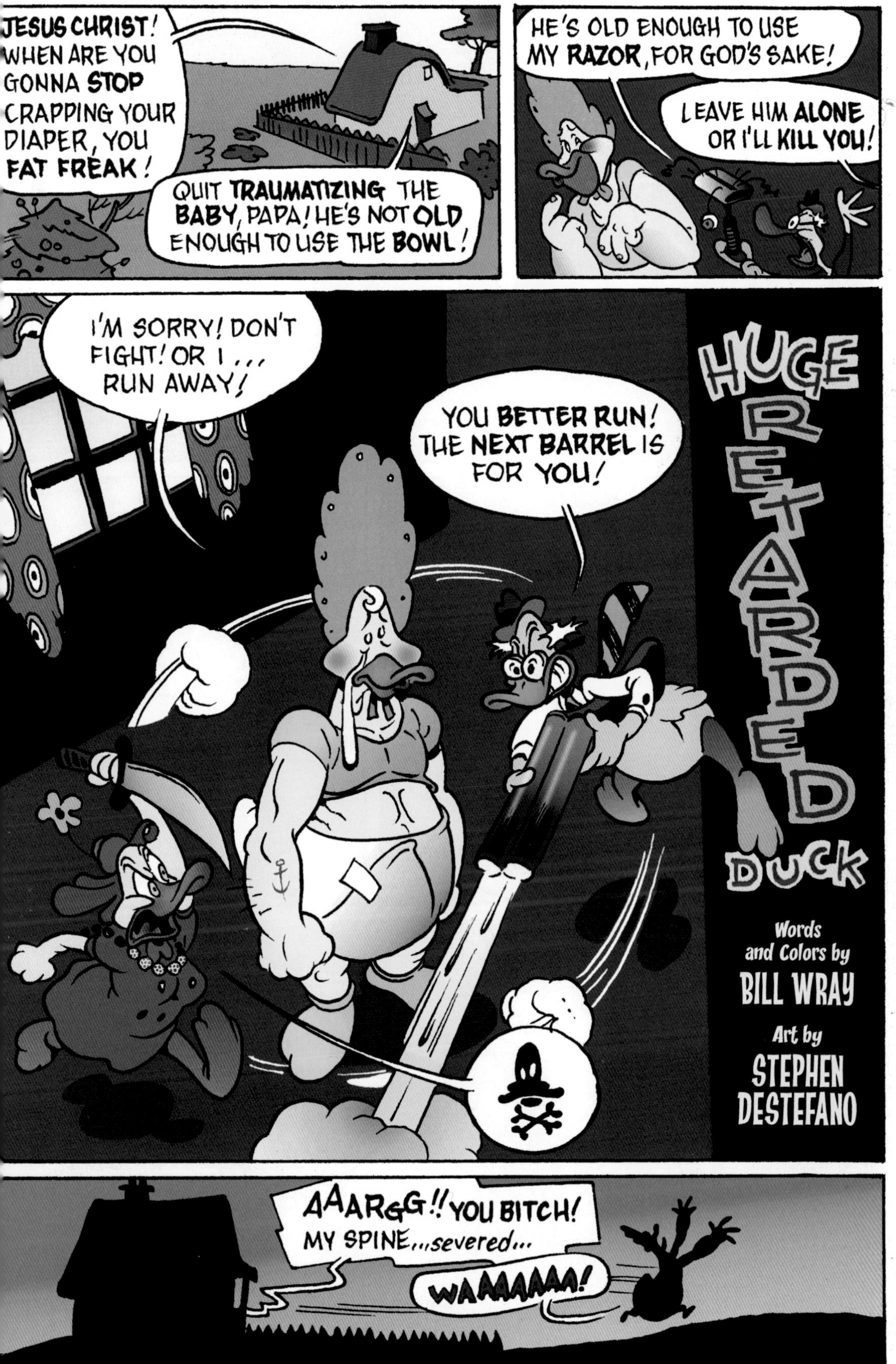

JESUS CHRIST! WHEN ARE YOU GONNA STOP CRAPPING YOUR DIAPER, YOU FAT FREAK!
QUIT TRAUMATIZING THE BABY, PAPA! HE'S NOT OLD ENOUGH TO USE THE BOWL!
HE'S OLD ENOUGH TO USE MY RAZOR, FOR GOD'S SAKE!
LEAVE HIM ALONE OR I'LL KILL YOU!
I'M SORRY! DON'T FIGHT! OR I... RUN AWAY!
YOU BETTER RUN! THE NEXT BARREL IS FOR YOU!
HUGE RETARDED DUCK
Words and Colors by
BILL WRAY
Art by
STEPHEN DESTEFANO
AAARGG!! YOU BITCH! MY SPINE...severed...
WAAAAAA!

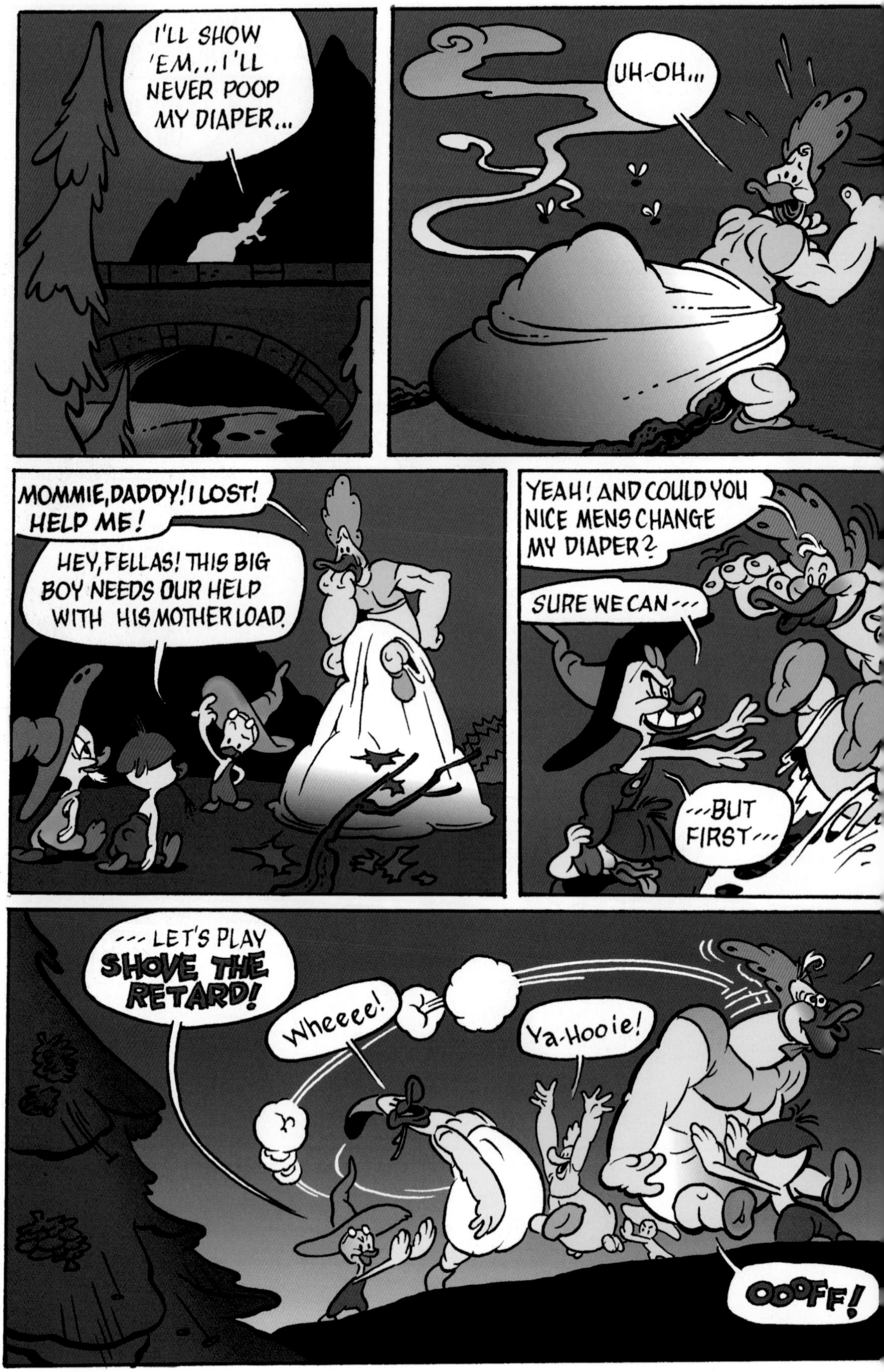
I'LL SHOW 'EM...I'LL NEVER POOP MY DIAPER...
UH-OH...
MOMMIE, DADDY! I LOST! HELP ME!
HEY, FELLAS! THIS BIG BOY NEEDS OUR HELP WITH HIS MOTHER LOAD.
YEAH! AND COULD YOU NICE MENS CHANGE MY DIAPER?
SURE WE CAN---
---BUT FIRST---
--- LET'S PLAY SHOVE THE RETARD!
Wheeee!
Ya-Hooie!
OOOFF!

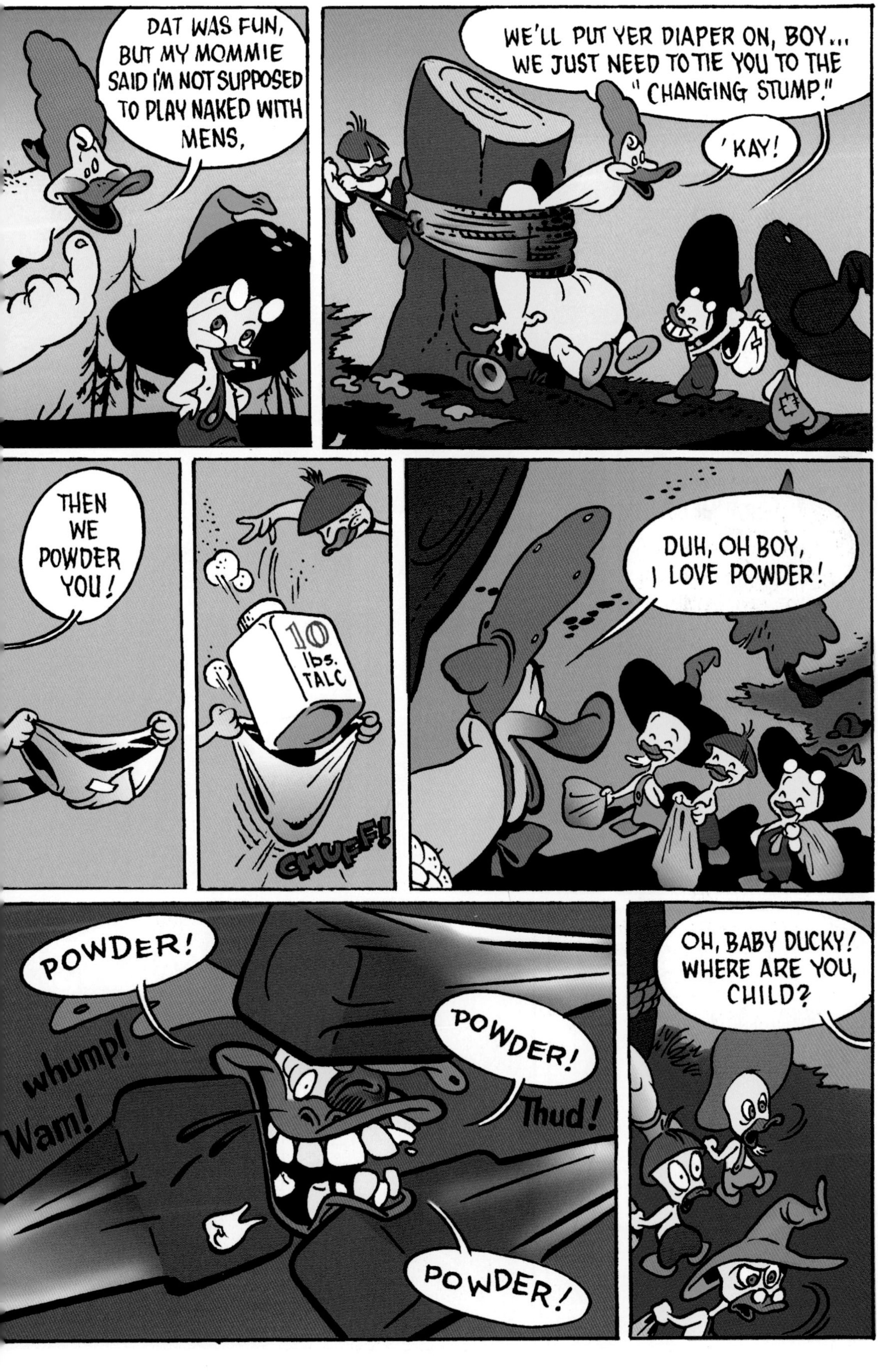
DAT WAS FUN, BUT MY MOMMIE SAID I'M NOT SUPPOSED TO PLAY NAKED WITH MENS,
WE'LL PUT YER DIAPER ON, BOY... WE JUST NEED TO TIE YOU TO THE "CHANGING STUMP."
'KAY!
THEN WE POWDER YOU!
10 lbs. TALC
CHUFF!
DUH, OH BOY, I LOVE POWDER!
POWDER!
whump!
Wam!
POWDER!
Thud!
POWDER!
OH, BABY DUCKY! WHERE ARE YOU, CHILD?

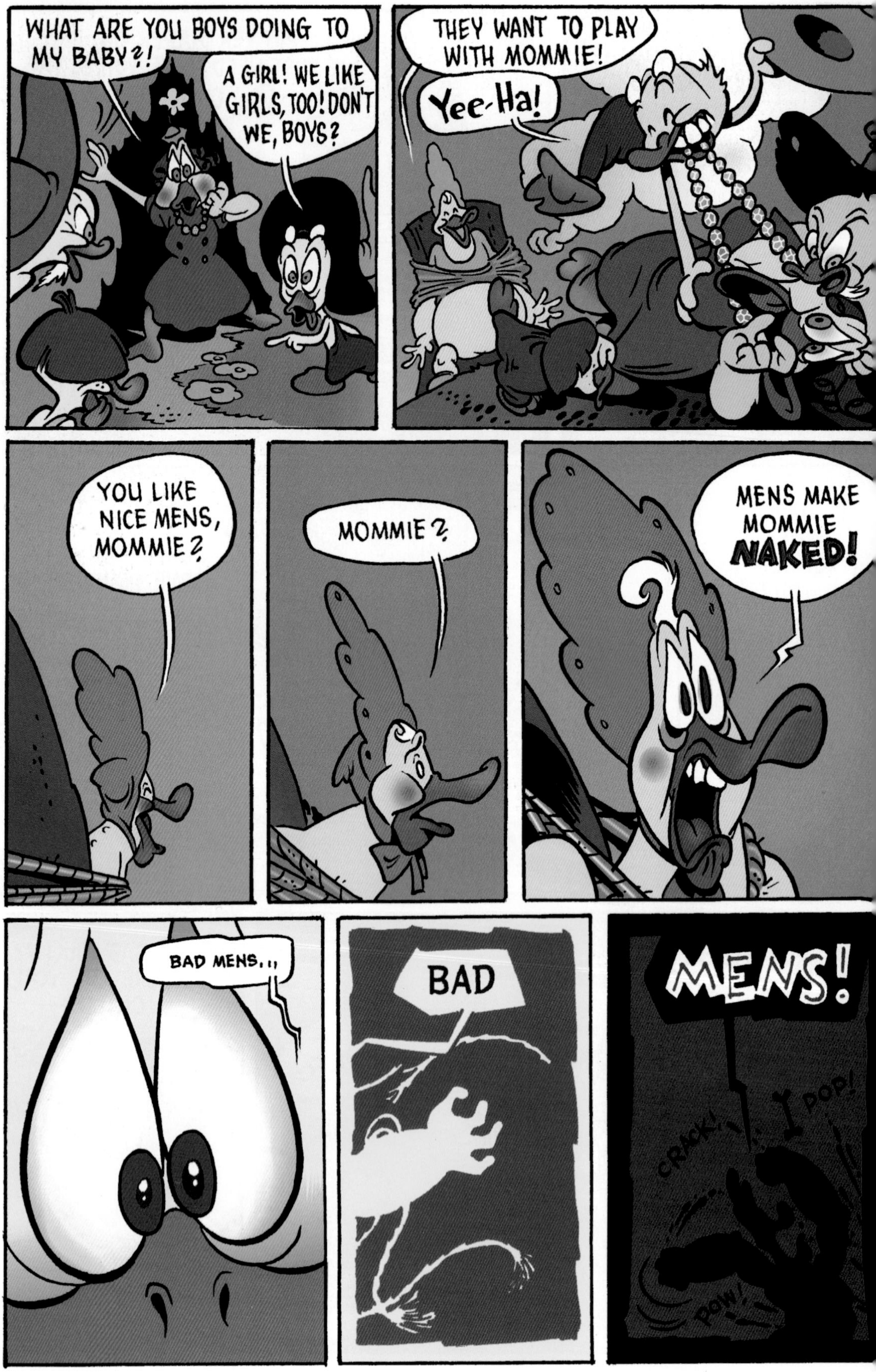
WHAT ARE YOU BOYS DOING TO MY BABY?!
A GIRL! WE LIKE GIRLS, TOO! DON'T WE, BOYS?
THEY WANT TO PLAY WITH MOMMIE!
Yee-Ha!
YOU LIKE NICE MENS, MOMMIE?
MOMMIE?
MENS MAKE MOMMIE NAKED!
BAD MENS...
BAD
MENS!
CRACK!
POP!
POW!

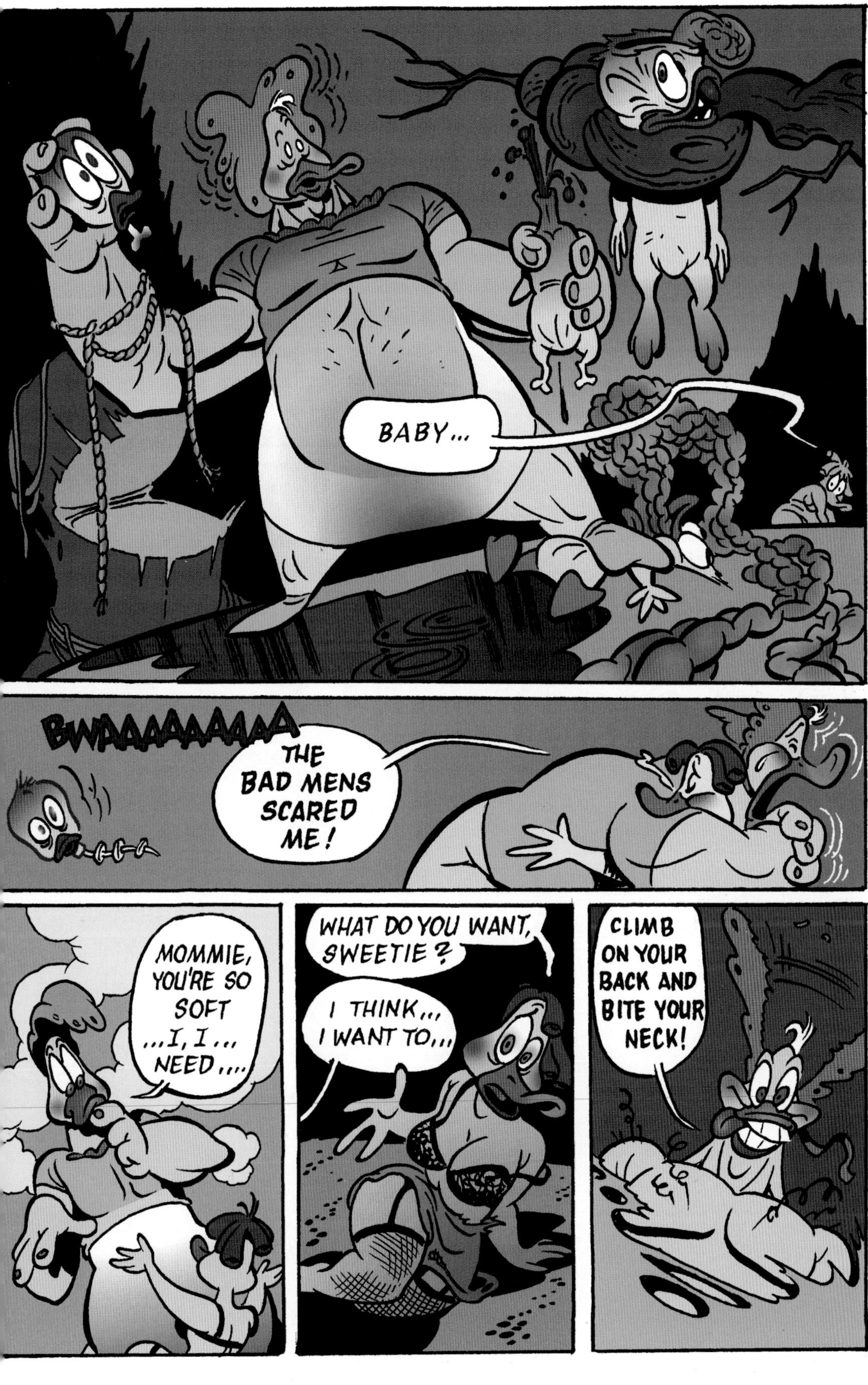
BABY...
BWAAAAAAAAA
THE BAD MENS SCARED ME!
MOMMIE, YOU'RE SO SOFT ...I, I... NEED....
WHAT DO YOU WANT, SWEETIE?
I THINK,,, I WANT TO,,,
CLIMB ON YOUR BACK AND BITE YOUR NECK!

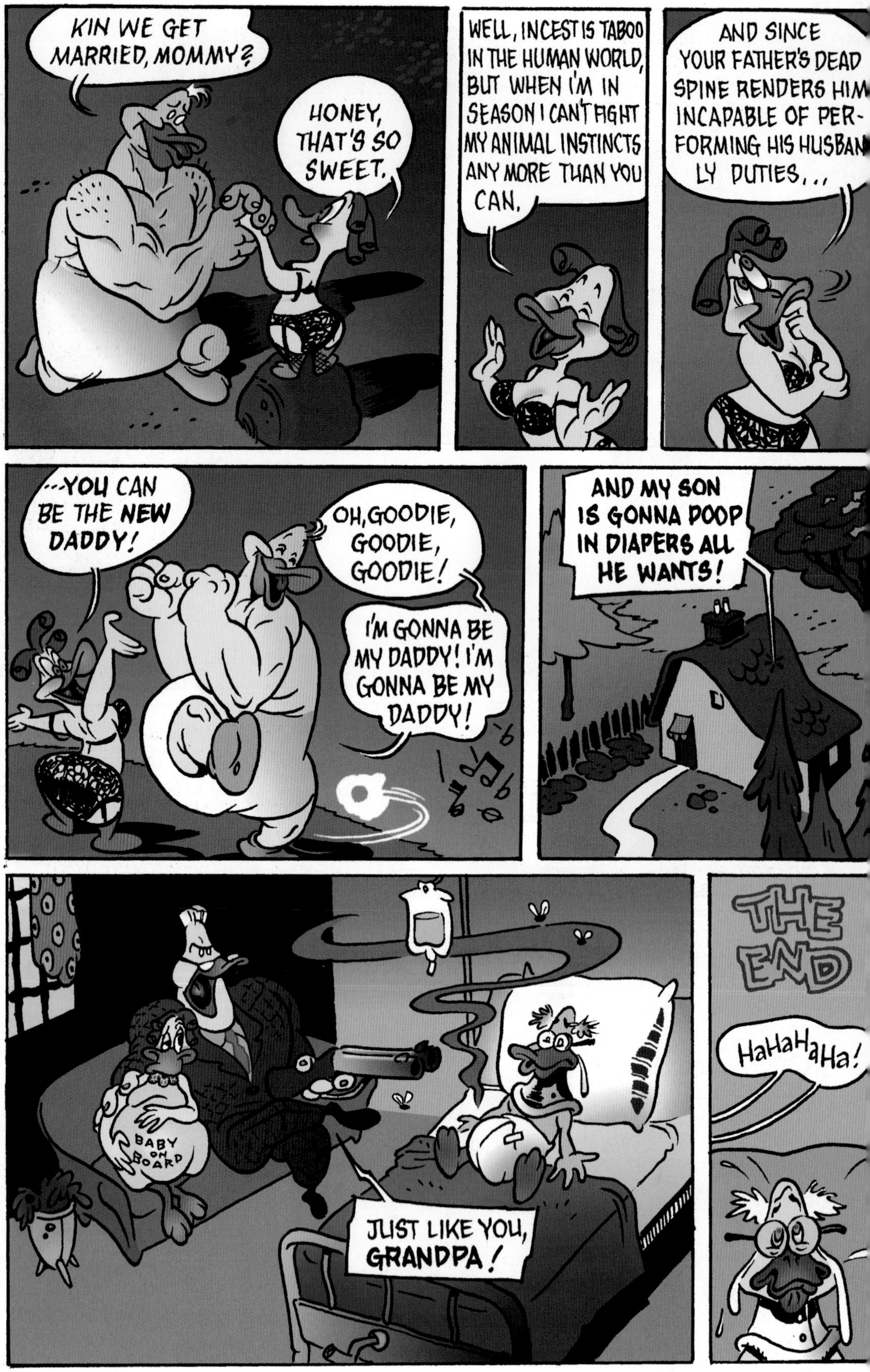
KIN WE GET MARRIED, MOMMY?
HONEY, THAT'S SO SWEET.
WELL, INCEST IS TABOO IN THE HUMAN WORLD, BUT WHEN I'M IN SEASON I CAN'T FIGHT MY ANIMAL INSTINCTS ANY MORE THAN YOU CAN.
AND SINCE YOUR FATHER'S DEAD SPINE RENDERS HIM INCAPABLE OF PERFORMING HIS HUSBAN-LY DUTIES...
--YOU CAN BE THE NEW DADDY!
OH, GOODIE, GOODIE, GOODIE!
I'M GONNA BE MY DADDY! I'M GONNA BE MY DADDY!
AND MY SON IS GONNA POOP IN DIAPERS ALL HE WANTS!
BABY ON BOARD
JUST LIKE YOU, GRANDPA!
THE END
HaHaHaHa!

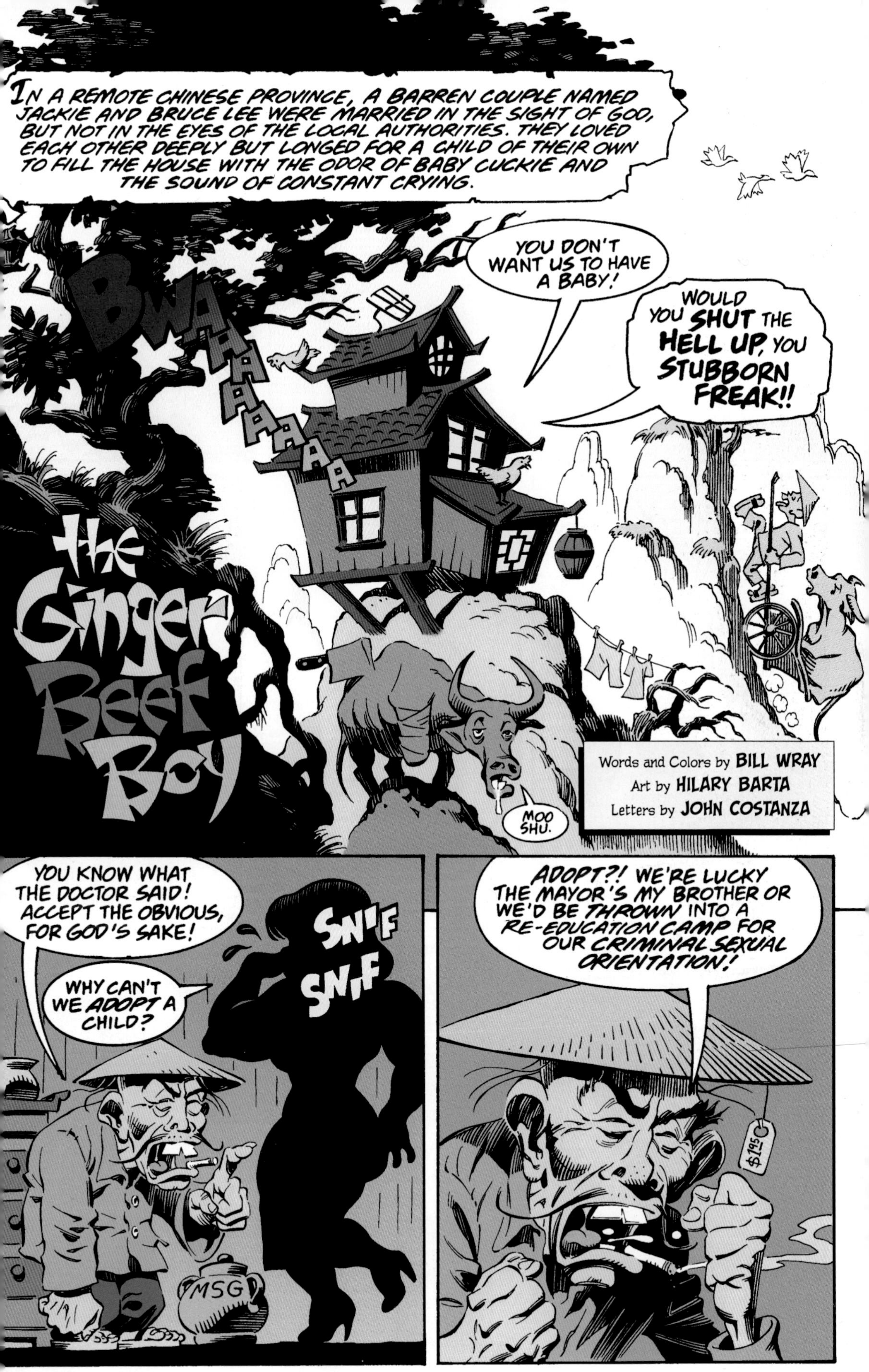
IN A REMOTE CHINESE PROVINCE, A BARREN COUPLE NAMED JACKIE AND BRUCE LEE WERE MARRIED IN THE SIGHT OF GOD, BUT NOT IN THE EYES OF THE LOCAL AUTHORITIES. THEY LOVED EACH OTHER DEEPLY BUT LONGED FOR A CHILD OF THEIR OWN TO FILL THE HOUSE WITH THE ODOR OF BABY CUCKIE AND THE SOUND OF CONSTANT CRYING.
BWAAAAAAAA
YOU DON'T WANT US TO HAVE A BABY!
WOULD YOU SHUT THE HELL UP, YOU STUBBORN FREAK!!
the Ginger Beef Boy
Words and Colors by BILL WRAY
Art by HILARY BARTA
Letters by JOHN COSTANZA
MOO SHU.
YOU KNOW WHAT THE DOCTOR SAID! ACCEPT THE OBVIOUS, FOR GOD'S SAKE!
SNIF SNIF
WHY CAN'T WE ADOPT A CHILD?
MSG
ADOPT?! WE'RE LUCKY THE MAYOR'S MY BROTHER OR WE'D BE THROWN INTO A RE-EDUCATION CAMP FOR OUR CRIMINAL SEXUAL ORIENTATION!
$1.95

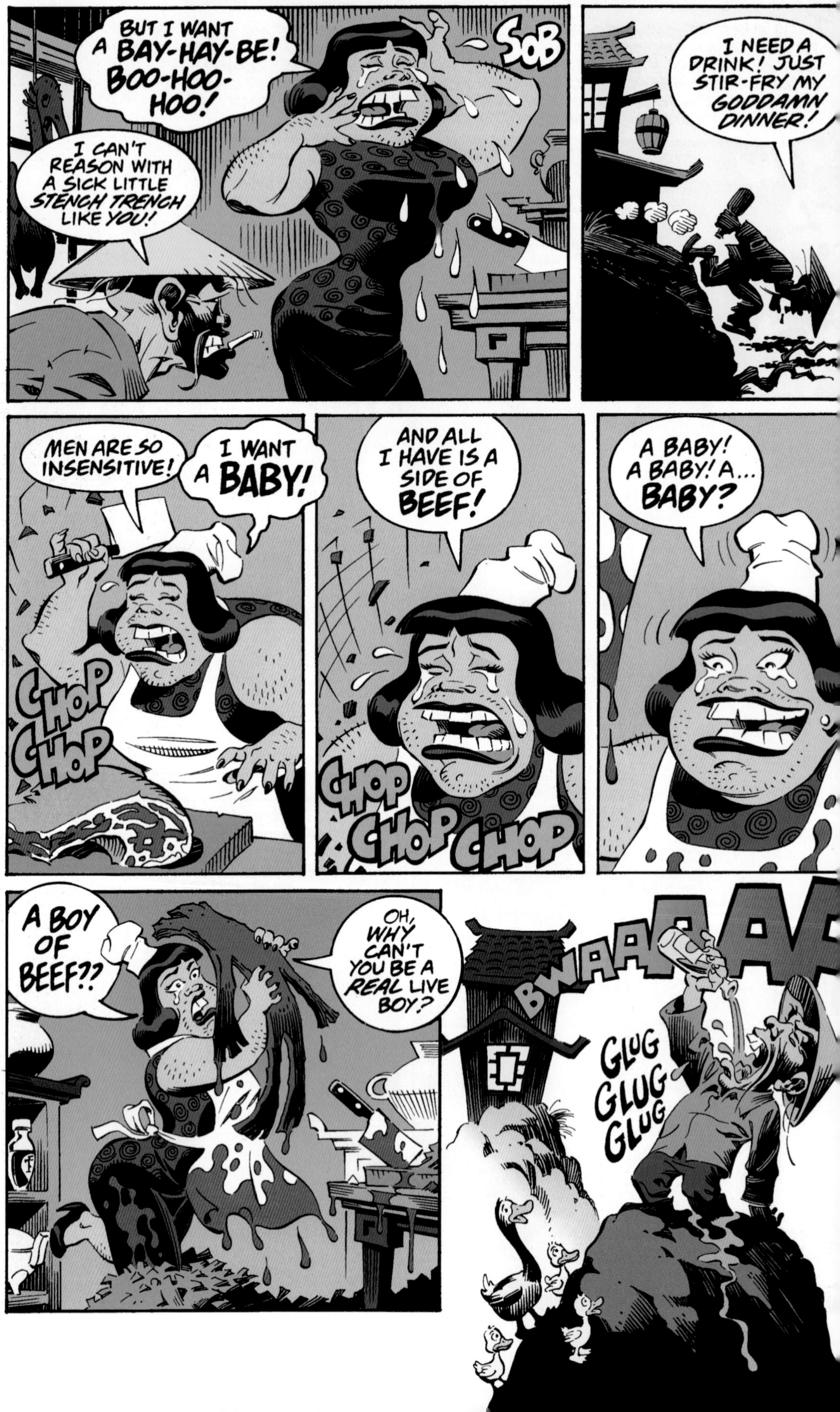
BUT I WANT A BAY-HAY-BE! BOO-HOO-HOO!
SOB
I CAN'T REASON WITH A SICK LITTLE STENCH TRENCH LIKE YOU!
I NEED A DRINK! JUST STIR-FRY MY GODDAMN DINNER!
MEN ARE SO INSENSITIVE!
I WANT A BABY!
CHOP CHOP
AND ALL I HAVE IS A SIDE OF BEEF!
CHOP CHOP CHOP
A BABY! A BABY! A... BABY?
A BOY OF BEEF??
OH, WHY CAN'T YOU BE A REAL LIVE BOY?
BWAAAAAA
GLUG GLUG GLUG

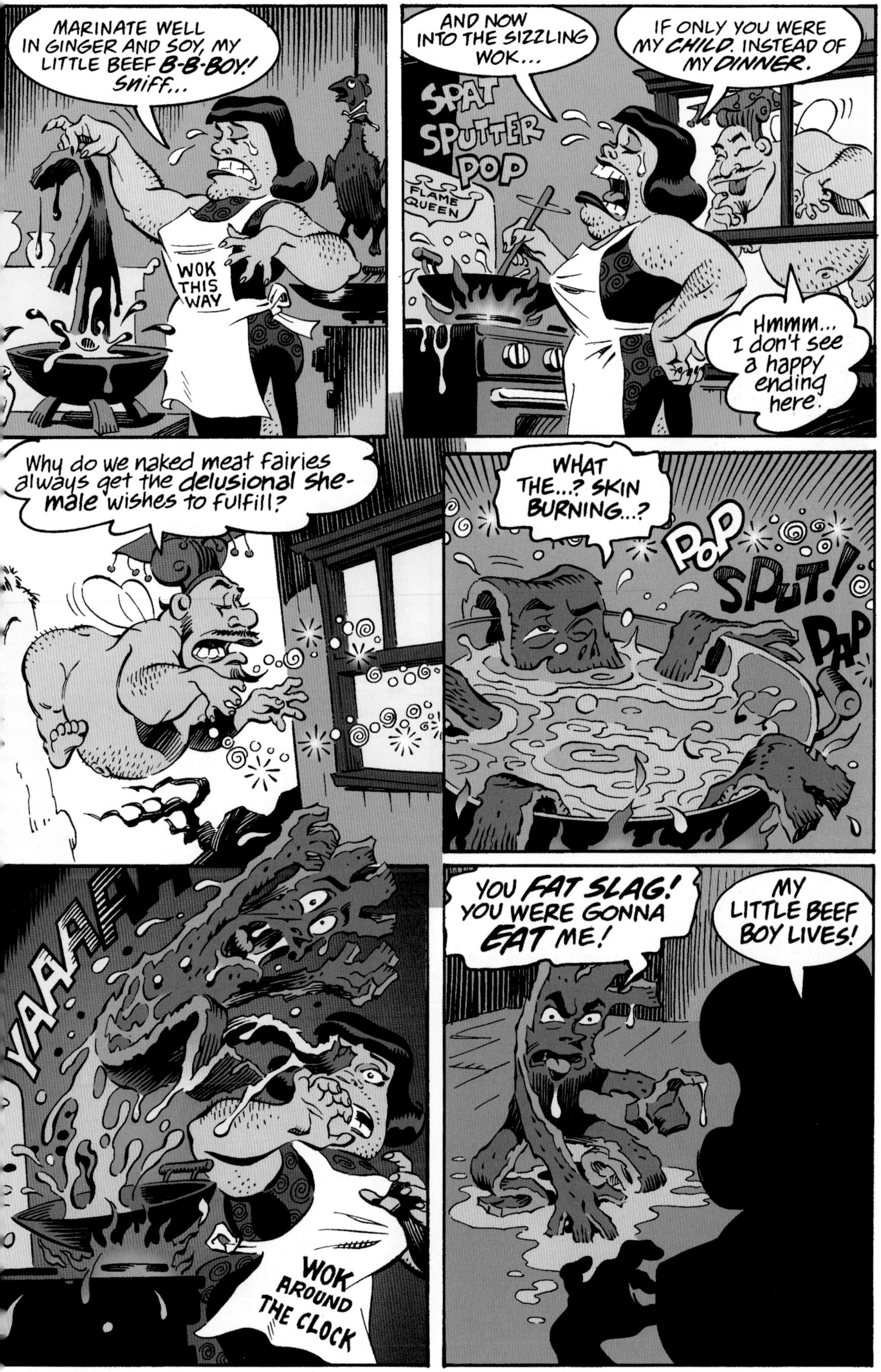
MARINATE WELL IN GINGER AND SOY, MY LITTLE BEEF B-B-BOY! Sniff...
WOK THIS WAY
AND NOW INTO THE SIZZLING WOK...
IF ONLY YOU WERE MY CHILD, INSTEAD OF MY DINNER.
SPAT SPUTTER POP
FLAME QUEEN
Hmmm... I don't see a happy ending here.
Why do we naked meat fairies always get the delusional she-male wishes to fulfill?
WHAT THE...? SKIN BURNING...?
POP SPUT! PAP
YAAAAH
WOK AROUND THE CLOCK
YOU FAT SLAG! YOU WERE GONNA EAT ME!
MY LITTLE BEEF BOY LIVES!

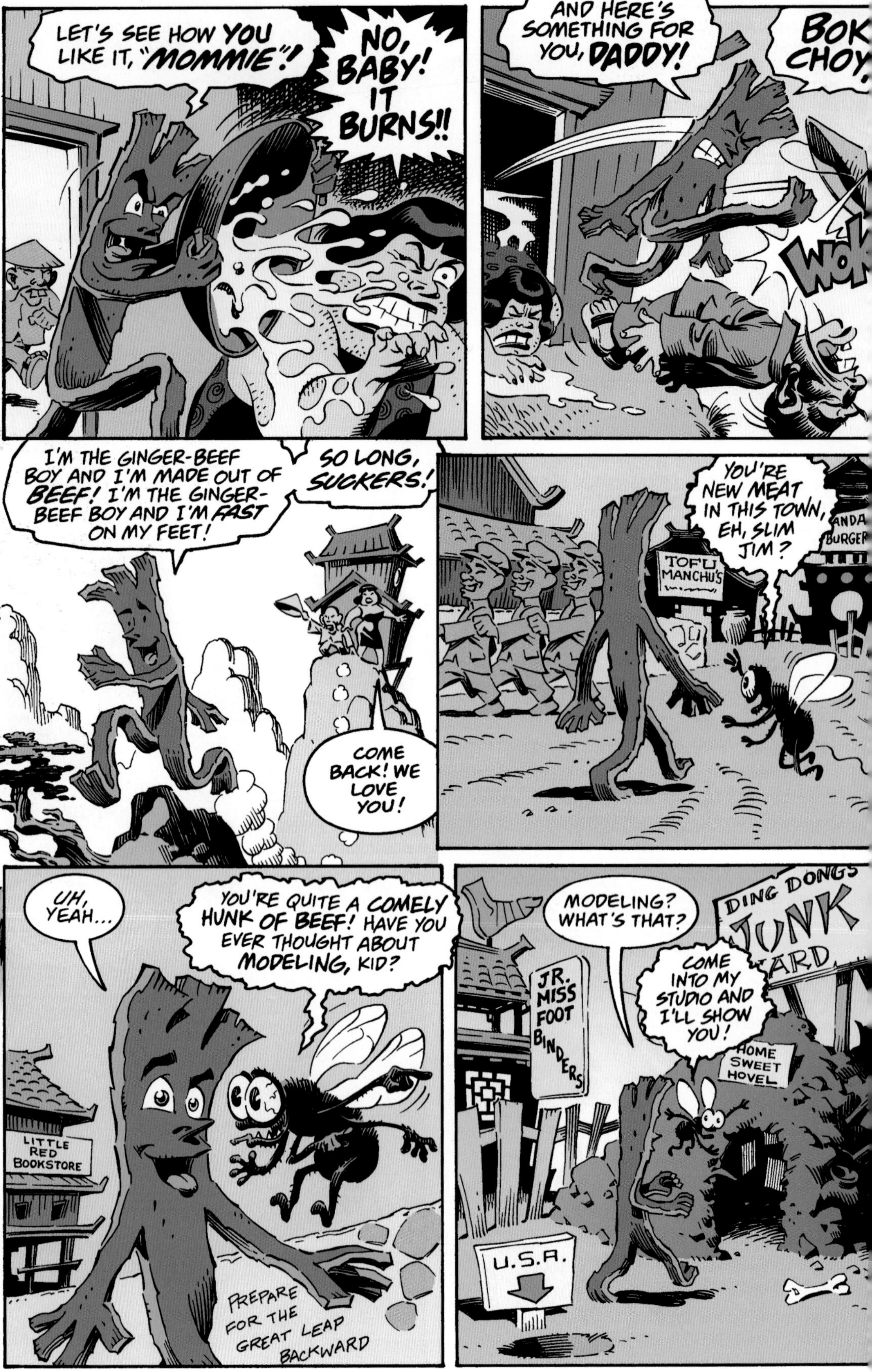
LET'S SEE HOW YOU LIKE IT, "MOMMIE"!
NO, BABY! IT BURNS!!
AND HERE'S SOMETHING FOR YOU, DADDY!
BOK CHOY
WOK
I'M THE GINGER-BEEF BOY AND I'M MADE OUT OF BEEF! I'M THE GINGER-BEEF BOY AND I'M FAST ON MY FEET!
SO LONG, SUCKERS!
COME BACK! WE LOVE YOU!
YOU'RE NEW MEAT IN THIS TOWN, EH, SLIM JIM?
TOFU MANCHU'S
BURGER
UH, YEAH...
YOU'RE QUITE A COMELY HUNK OF BEEF! HAVE YOU EVER THOUGHT ABOUT MODELING, KID?
LITTLE RED BOOKSTORE
PREPARE FOR THE GREAT LEAP BACKWARD
MODELING? WHAT'S THAT?
COME INTO MY STUDIO AND I'LL SHOW YOU!
DING DONGS JUNK
JR. MISS FOOT BINDERS
HOME SWEET HOVEL
U.S.A.

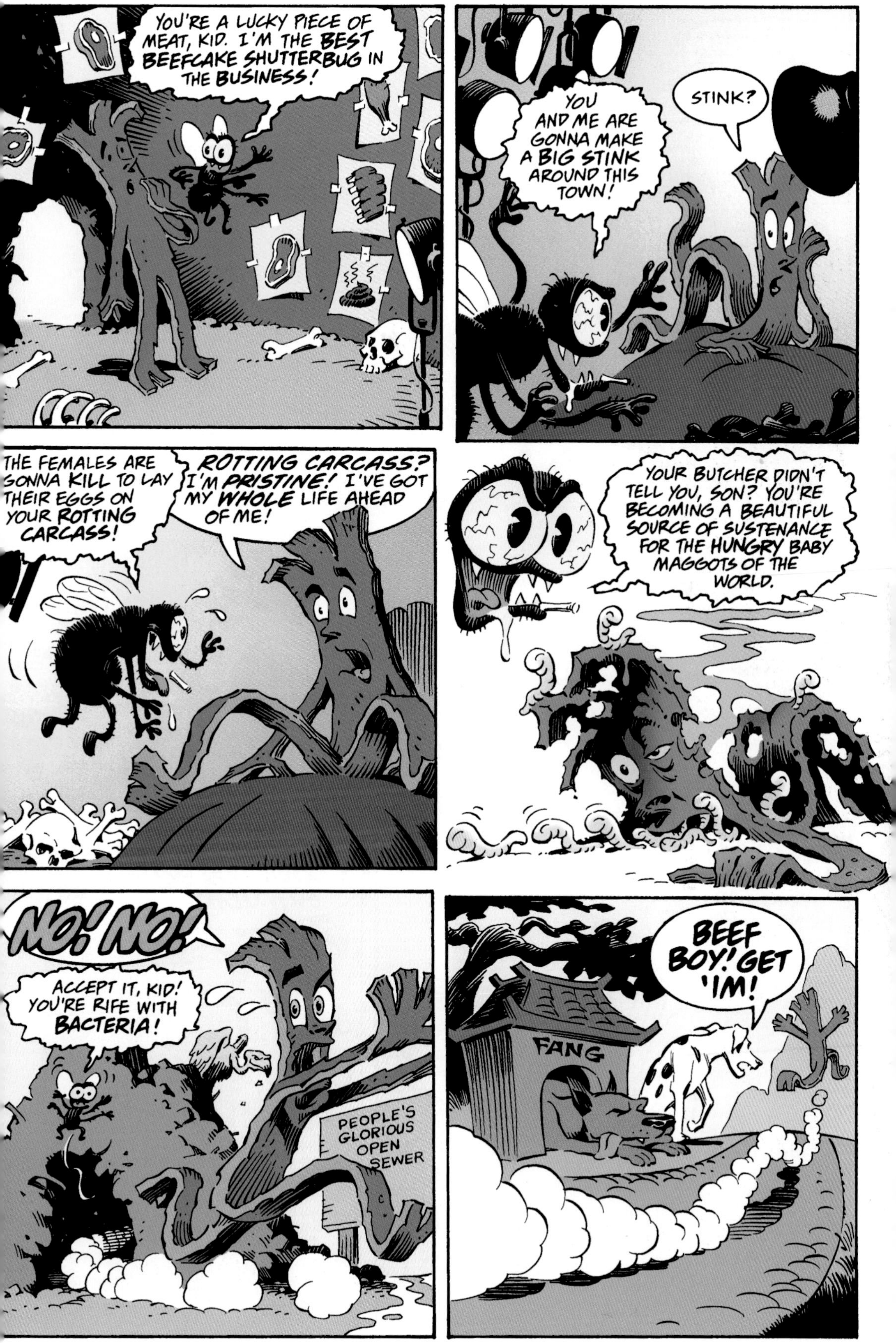
YOU'RE A LUCKY PIECE OF MEAT, KID. I'M THE BEST BEEFCAKE SHUTTERBUG IN THE BUSINESS!
YOU AND ME ARE GONNA MAKE A BIG STINK AROUND THIS TOWN!
STINK?
THE FEMALES ARE GONNA KILL TO LAY THEIR EGGS ON YOUR ROTTING CARCASS!
ROTTING CARCASS? I'M PRISTINE! I'VE GOT MY WHOLE LIFE AHEAD OF ME!
YOUR BUTCHER DIDN'T TELL YOU, SON? YOU'RE BECOMING A BEAUTIFUL SOURCE OF SUSTENANCE FOR THE HUNGRY BABY MAGGOTS OF THE WORLD.
NO! NO!
ACCEPT IT, KID! YOU'RE RIFE WITH BACTERIA!
PEOPLE'S GLORIOUS OPEN SEWER
FANG
BEEF BOY! GET 'IM!

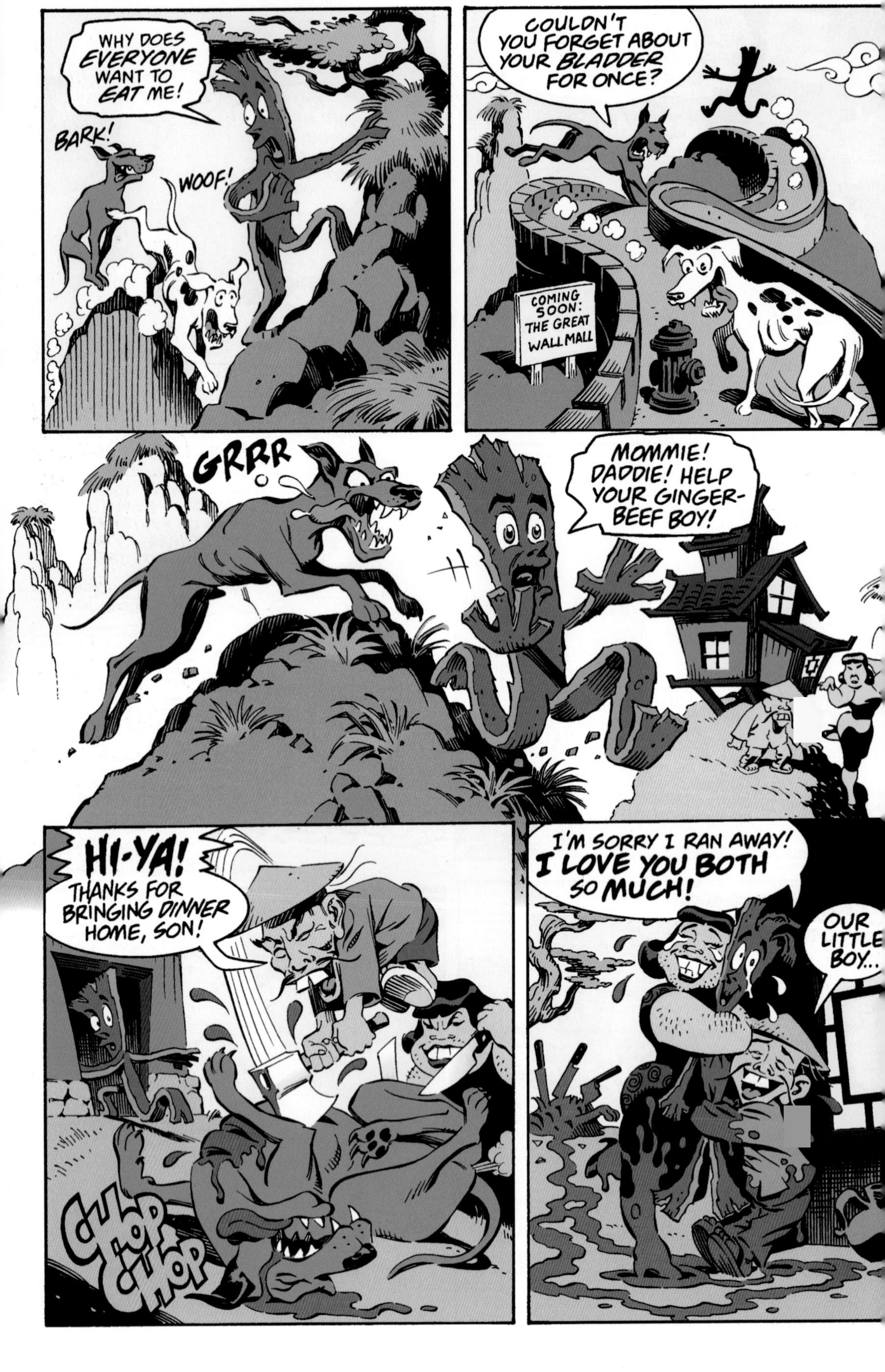

WHY DOES EVERYONE WANT TO EAT ME!
BARK!
WOOF!
COULDN'T YOU FORGET ABOUT YOUR BLADDER FOR ONCE?
COMING SOON: THE GREAT WALL MALL
GRRR
MOMMIE! DADDIE! HELP YOUR GINGER-BEEF BOY!
HI-YA!
THANKS FOR BRINGING DINNER HOME, SON!
CHOP CHOP
I'M SORRY I RAN AWAY! I LOVE YOU BOTH SO MUCH!
OUR LITTLE BOY...

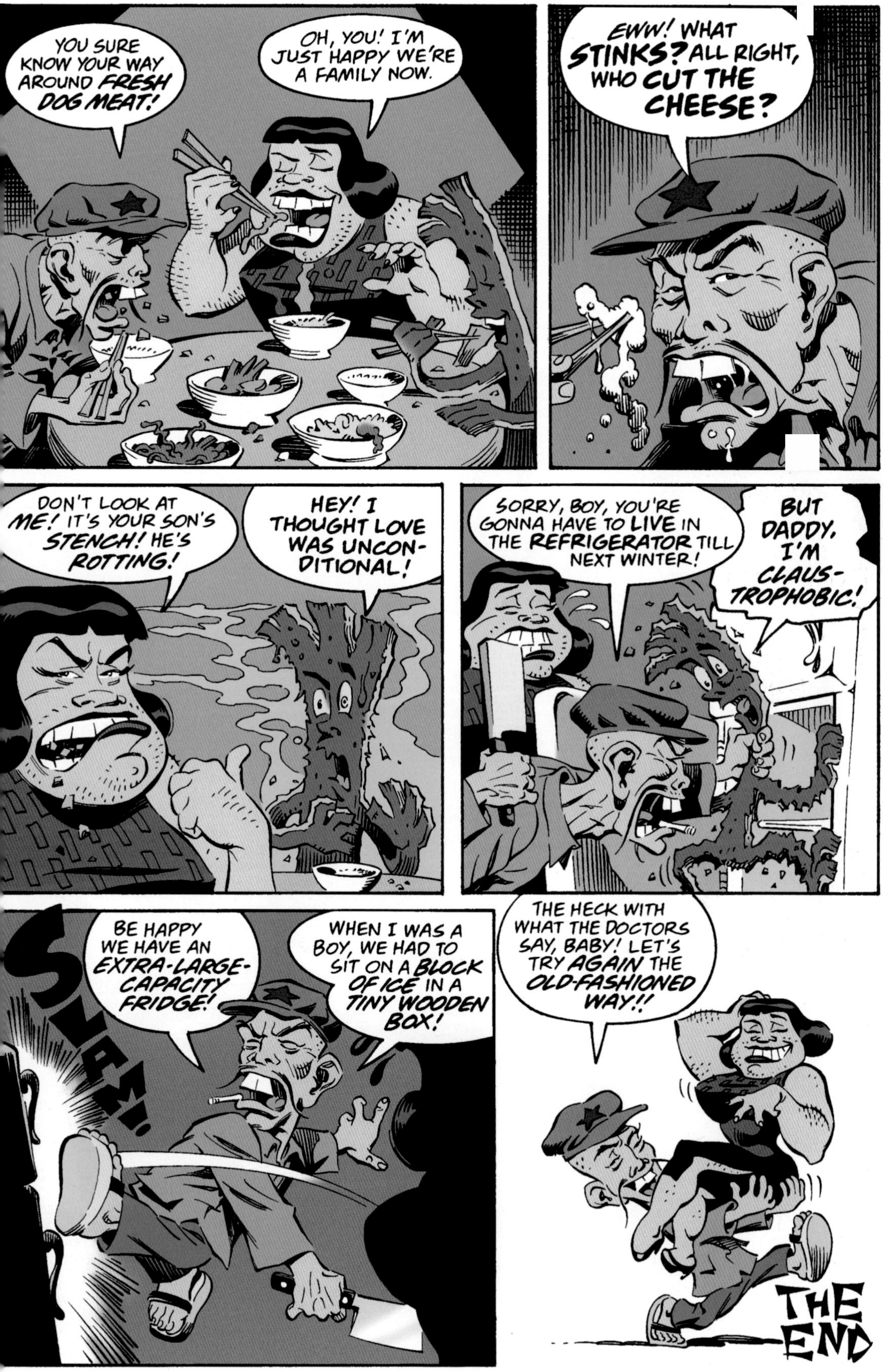
YOU SURE KNOW YOUR WAY AROUND FRESH DOG MEAT!
OH, YOU! I'M JUST HAPPY WE'RE A FAMILY NOW.
EWW! WHAT STINKS? ALL RIGHT, WHO CUT THE CHEESE?
DON'T LOOK AT ME! IT'S YOUR SON'S STENCH! HE'S ROTTING!
HEY! I THOUGHT LOVE WAS UNCONDITIONAL!
SORRY, BOY, YOU'RE GONNA HAVE TO LIVE IN THE REFRIGERATOR TILL NEXT WINTER!
BUT DADDY, I'M CLAUSTROPHOBIC!
SLAM!
BE HAPPY WE HAVE AN EXTRA-LARGE-CAPACITY FRIDGE!
WHEN I WAS A BOY, WE HAD TO SIT ON A BLOCK OF ICE IN A TINY WOODEN BOX!
THE HECK WITH WHAT THE DOCTORS SAY, BABY! LET'S TRY AGAIN THE OLD-FASHIONED WAY!!
THE END

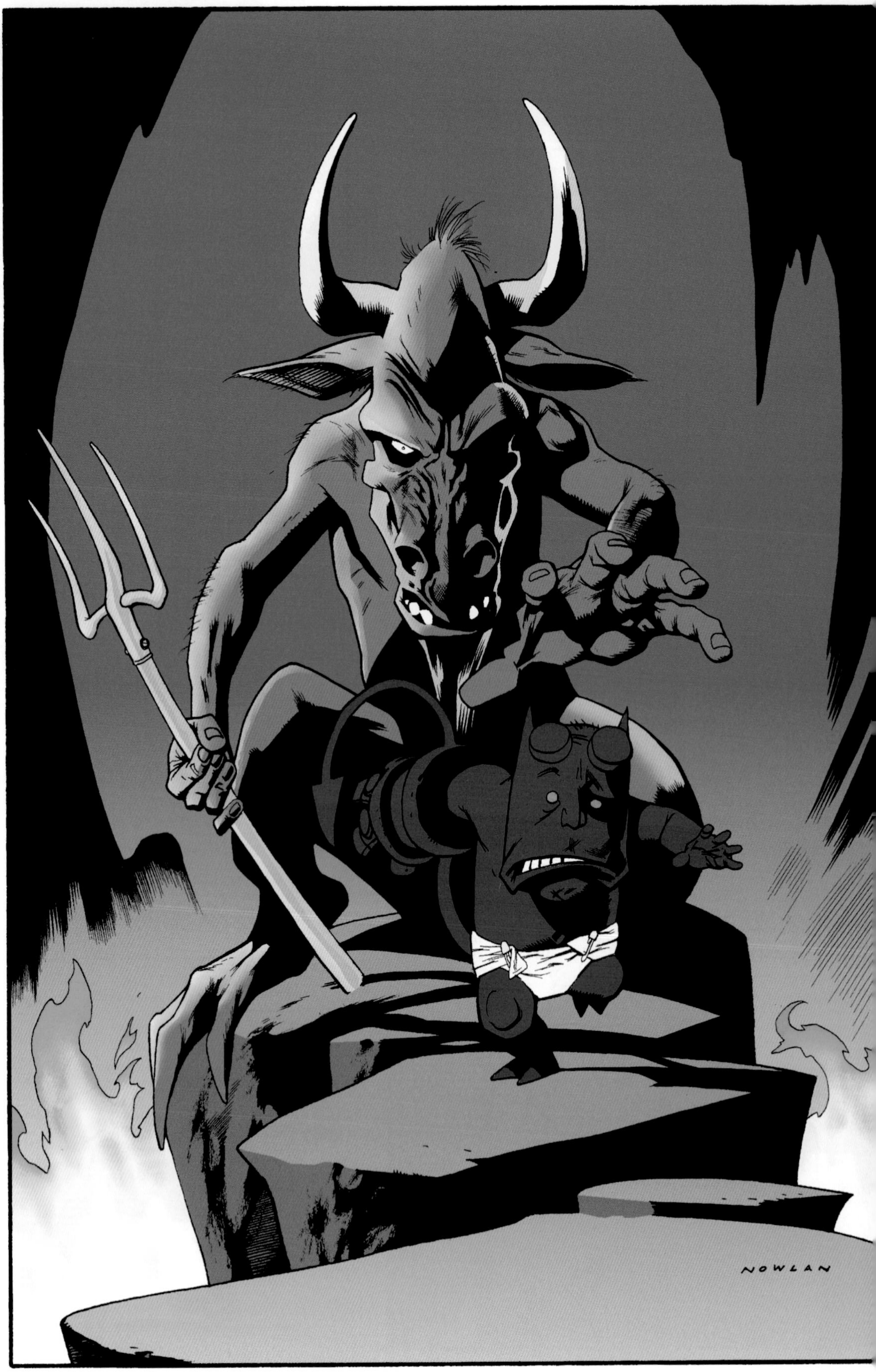
NOWLAN

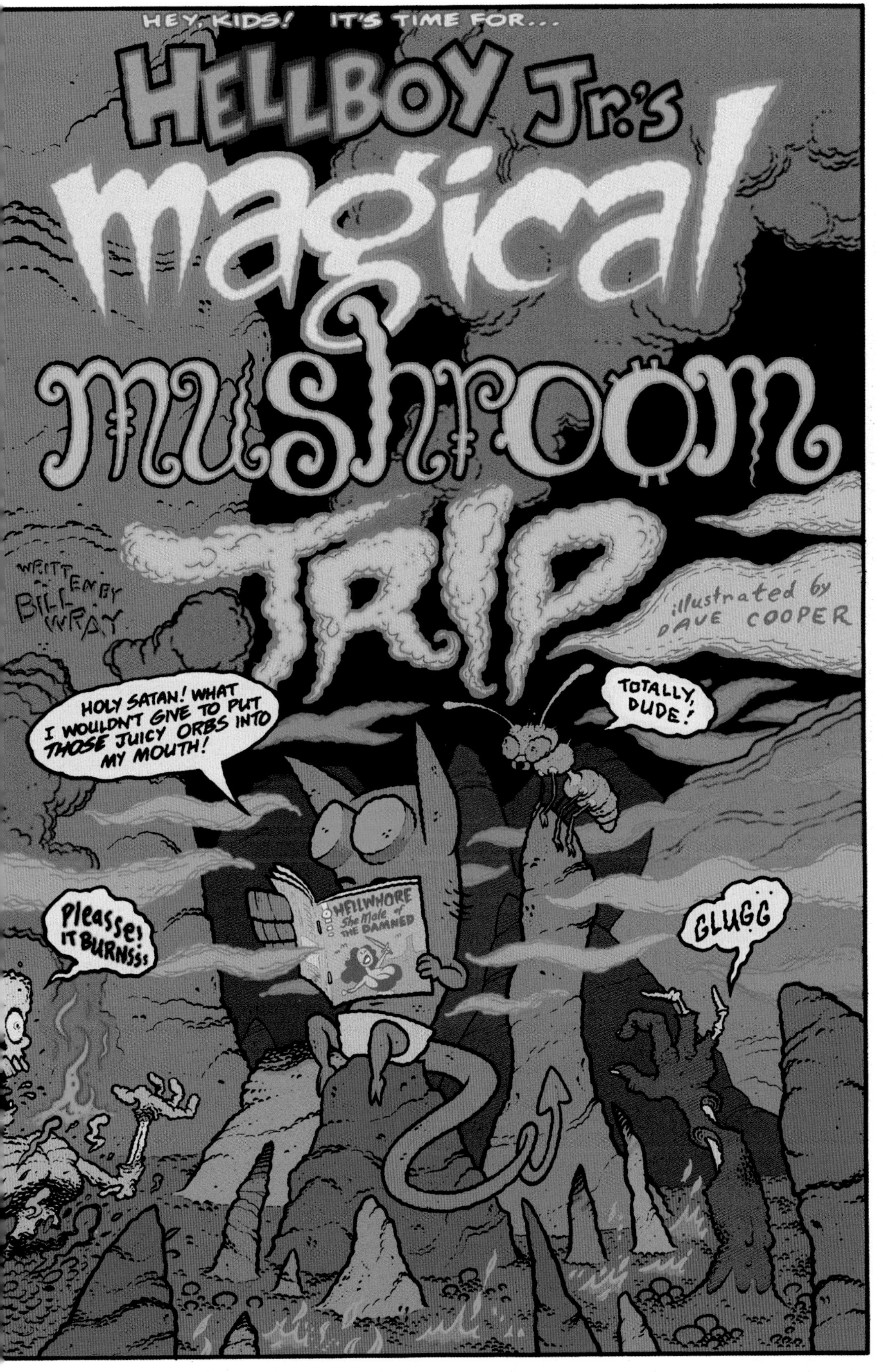
HEY, KIDS! IT'S TIME FOR...
HELLBOY Jr.'s magical mushroom TRIP
WRITTEN BY BILL WRAY
illustrated by DAVE COOPER
HOLY SATAN! WHAT I WOULDN'T GIVE TO PUT THOSE JUICY ORBS INTO MY MOUTH!
TOTALLY, DUDE!
HELLWHORE She Male of THE DAMNED
Pleassse! IT BURNSsss
GLUGG

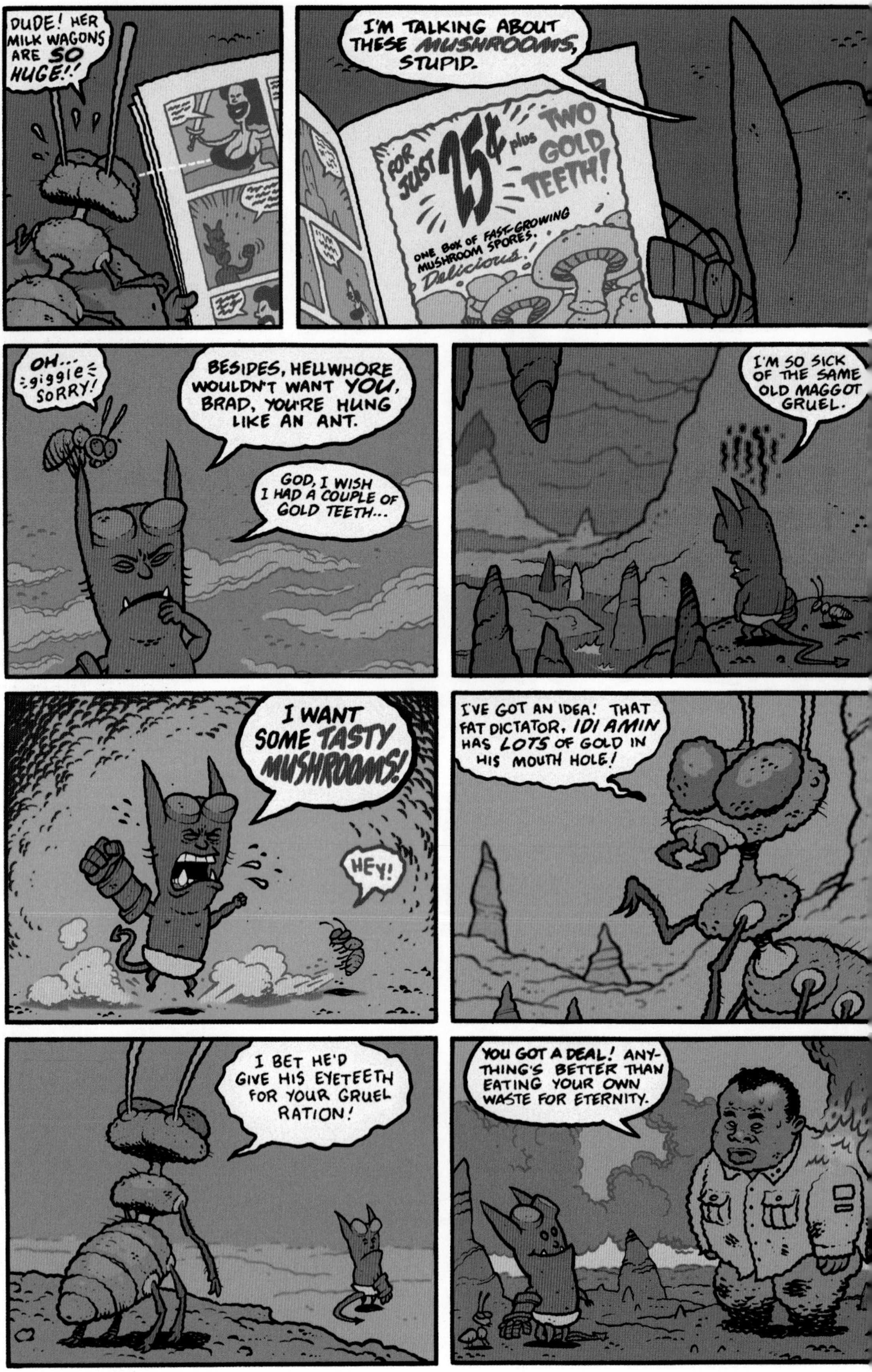
DUDE! HER MILK WAGONS ARE SO HUGE!!
I'M TALKING ABOUT THESE MUSHROOMS, STUPID.
FOR JUST 25¢ plus TWO GOLD TEETH!
ONE BOX OF FAST-GROWING MUSHROOM SPORES.
Delicious.
OH... giggle SORRY!
BESIDES, HELLWHORE WOULDN'T WANT YOU, BRAD, YOU'RE HUNG LIKE AN ANT.
GOD, I WISH I HAD A COUPLE OF GOLD TEETH...
I'M SO SICK OF THE SAME OLD MAGGOT GRUEL.
I WANT SOME TASTY MUSHROOMS!
HEY!
I'VE GOT AN IDEA! THAT FAT DICTATOR, IDI AMIN HAS LOTS OF GOLD IN HIS MOUTH HOLE!
I BET HE'D GIVE HIS EYETEETH FOR YOUR GRUEL RATION!
YOU GOT A DEAL! ANYTHING'S BETTER THAN EATING YOUR OWN WASTE FOR ETERNITY.

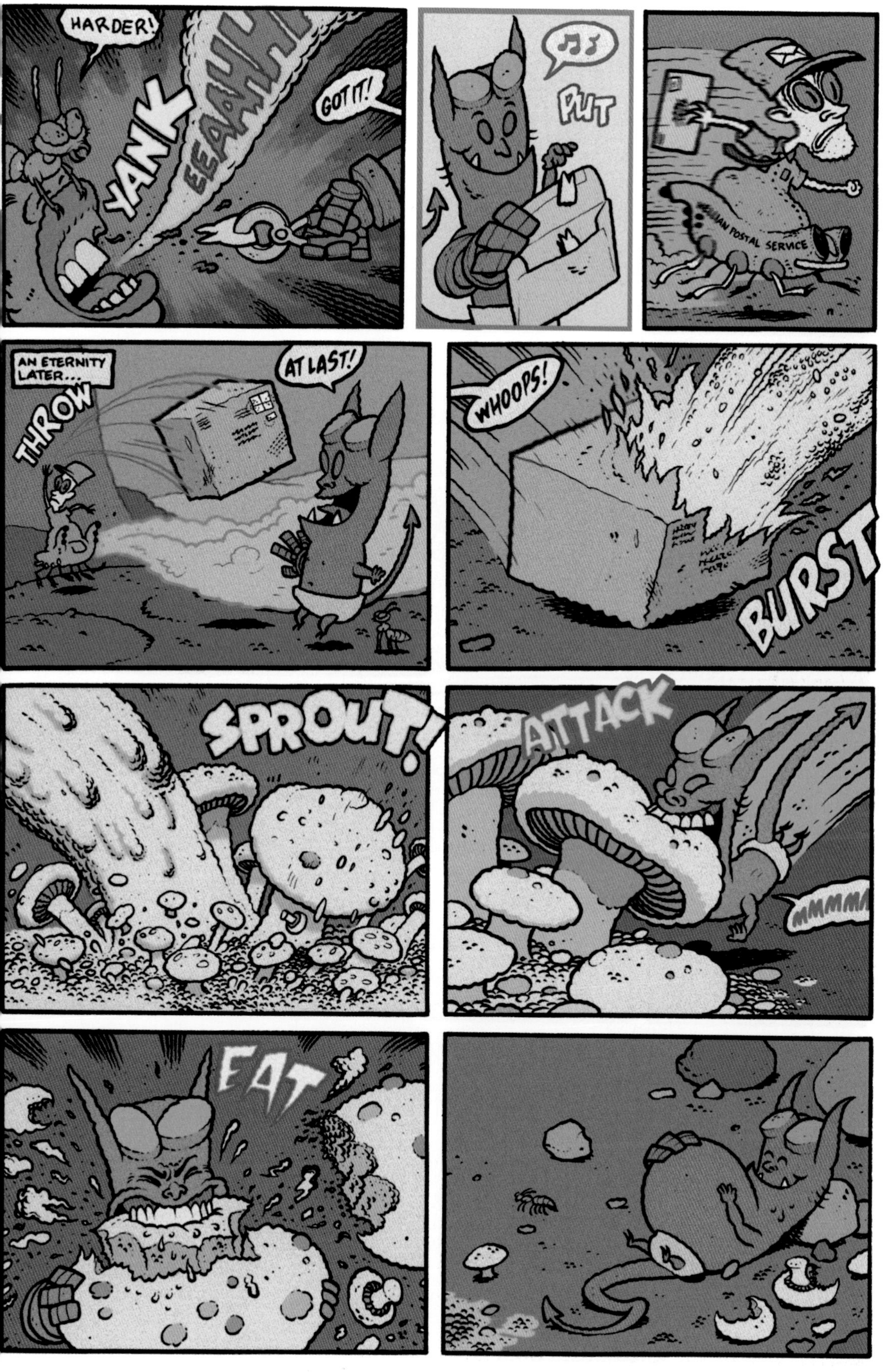
HARDER!
YANK
EEAAH!!
GOT IT!
PUT
AN ETERNITY LATER...
THROW
AT LAST!
WHOOPS!
BURST
SPROUT!
ATTACK
MMMMM
EAT

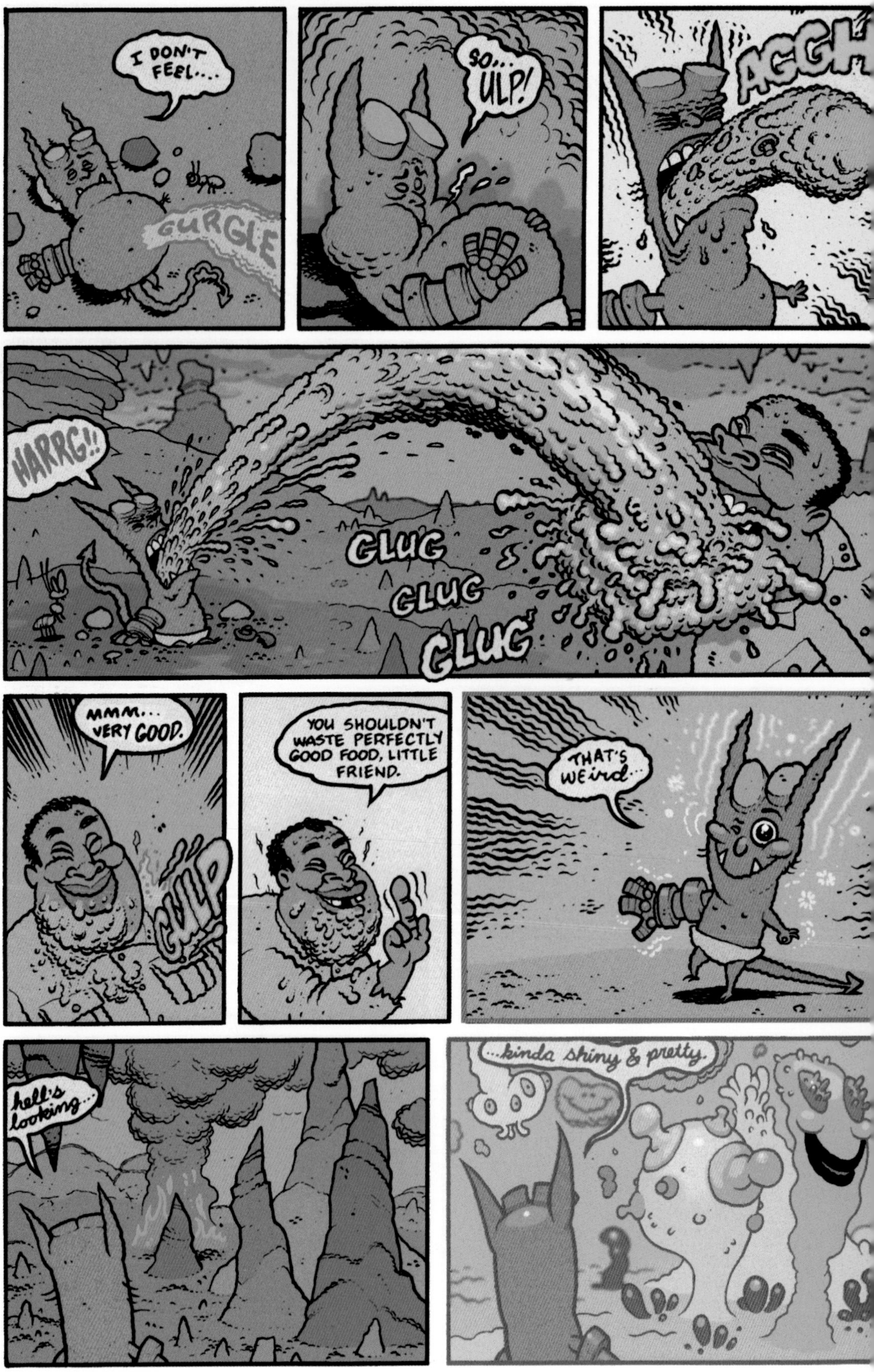
I DON'T FEEL...
GURGLE
SO... ULP!
AGGH
HARRG!!
GLUG
GLUG
GLUG
MMM... VERY GOOD.
GULP
YOU SHOULDN'T WASTE PERFECTLY GOOD FOOD, LITTLE FRIEND.
THAT'S WEird...
hell's looking...
...kinda shiny & pretty.

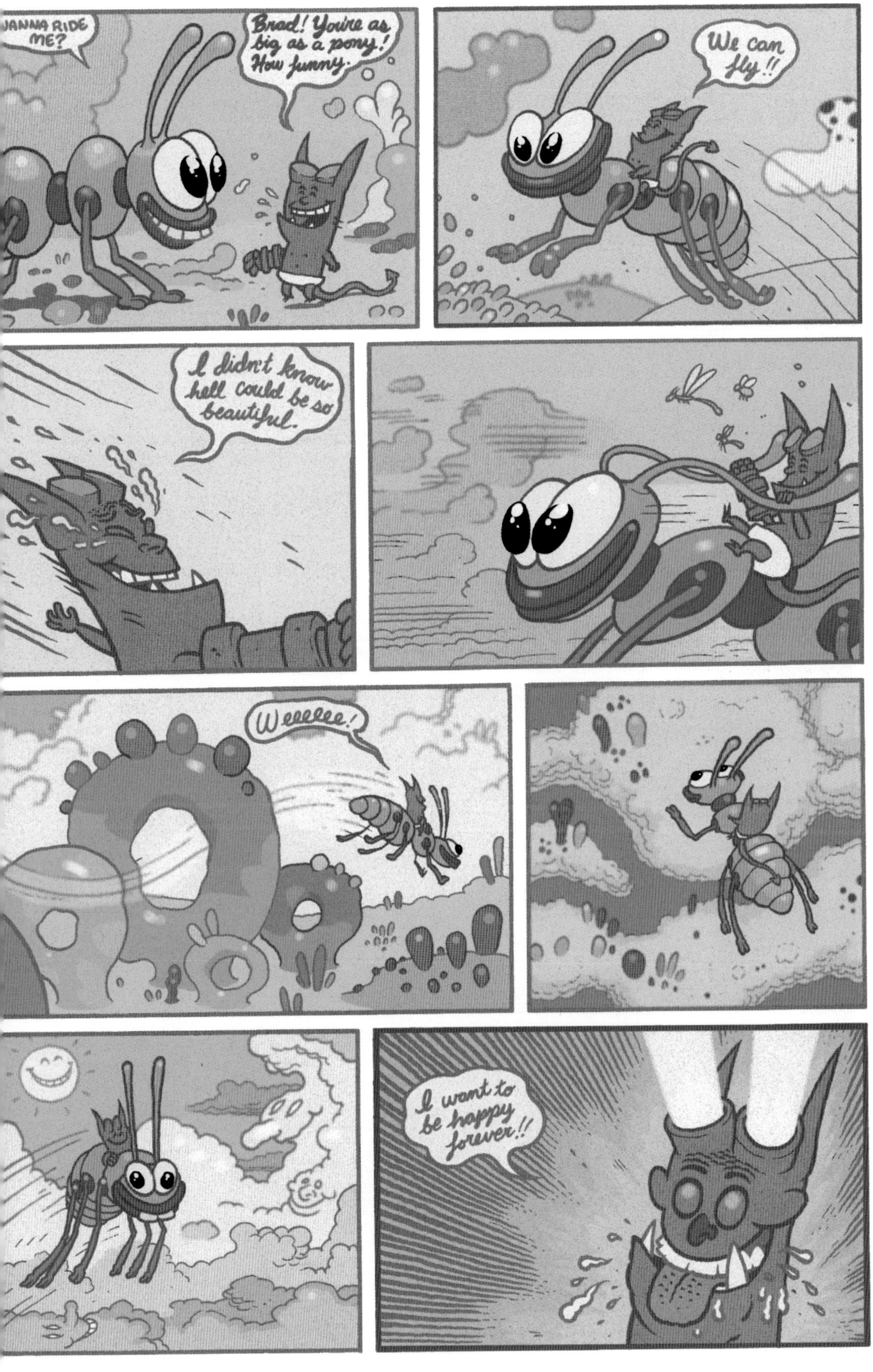
WANNA RIDE ME?
Brad! You're as big as a pony! How funny.
We can fly!!
I didn't know hell could be so beautiful.
Weeeeee!
I want to be happy forever!!

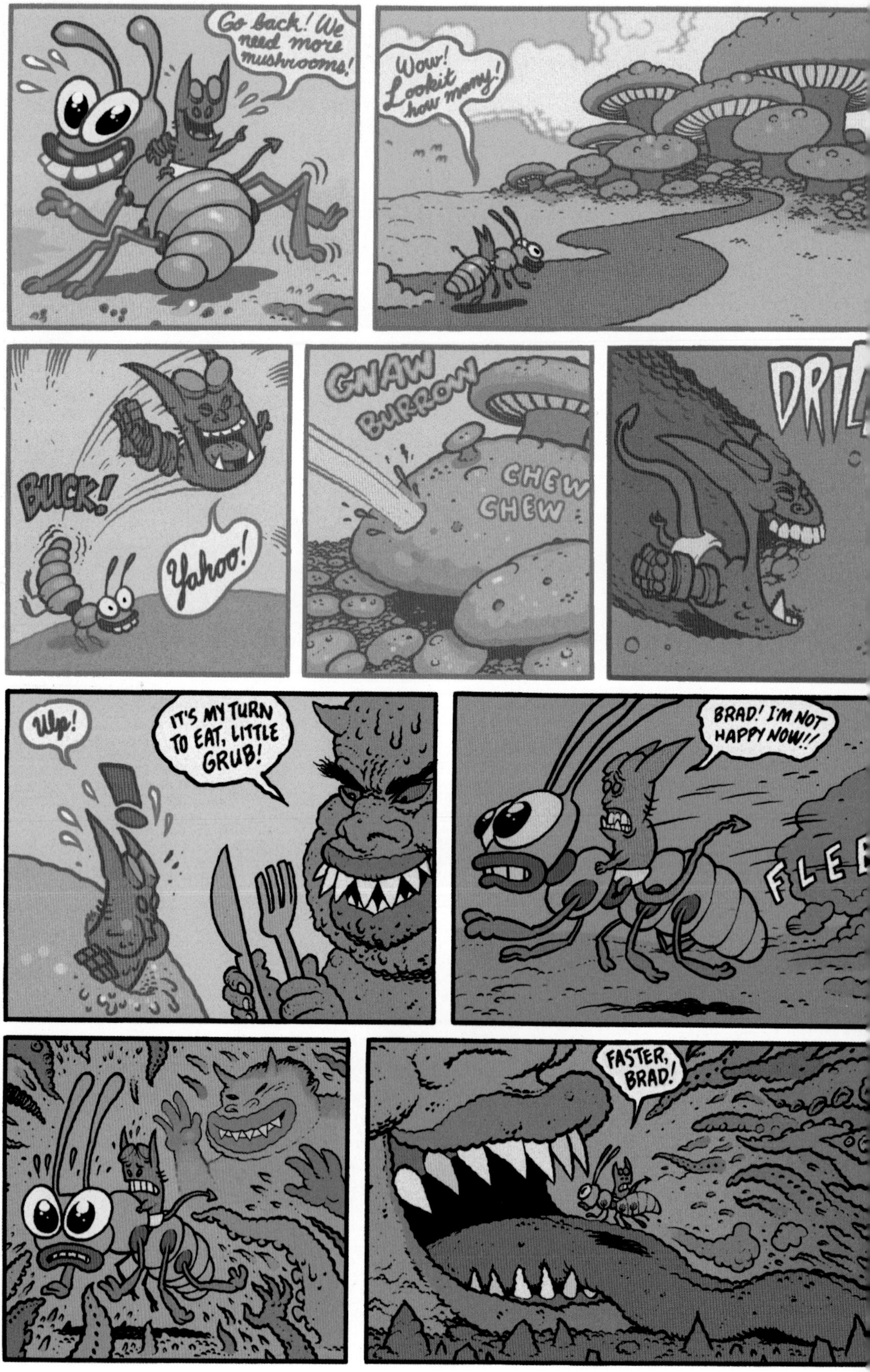

Go back! We need more mushrooms!
Wow! Lookit how many!
BUCK!
Yahoo!
GNAW
BURROW
CHEW CHEW
DRI
Ulp!
IT'S MY TURN TO EAT, LITTLE GRUB!
BRAD! I'M NOT HAPPY NOW!!
FLEE
FASTER, BRAD!

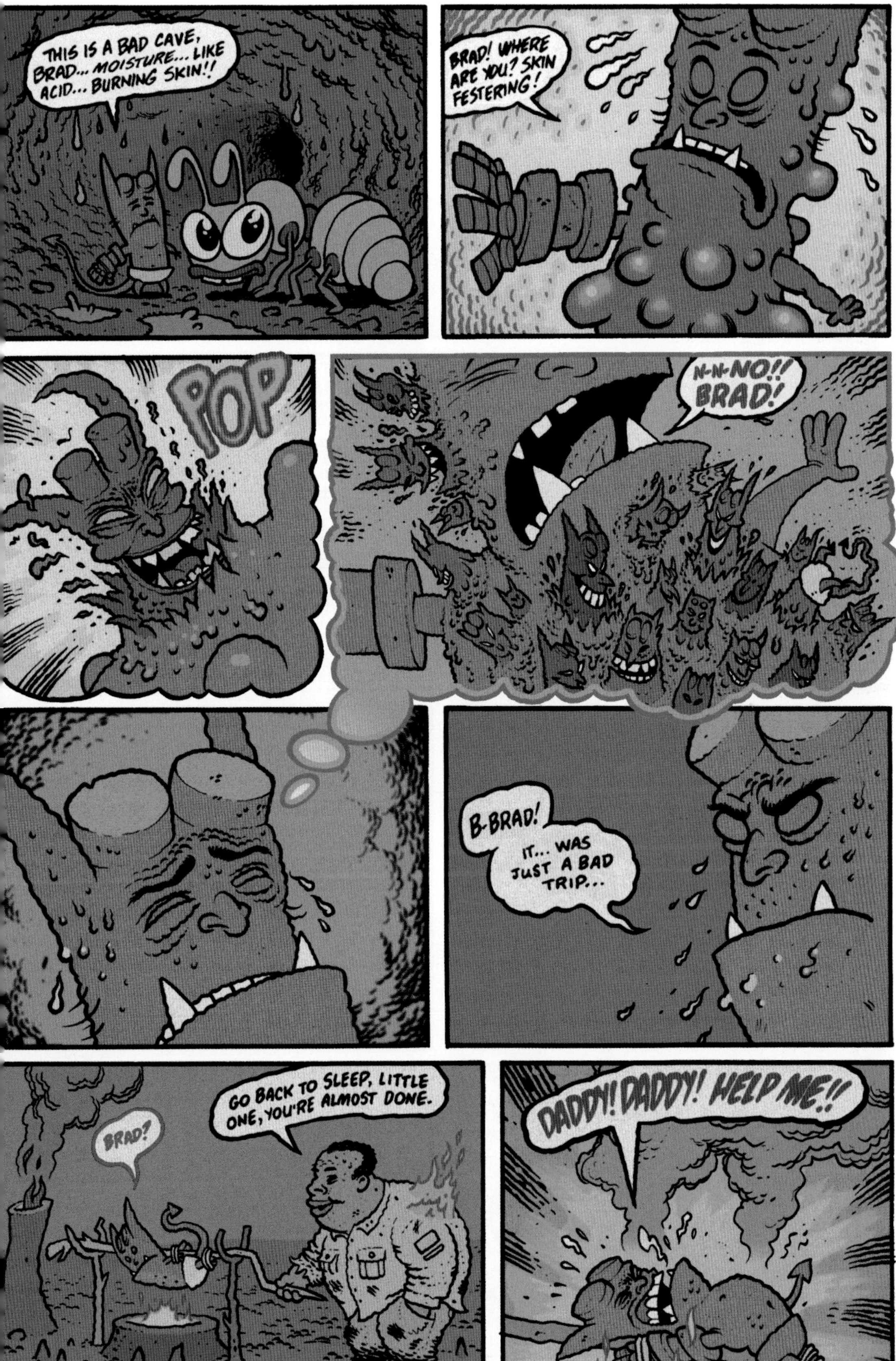
THIS IS A BAD CAVE, BRAD... MOISTURE... LIKE ACID... BURNING SKIN!!
BRAD! WHERE ARE YOU? SKIN FESTERING!
POP
N-N-NO!! BRAD!
B-BRAD!
IT... WAS JUST A BAD TRIP...
BRAD?
GO BACK TO SLEEP, LITTLE ONE, YOU'RE ALMOST DONE.
DADDY! DADDY! HELP ME!!

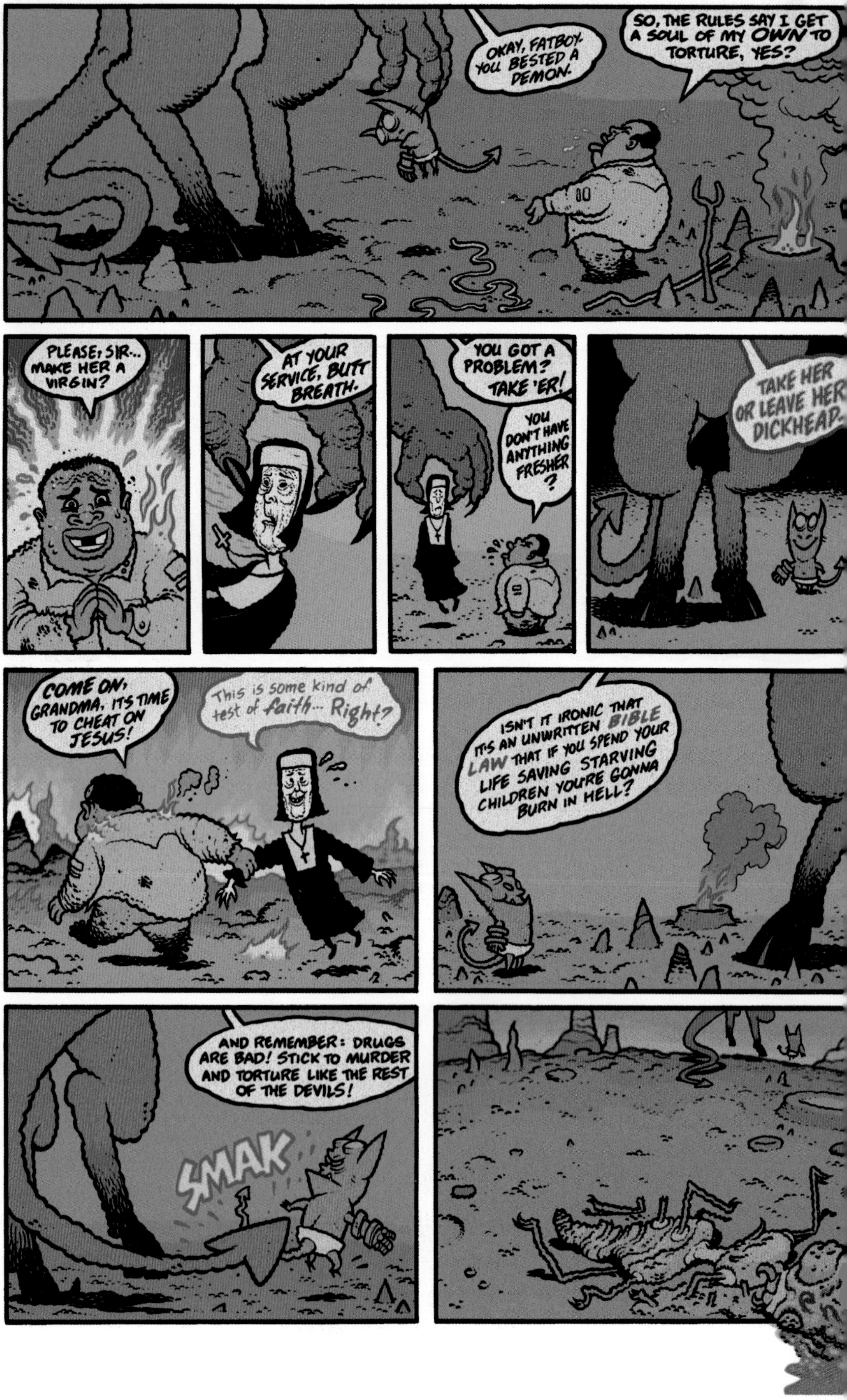
OKAY, FATBOY. YOU BESTED A DEMON.
SO, THE RULES SAY I GET A SOUL OF MY OWN TO TORTURE, YES?
PLEASE, SIR... MAKE HER A VIRGIN?
AT YOUR SERVICE, BUTT BREATH.
YOU GOT A PROBLEM? TAKE 'ER!
YOU DON'T HAVE ANYTHING FRESHER?
TAKE HER OR LEAVE HER DICKHEAD.
COME ON, GRANDMA, IT'S TIME TO CHEAT ON JESUS!
This is some kind of test of faith... Right?
ISN'T IT IRONIC THAT IT'S AN UNWRITTEN BIBLE LAW THAT IF YOU SPEND YOUR LIFE SAVING STARVING CHILDREN YOU'RE GONNA BURN IN HELL?
AND REMEMBER: DRUGS ARE BAD! STICK TO MURDER AND TORTURE LIKE THE REST OF THE DEVILS!
SMAK

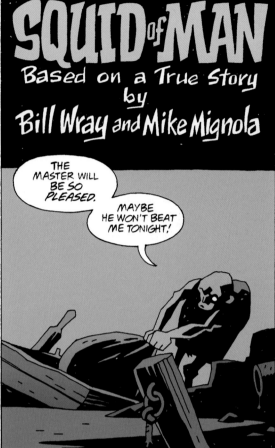

SQUID of MAN
Based on a True Story
by
Bill Wray and Mike Mignola

THE MASTER WILL BE SO PLEASED.

MAYBE HE WON'T BEAT ME TONIGHT!

PLANKTON DEPOOL ROGUE ICTHYOLOGIST

DO NOT ENTER

DID YOU GET ONE?

NICE AND FRESH, MASTER!

SPLOSH!

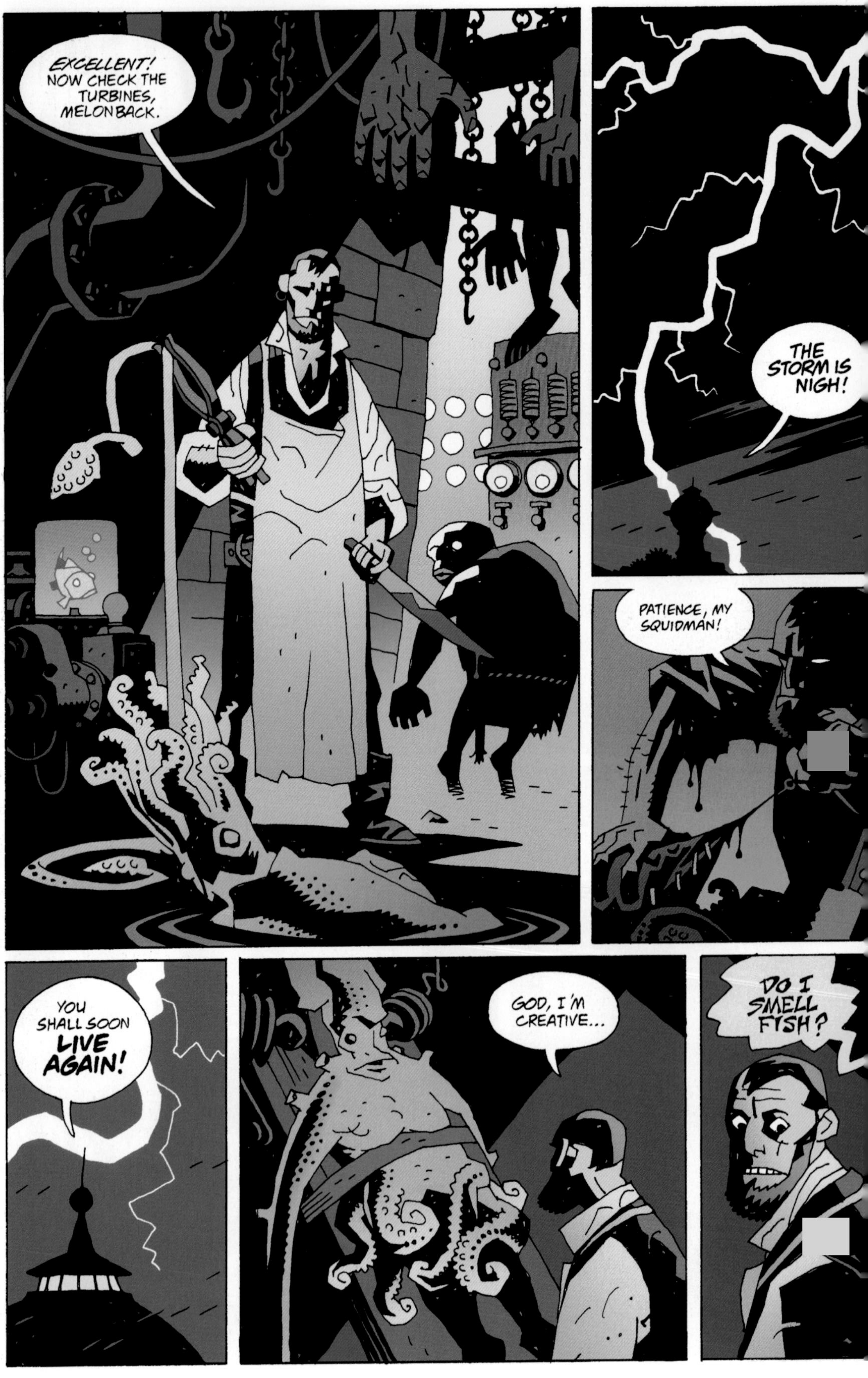
EXCELLENT! NOW CHECK THE TURBINES, MELONBACK.
THE STORM IS NIGH!
PATIENCE, MY SQUIDMAN!
YOU SHALL SOON LIVE AGAIN!
GOD, I'M CREATIVE...
DO I SMELL FISH?

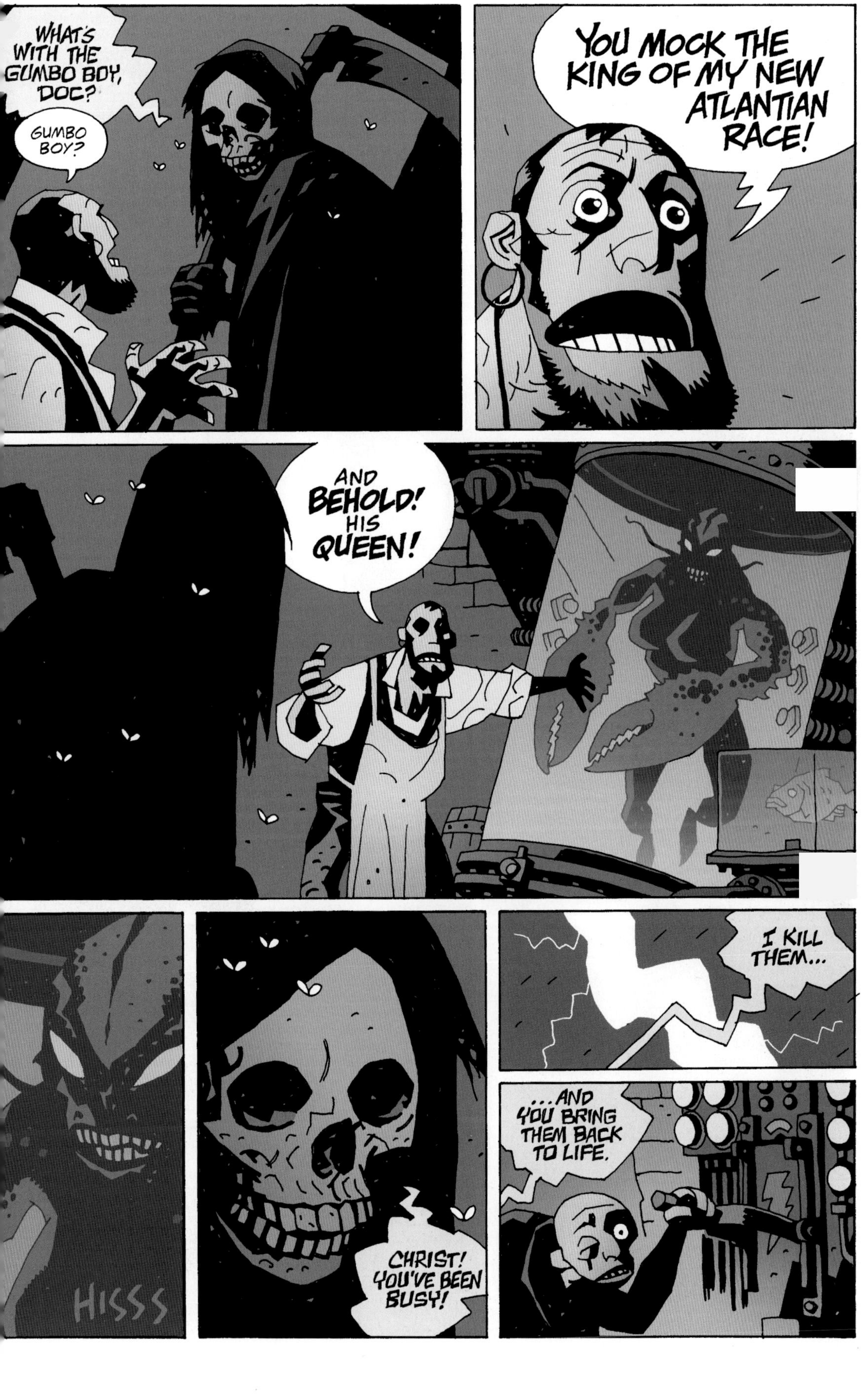
WHAT'S WITH THE GUMBO BOY, DOC?
GUMBO BOY?
YOU MOCK THE KING OF MY NEW ATLANTIAN RACE!
AND BEHOLD! HIS QUEEN!
HISSS
CHRIST! YOU'VE BEEN BUSY!
I KILL THEM...
...AND YOU BRING THEM BACK TO LIFE.

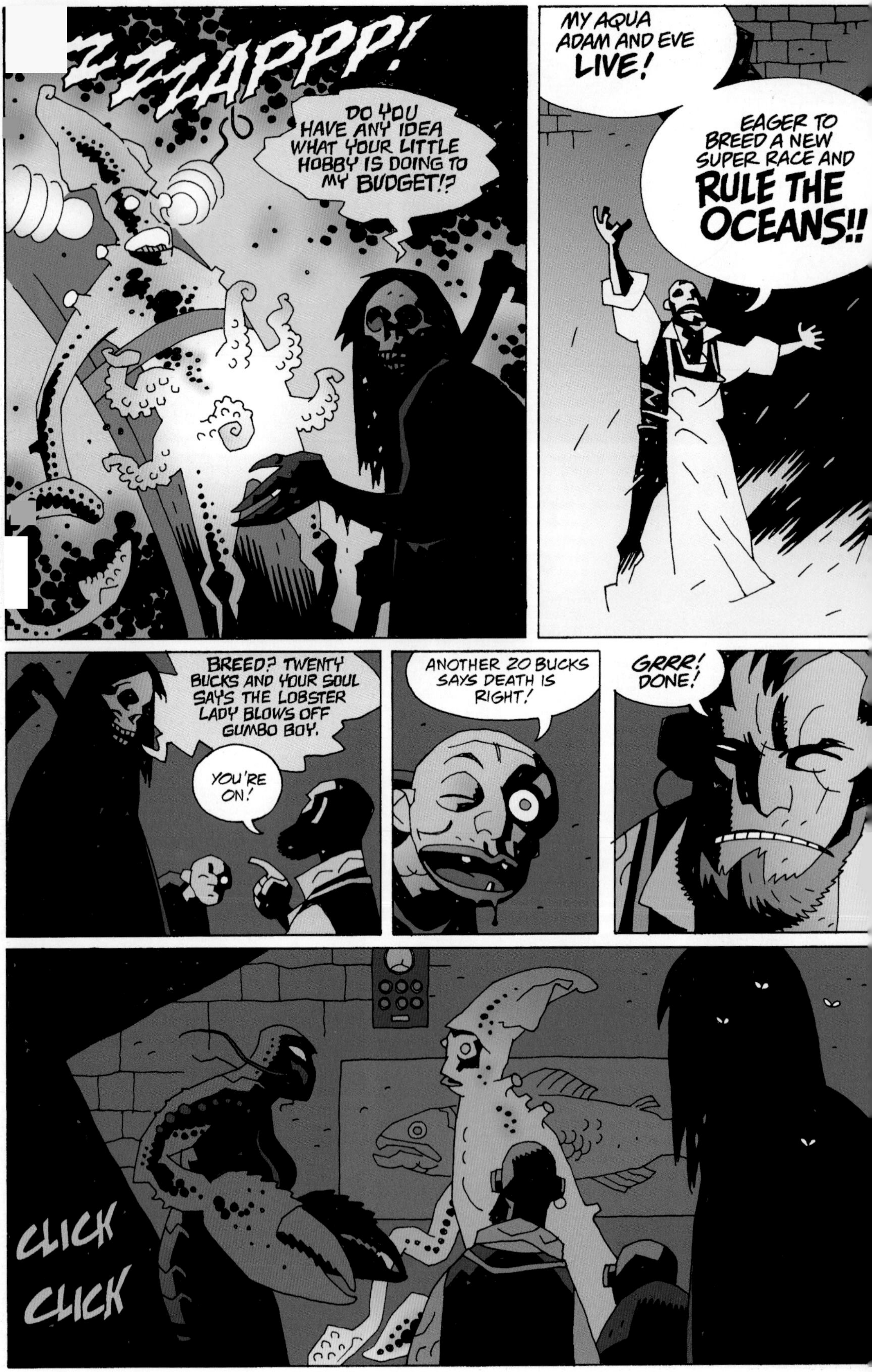
ZZZZAPPPP!
DO YOU HAVE ANY IDEA WHAT YOUR LITTLE HOBBY IS DOING TO MY BUDGET!?
MY AQUA ADAM AND EVE LIVE!
EAGER TO BREED A NEW SUPER RACE AND RULE THE OCEANS!!
BREED? TWENTY BUCKS AND YOUR SOUL SAYS THE LOBSTER LADY BLOWS OFF GUMBO BOY.
YOU'RE ON!
ANOTHER 20 BUCKS SAYS DEATH IS RIGHT!
GRRR! DONE!
CLICK
CLICK

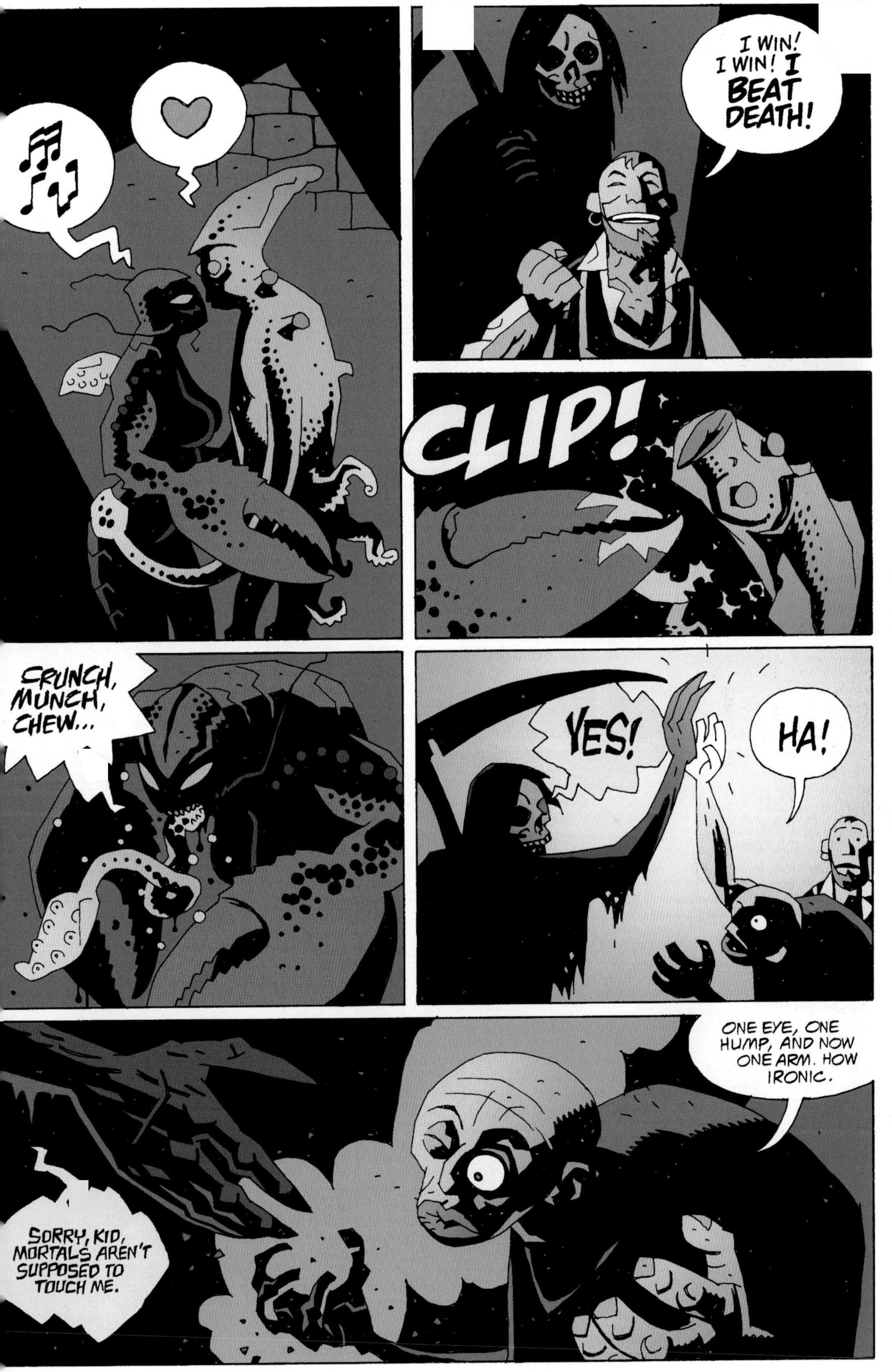

I WIN! I WIN! I BEAT DEATH!
CLIP!
CRUNCH, MUNCH, CHEW...
YES!
HA!
ONE EYE, ONE HUMP, AND NOW ONE ARM. HOW IRONIC.
SORRY, KID, MORTALS AREN'T SUPPOSED TO TOUCH ME.

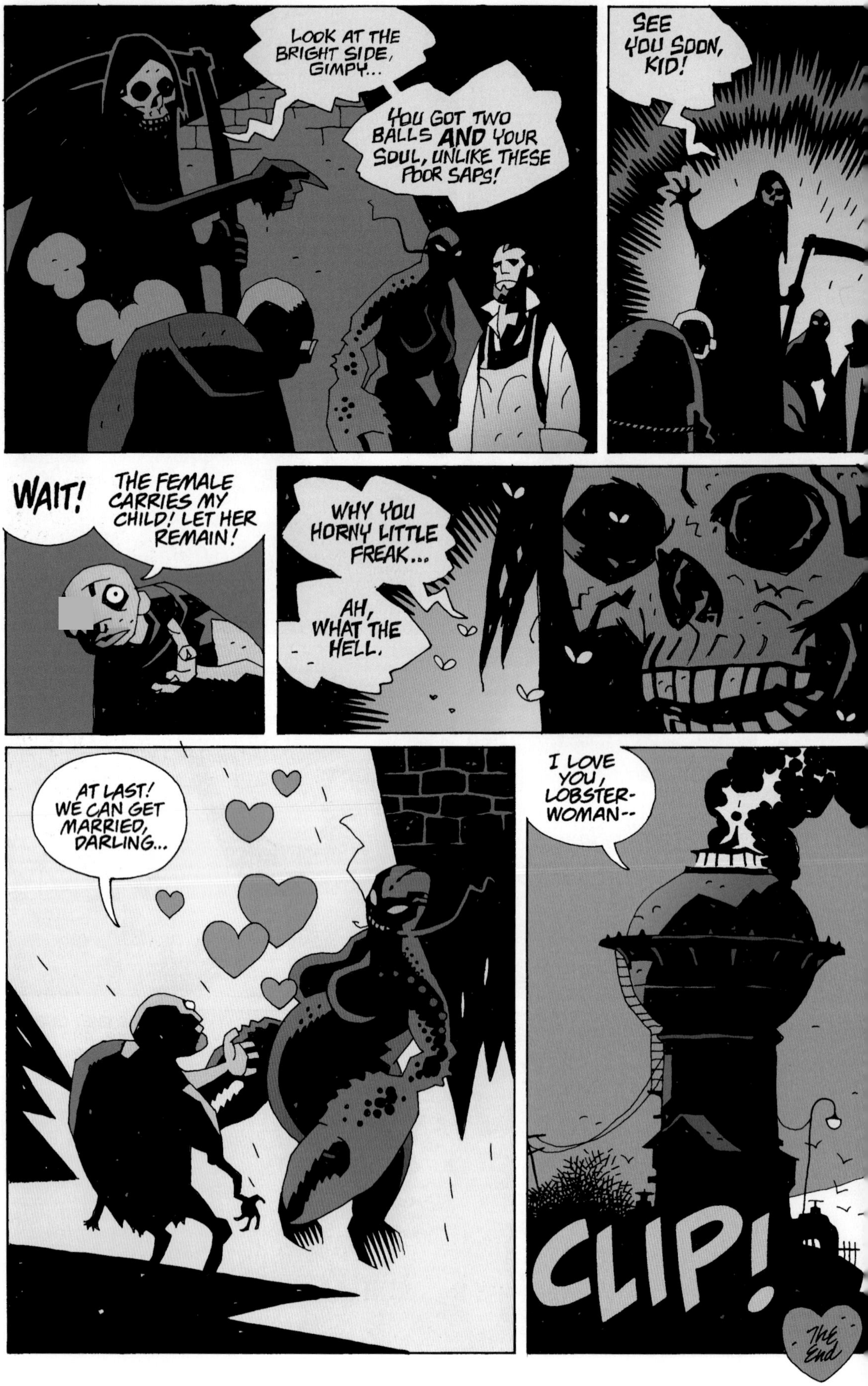

LOOK AT THE BRIGHT SIDE, GIMPY...
YOU GOT TWO BALLS AND YOUR SOUL, UNLIKE THESE POOR SAPS!
SEE YOU SOON, KID!
WAIT!
THE FEMALE CARRIES MY CHILD! LET HER REMAIN!
WHY YOU HORNY LITTLE FREAK...
AH, WHAT THE HELL.
AT LAST! WE CAN GET MARRIED, DARLING...
I LOVE YOU, LOBSTER-WOMAN--
CLIP!
The End

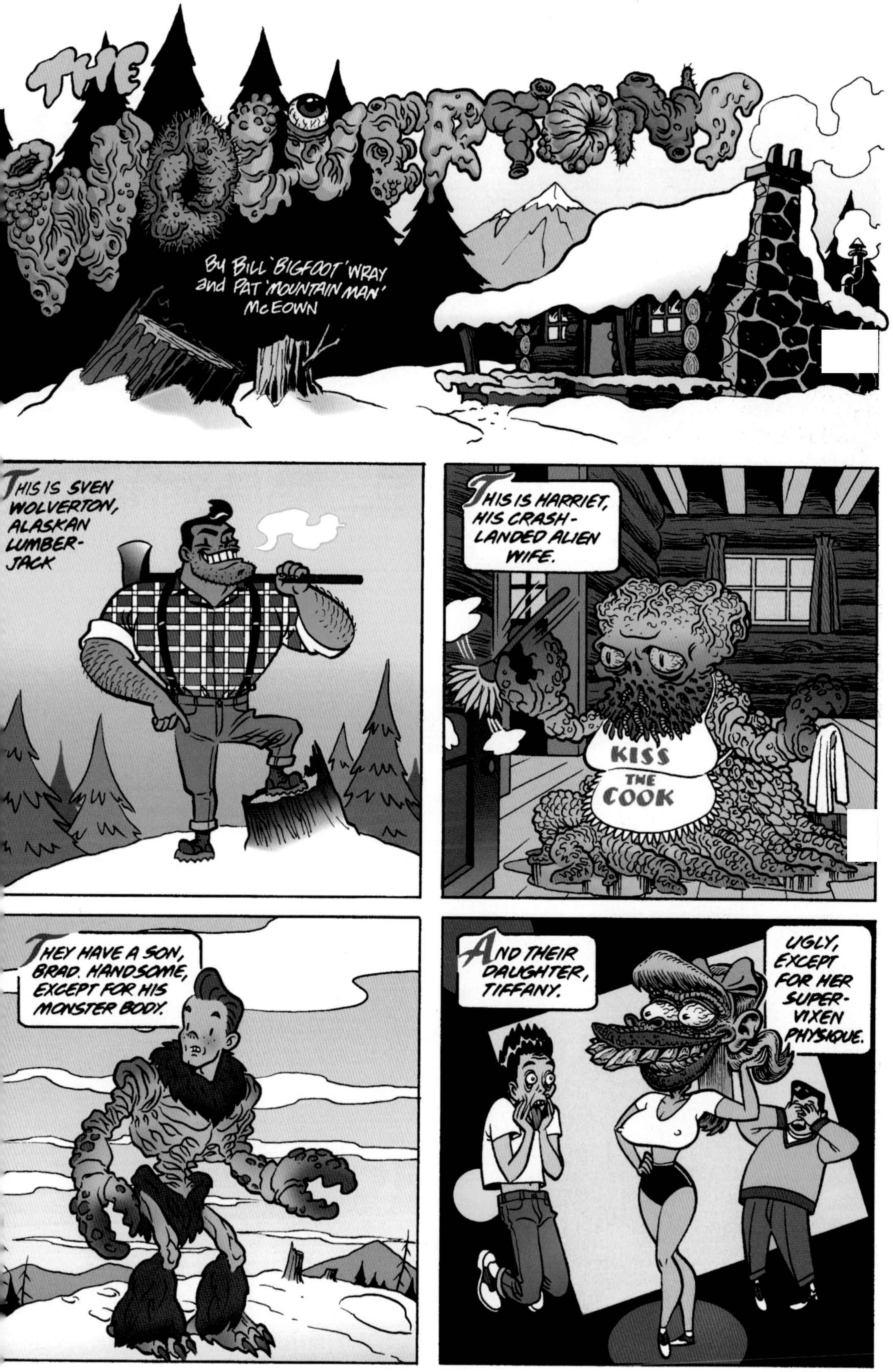
THE
By BILL 'BIGFOOT' WRAY and PAT 'MOUNTAIN MAN' McEOWN
THIS IS SVEN WOLVERTON, ALASKAN LUMBER-JACK
THIS IS HARRIET, HIS CRASH-LANDED ALIEN WIFE.
KISS THE COOK
THEY HAVE A SON, BRAD. HANDSOME, EXCEPT FOR HIS MONSTER BODY.
AND THEIR DAUGHTER, TIFFANY.
UGLY, EXCEPT FOR HER SUPER-VIXEN PHYSIQUE.

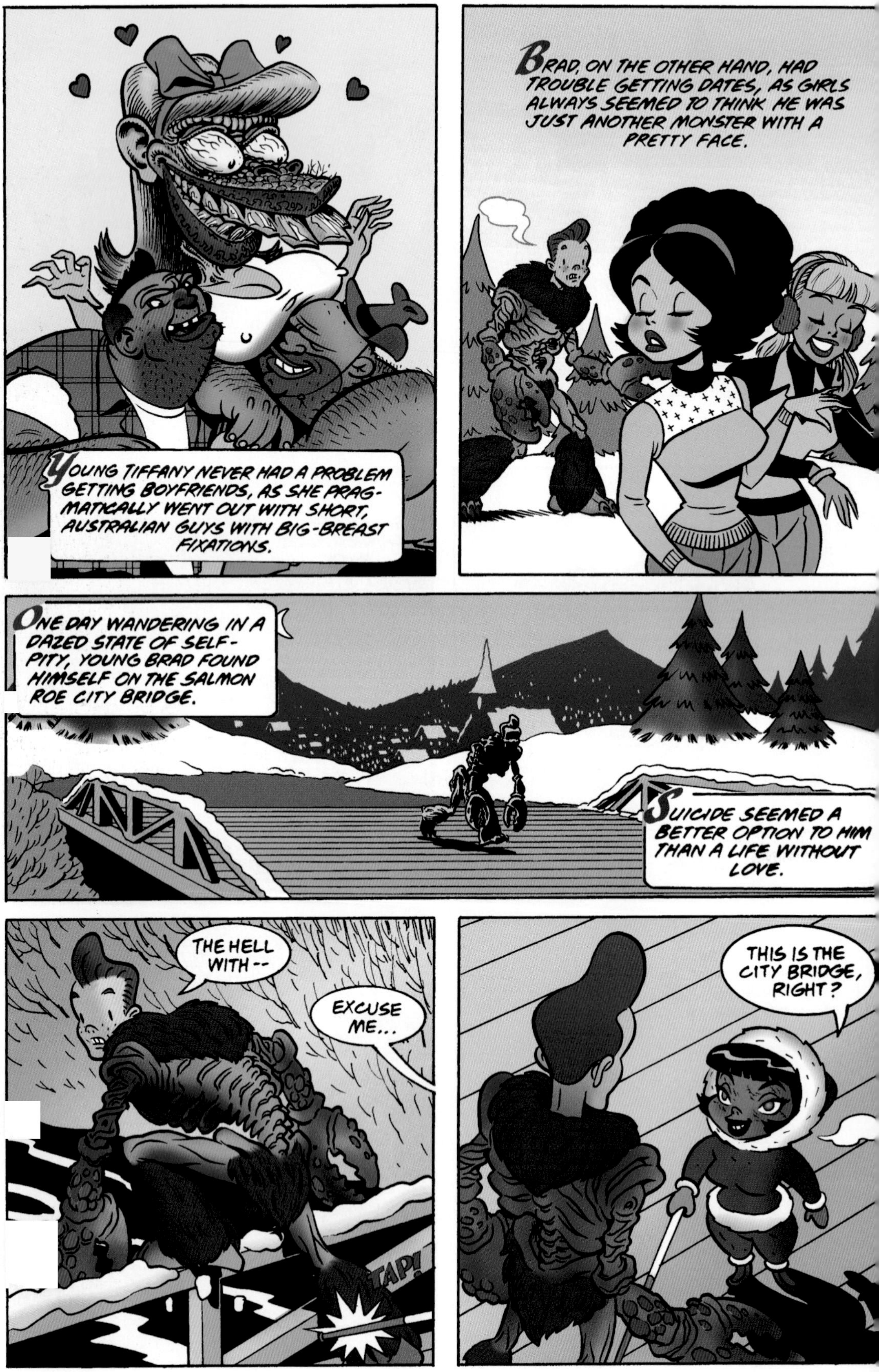
YOUNG TIFFANY NEVER HAD A PROBLEM GETTING BOYFRIENDS, AS SHE PRAG-MATICALLY WENT OUT WITH SHORT, AUSTRALIAN GUYS WITH BIG-BREAST FIXATIONS.
BRAD, ON THE OTHER HAND, HAD TROUBLE GETTING DATES, AS GIRLS ALWAYS SEEMED TO THINK HE WAS JUST ANOTHER MONSTER WITH A PRETTY FACE.
ONE DAY WANDERING IN A DAZED STATE OF SELF-PITY, YOUNG BRAD FOUND HIMSELF ON THE SALMON ROE CITY BRIDGE.
SUICIDE SEEMED A BETTER OPTION TO HIM THAN A LIFE WITHOUT LOVE.
THE HELL WITH --
EXCUSE ME...
TAP!
THIS IS THE CITY BRIDGE, RIGHT?

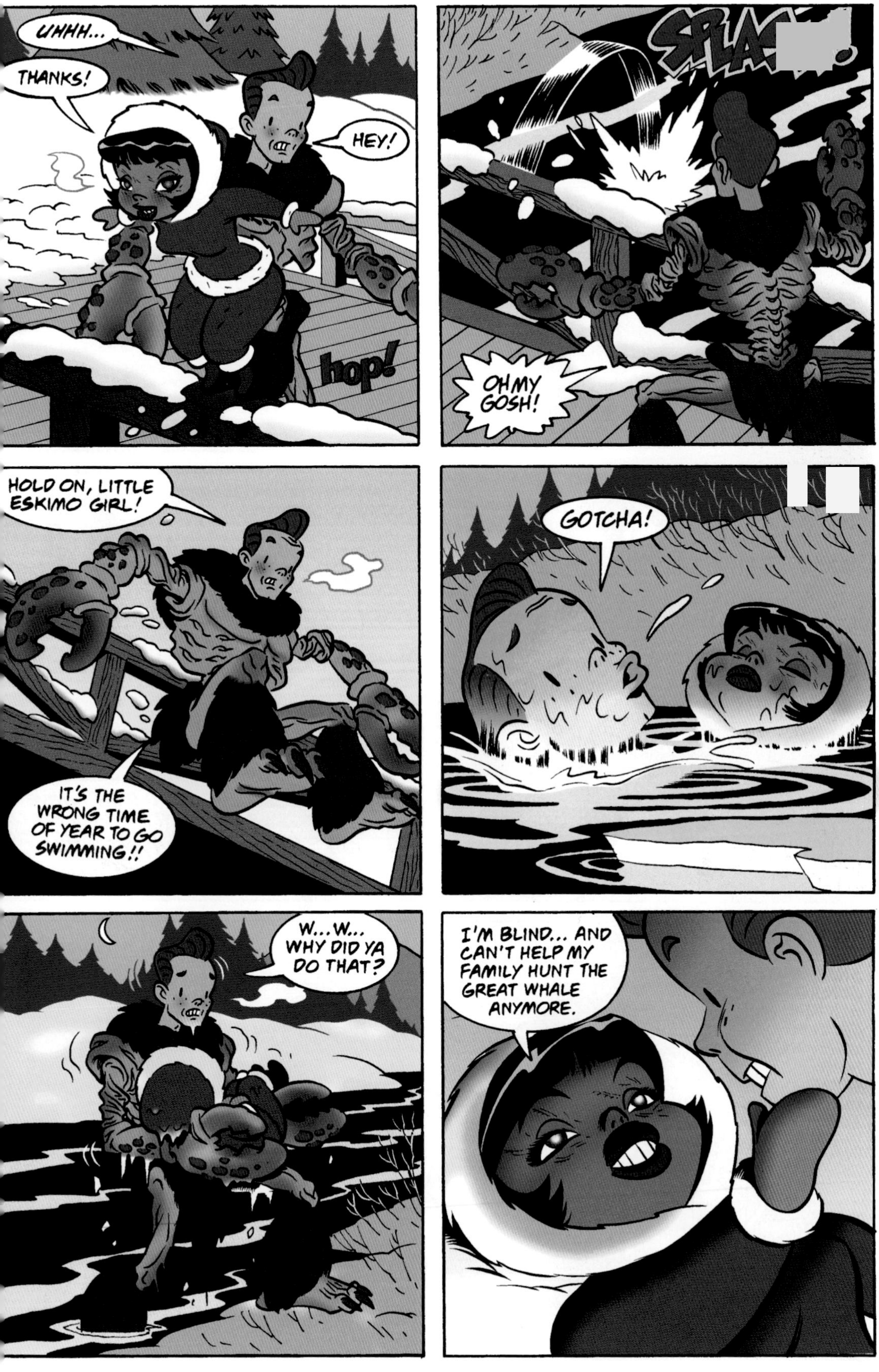
UHHH...
THANKS!
HEY!
hop!
OH MY GOSH!
HOLD ON, LITTLE ESKIMO GIRL!
IT'S THE WRONG TIME OF YEAR TO GO SWIMMING!!
GOTCHA!
W...W... WHY DID YA DO THAT?
I'M BLIND... AND CAN'T HELP MY FAMILY HUNT THE GREAT WHALE ANYMORE.

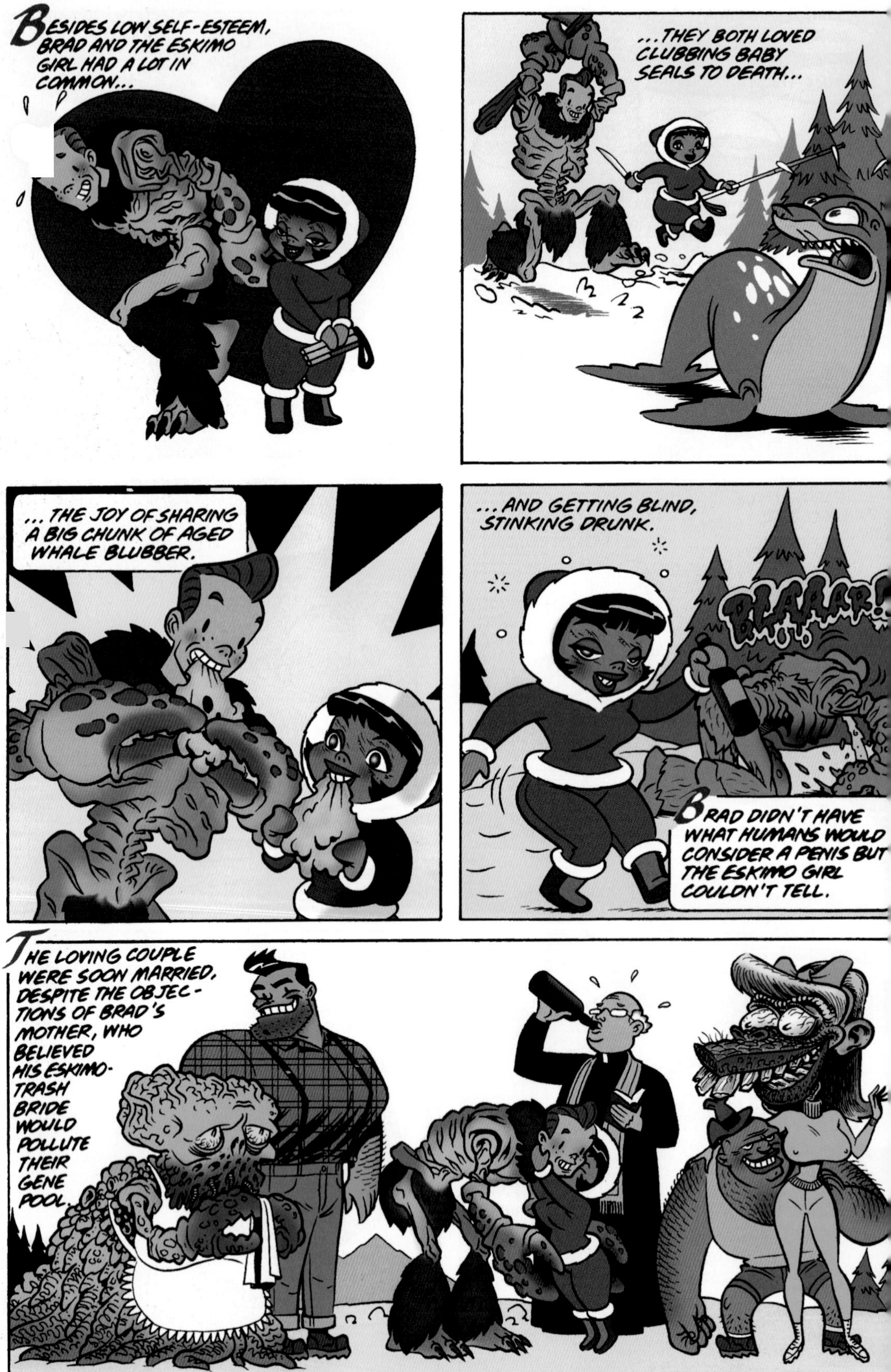
BESIDES LOW SELF-ESTEEM, BRAD AND THE ESKIMO GIRL HAD A LOT IN COMMON...
...THEY BOTH LOVED CLUBBING BABY SEALS TO DEATH...
...THE JOY OF SHARING A BIG CHUNK OF AGED WHALE BLUBBER.
...AND GETTING BLIND, STINKING DRUNK.
BRAD DIDN'T HAVE WHAT HUMANS WOULD CONSIDER A PENIS BUT THE ESKIMO GIRL COULDN'T TELL.
THE LOVING COUPLE WERE SOON MARRIED, DESPITE THE OBJECTIONS OF BRAD'S MOTHER, WHO BELIEVED HIS ESKIMO-TRASH BRIDE WOULD POLLUTE THEIR GENE POOL.

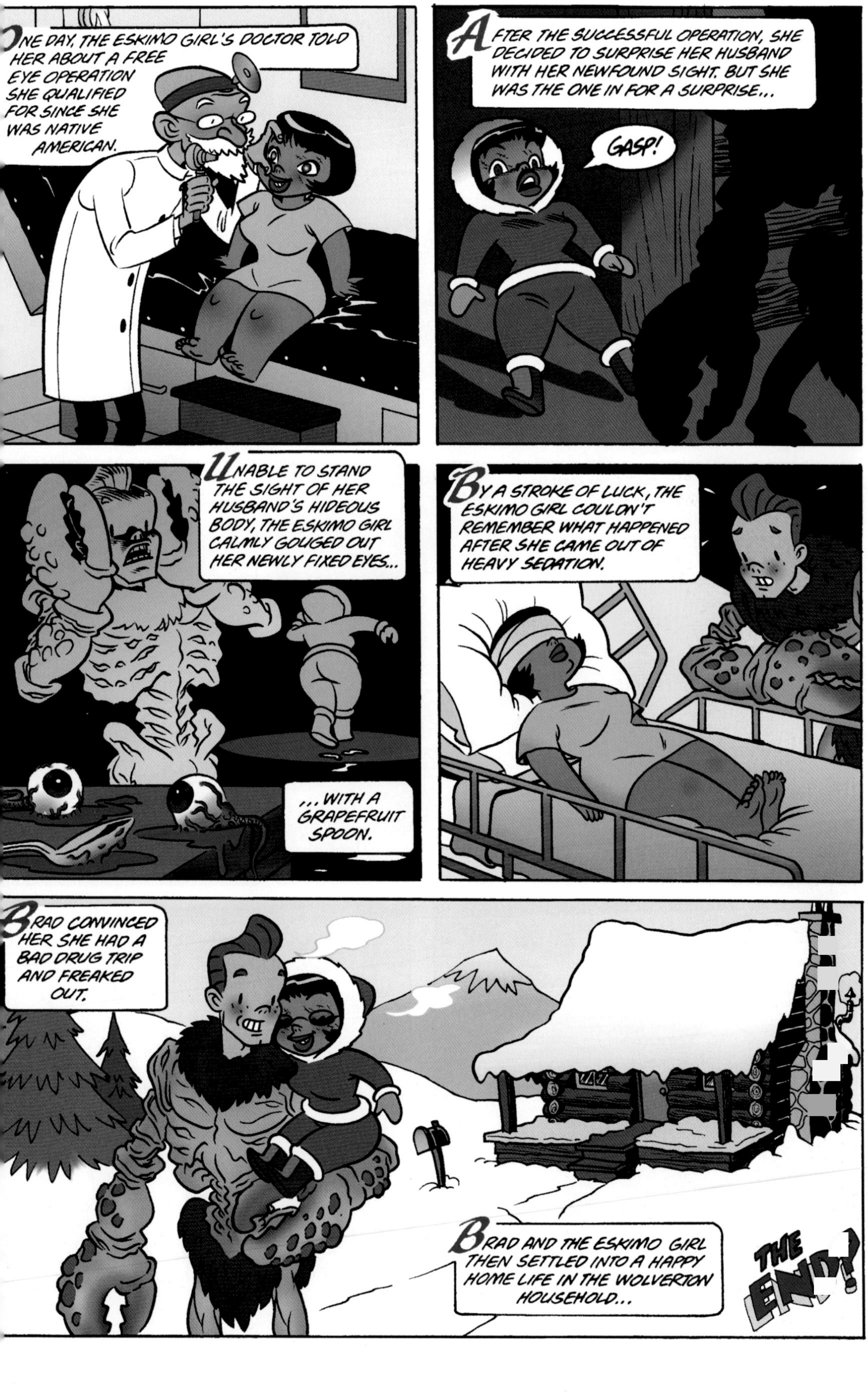
ONE DAY, THE ESKIMO GIRL'S DOCTOR TOLD HER ABOUT A FREE EYE OPERATION SHE QUALIFIED FOR SINCE SHE WAS NATIVE AMERICAN.
AFTER THE SUCCESSFUL OPERATION, SHE DECIDED TO SURPRISE HER HUSBAND WITH HER NEWFOUND SIGHT. BUT SHE WAS THE ONE IN FOR A SURPRISE...
GASP!
UNABLE TO STAND THE SIGHT OF HER HUSBAND'S HIDEOUS BODY, THE ESKIMO GIRL CALMLY GOUGED OUT HER NEWLY FIXED EYES...
...WITH A GRAPEFRUIT SPOON.
BY A STROKE OF LUCK, THE ESKIMO GIRL COULDN'T REMEMBER WHAT HAPPENED AFTER SHE CAME OUT OF HEAVY SEDATION.
BRAD CONVINCED HER SHE HAD A BAD DRUG TRIP AND FREAKED OUT.
BRAD AND THE ESKIMO GIRL THEN SETTLED INTO A HAPPY HOME LIFE IN THE WOLVERTON HOUSEHOLD...
THE END!

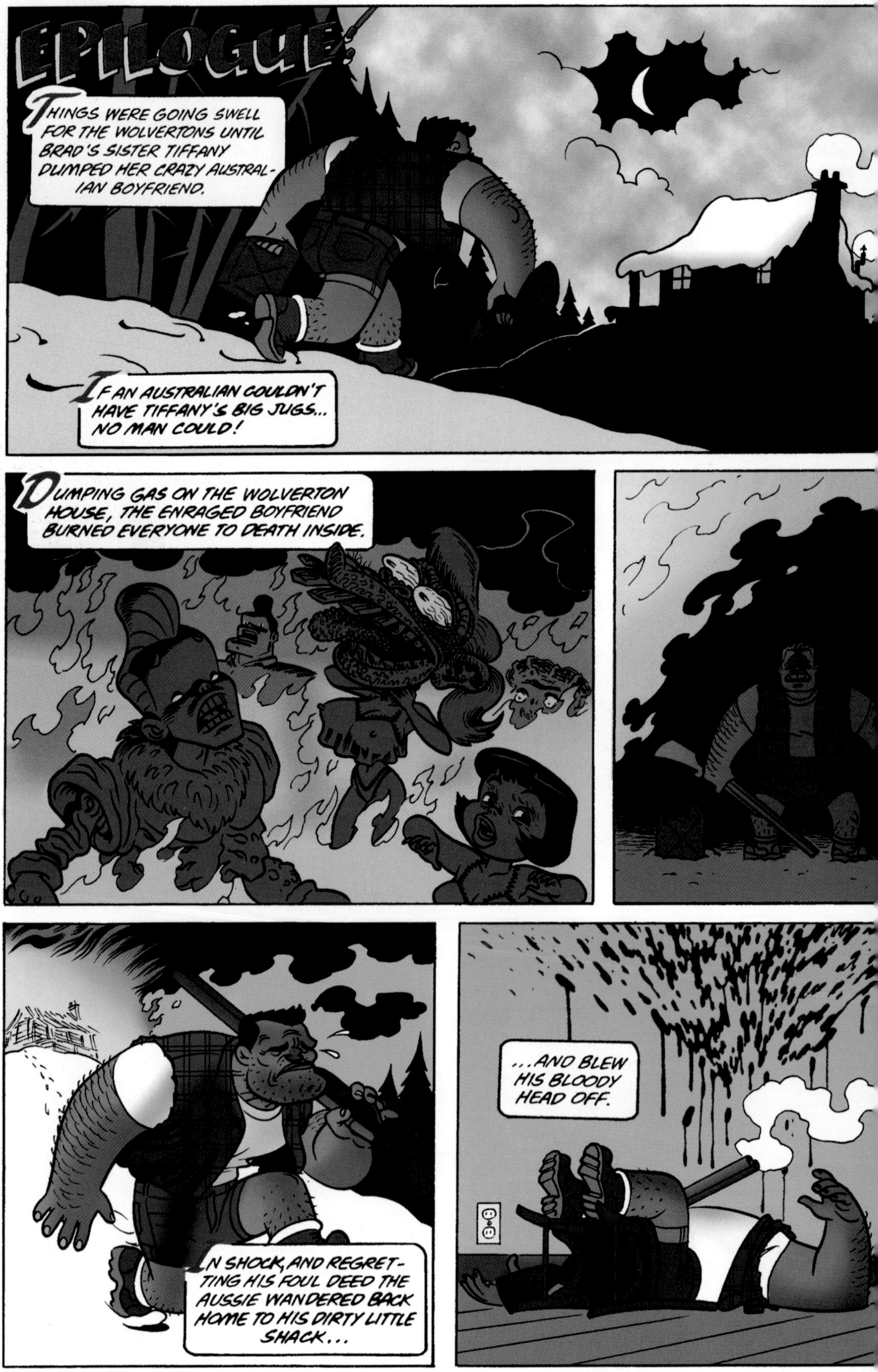
EPILOGUE
THINGS WERE GOING SWELL FOR THE WOLVERTONS UNTIL BRAD'S SISTER TIFFANY DUMPED HER CRAZY AUSTRALIAN BOYFRIEND.
IF AN AUSTRALIAN COULDN'T HAVE TIFFANY'S BIG JUGS... NO MAN COULD!
DUMPING GAS ON THE WOLVERTON HOUSE, THE ENRAGED BOYFRIEND BURNED EVERYONE TO DEATH INSIDE.
IN SHOCK, AND REGRETTING HIS FOUL DEED THE AUSSIE WANDERED BACK HOME TO HIS DIRTY LITTLE SHACK...
...AND BLEW HIS BLOODY HEAD OFF.

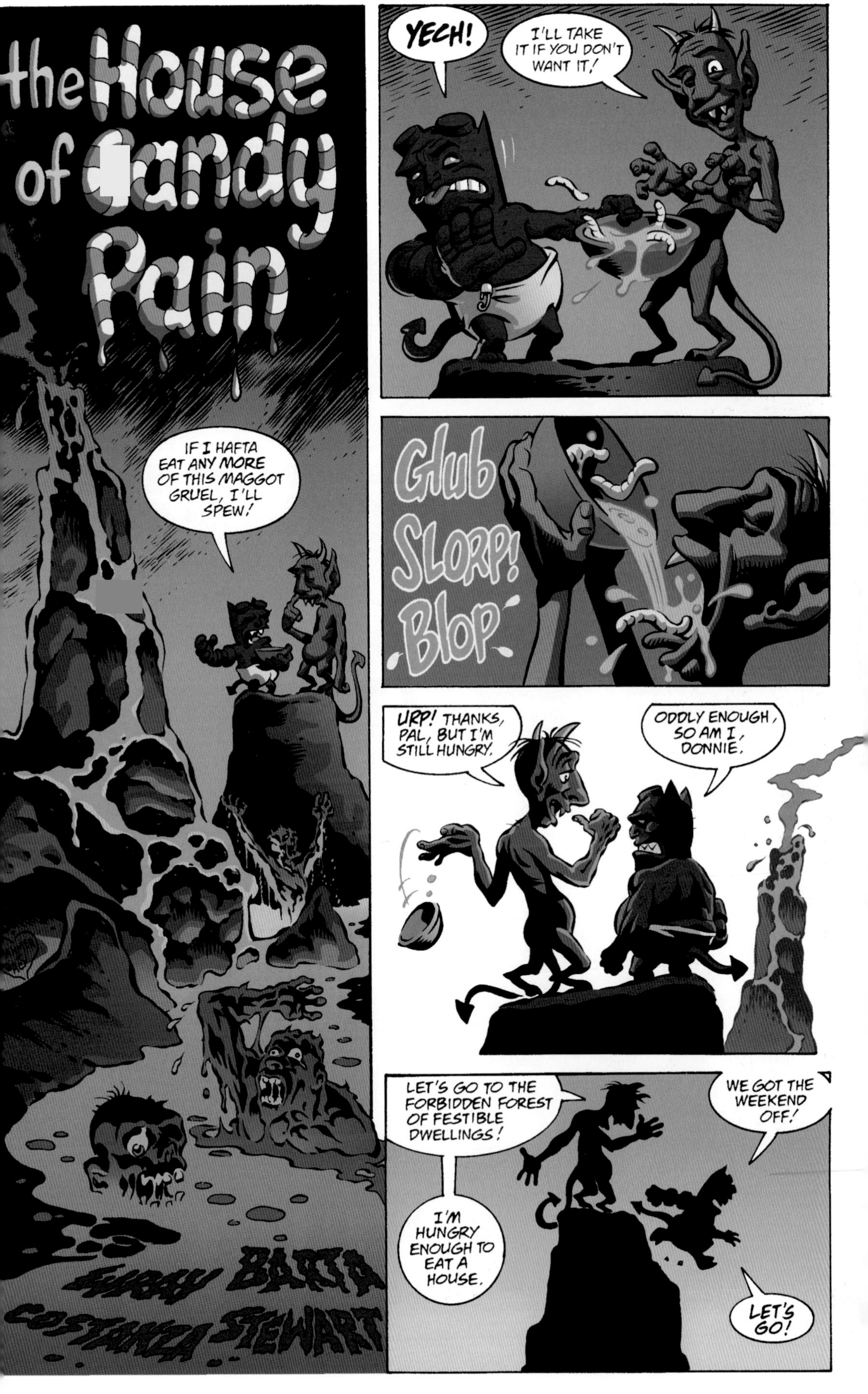

the House of Candy Pain
IF I HAFTA EAT ANY MORE OF THIS MAGGOT GRUEL, I'LL SPEW!
BATTA
COSTANZA
STEWART
YECH!
I'LL TAKE IT IF YOU DON'T WANT IT!
Glub
SLORP!
Blop
URP! THANKS, PAL, BUT I'M STILL HUNGRY.
ODDLY ENOUGH, SO AM I, DONNIE.
LET'S GO TO THE FORBIDDEN FOREST OF FESTIBLE DWELLINGS!
I'M HUNGRY ENOUGH TO EAT A HOUSE.
WE GOT THE WEEKEND OFF!
LET'S GO!

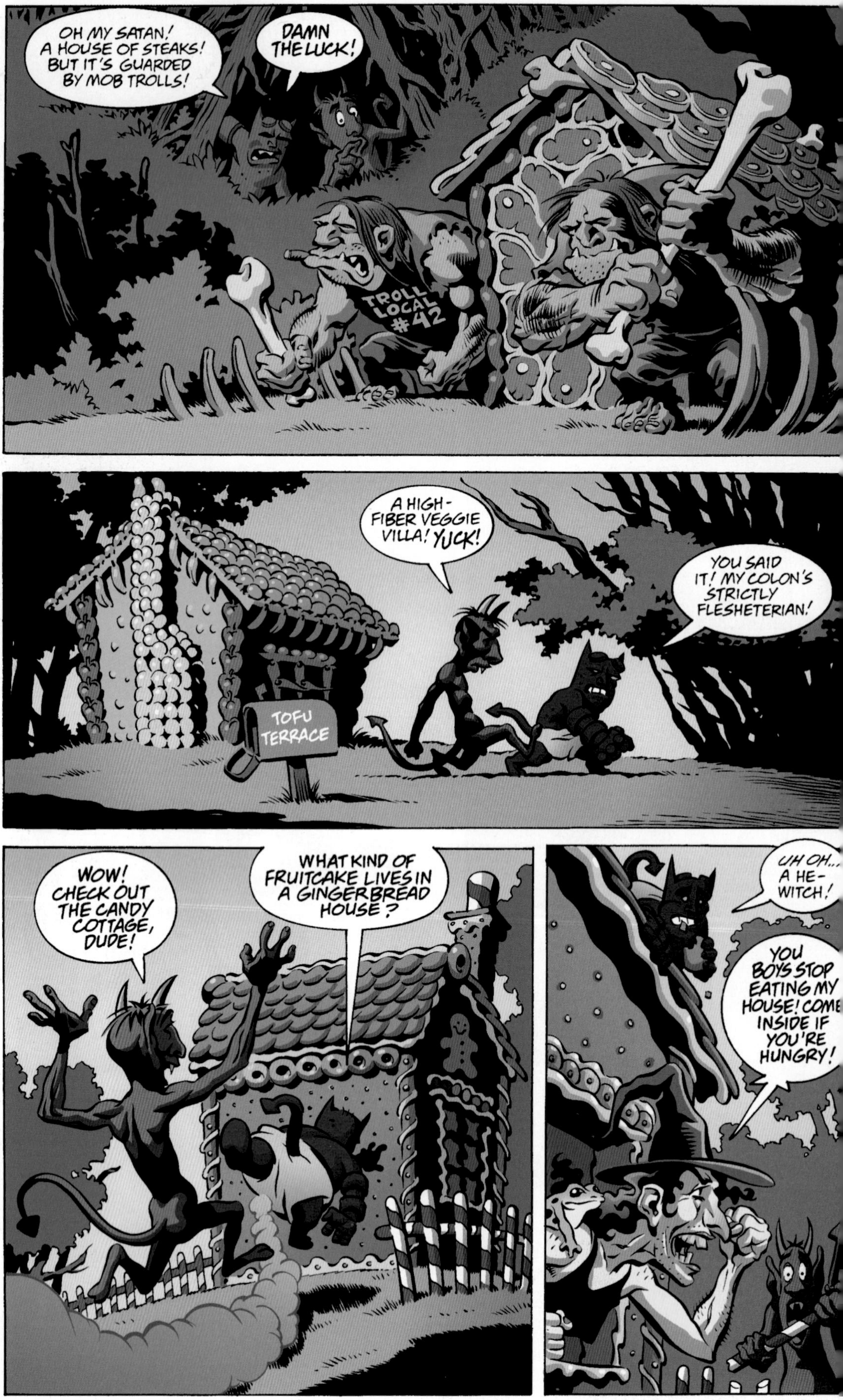
OH MY SATAN! A HOUSE OF STEAKS! BUT IT'S GUARDED BY MOB TROLLS!
DAMN THE LUCK!
TROLL LOCAL #42
A HIGH-FIBER VEGGIE VILLA! YUCK!
YOU SAID IT! MY COLON'S STRICTLY FLESHETERIAN!
TOFU TERRACE
WOW! CHECK OUT THE CANDY COTTAGE, DUDE!
WHAT KIND OF FRUITCAKE LIVES IN A GINGERBREAD HOUSE?
UH OH... A HE-WITCH!
YOU BOYS STOP EATING MY HOUSE! COME INSIDE IF YOU'RE HUNGRY!

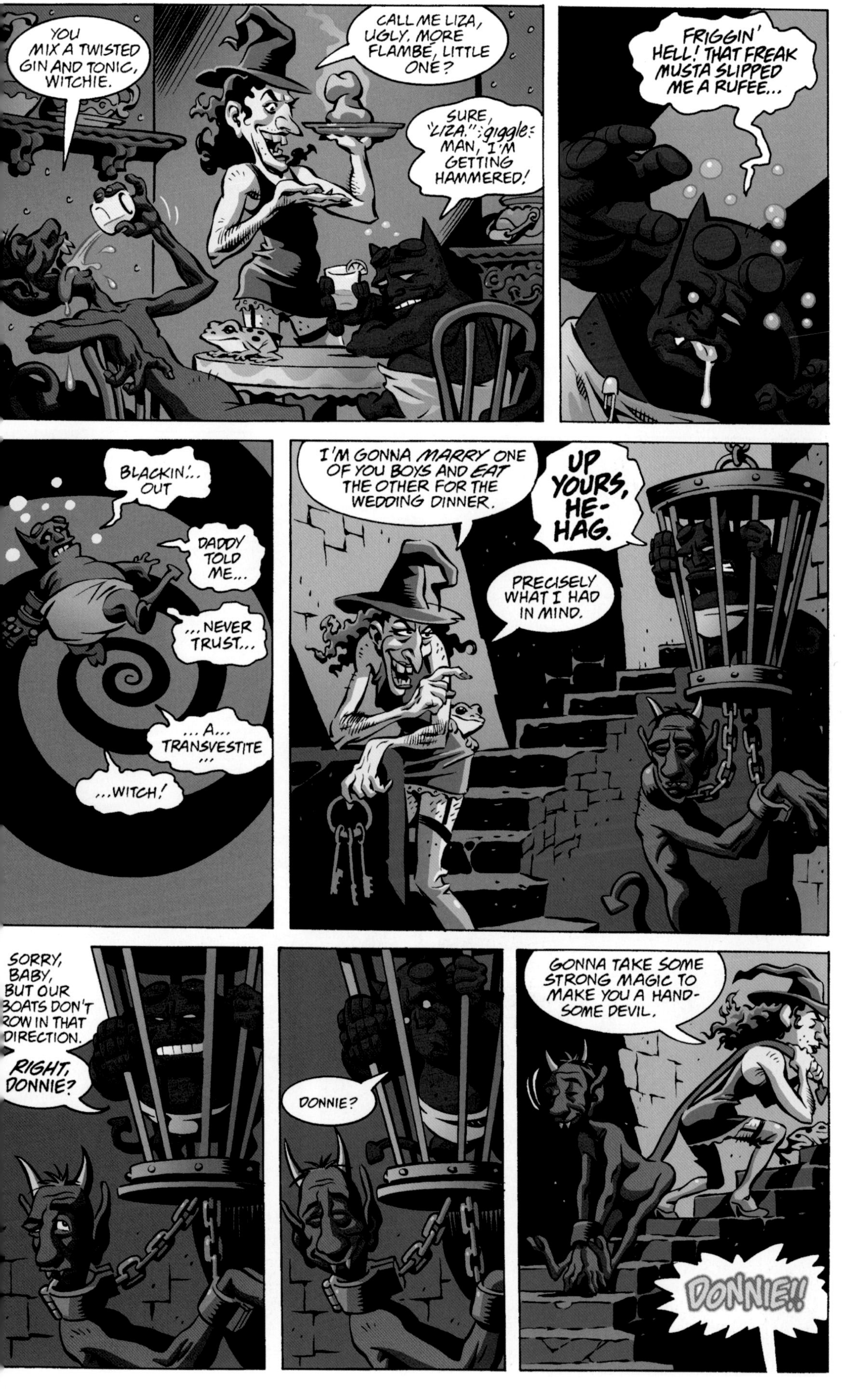
YOU MIX A TWISTED GIN AND TONIC, WITCHIE.
CALL ME LIZA, UGLY. MORE FLAMBE, LITTLE ONE?
SURE, "LIZA." :giggle: MAN, I'M GETTING HAMMERED!
FRIGGIN' HELL! THAT FREAK MUSTA SLIPPED ME A RUFEE...
BLACKIN'... OUT
DADDY TOLD ME...
...NEVER TRUST...
...A... TRANSVESTITE ...
...WITCH!
I'M GONNA MARRY ONE OF YOU BOYS AND EAT THE OTHER FOR THE WEDDING DINNER.
UP YOURS, HE-HAG.
PRECISELY WHAT I HAD IN MIND.
SORRY, BABY, BUT OUR BOATS DON'T ROW IN THAT DIRECTION.
RIGHT, DONNIE?
DONNIE?
GONNA TAKE SOME STRONG MAGIC TO MAKE YOU A HAND-SOME DEVIL.
DONNIE!!

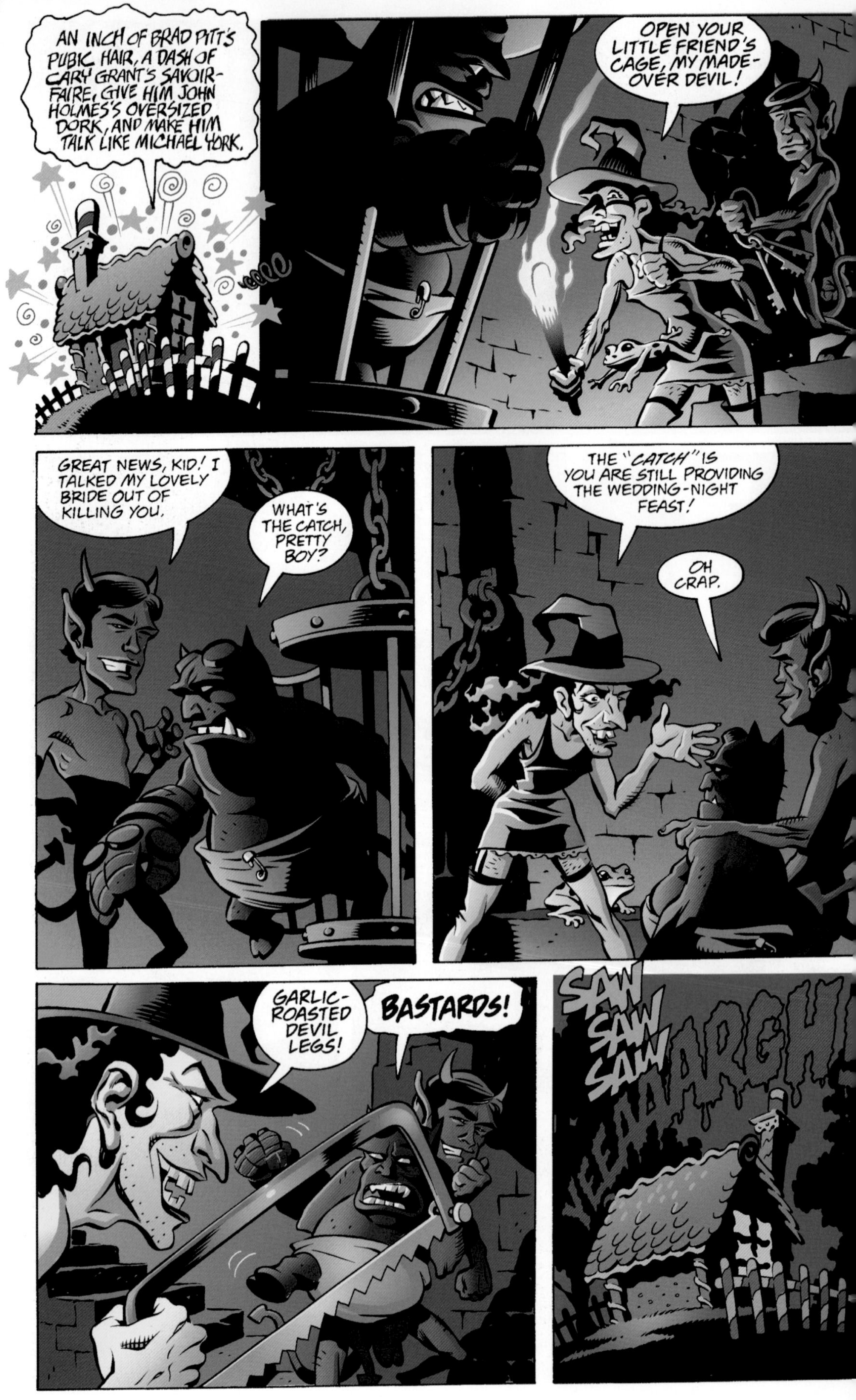
AN INCH OF BRAD PITT'S PUBIC HAIR, A DASH OF CARY GRANT'S SAVOIR-FAIRE, GIVE HIM JOHN HOLMES'S OVERSIZED DORK, AND MAKE HIM TALK LIKE MICHAEL YORK.
OPEN YOUR LITTLE FRIEND'S CAGE, MY MADE-OVER DEVIL!
GREAT NEWS, KID! I TALKED MY LOVELY BRIDE OUT OF KILLING YOU.
WHAT'S THE CATCH, PRETTY BOY?
THE "CATCH" IS YOU ARE STILL PROVIDING THE WEDDING-NIGHT FEAST!
OH CRAP.
GARLIC-ROASTED DEVIL LEGS!
BASTARDS!
SAW SAW SAW

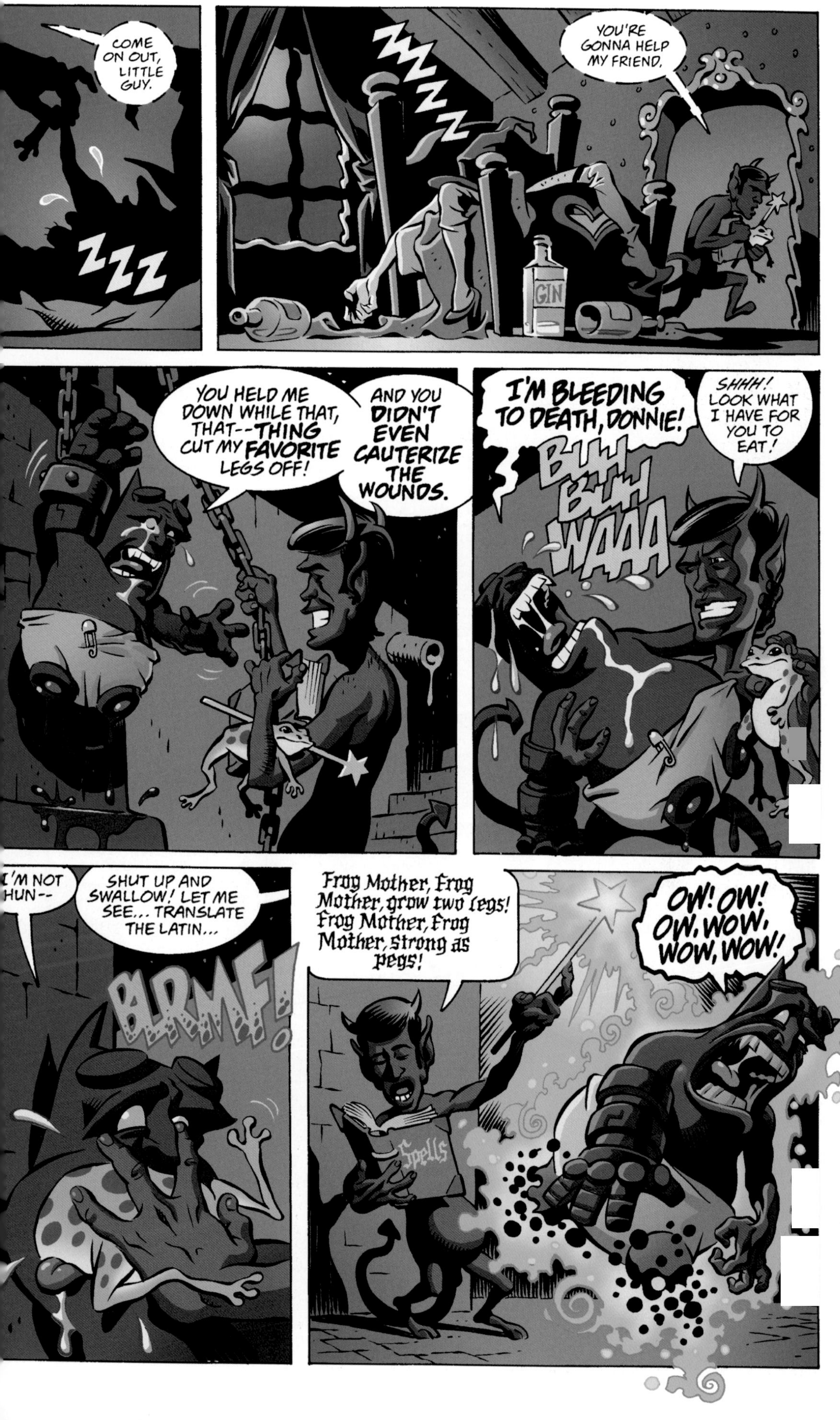
COME ON OUT, LITTLE GUY.
ZZZ
ZZZZ
YOU'RE GONNA HELP MY FRIEND.
GIN
YOU HELD ME DOWN WHILE THAT, THAT--THING CUT MY FAVORITE LEGS OFF!
AND YOU DIDN'T EVEN CAUTERIZE THE WOUNDS.
I'M BLEEDING TO DEATH, DONNIE!
SHHH! LOOK WHAT I HAVE FOR YOU TO EAT!
BUH BUH WAAA
I'M NOT HUN--
SHUT UP AND SWALLOW! LET ME SEE... TRANSLATE THE LATIN...
BLRMF!
Frog Mother, Frog Mother, grow two legs! Frog Mother, Frog Mother, strong as pegs!
OW! OW! OW, WOW, WOW, WOW!
Spells

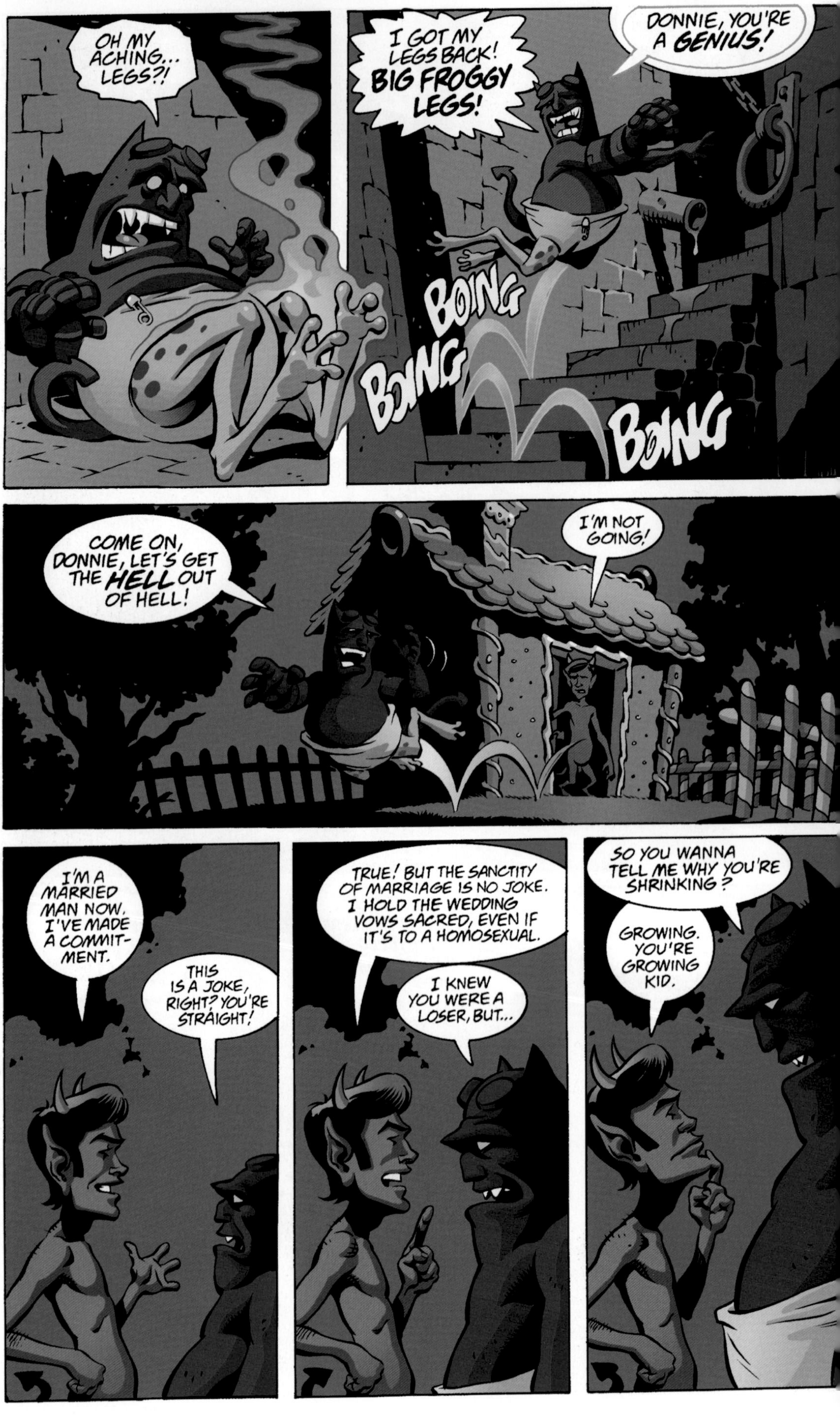

OH MY ACHING... LEGS?!
I GOT MY LEGS BACK! BIG FROGGY LEGS!
DONNIE, YOU'RE A GENIUS!
BOING
BOING
BOING
COME ON, DONNIE, LET'S GET THE HELL OUT OF HELL!
I'M NOT GOING!
I'M A MARRIED MAN NOW. I'VE MADE A COMMIT-MENT.
THIS IS A JOKE, RIGHT? YOU'RE STRAIGHT!
TRUE! BUT THE SANCTITY OF MARRIAGE IS NO JOKE. I HOLD THE WEDDING VOWS SACRED, EVEN IF IT'S TO A HOMOSEXUAL.
I KNEW YOU WERE A LOSER, BUT...
SO YOU WANNA TELL ME WHY YOU'RE SHRINKING?
GROWING. YOU'RE GROWING KID.

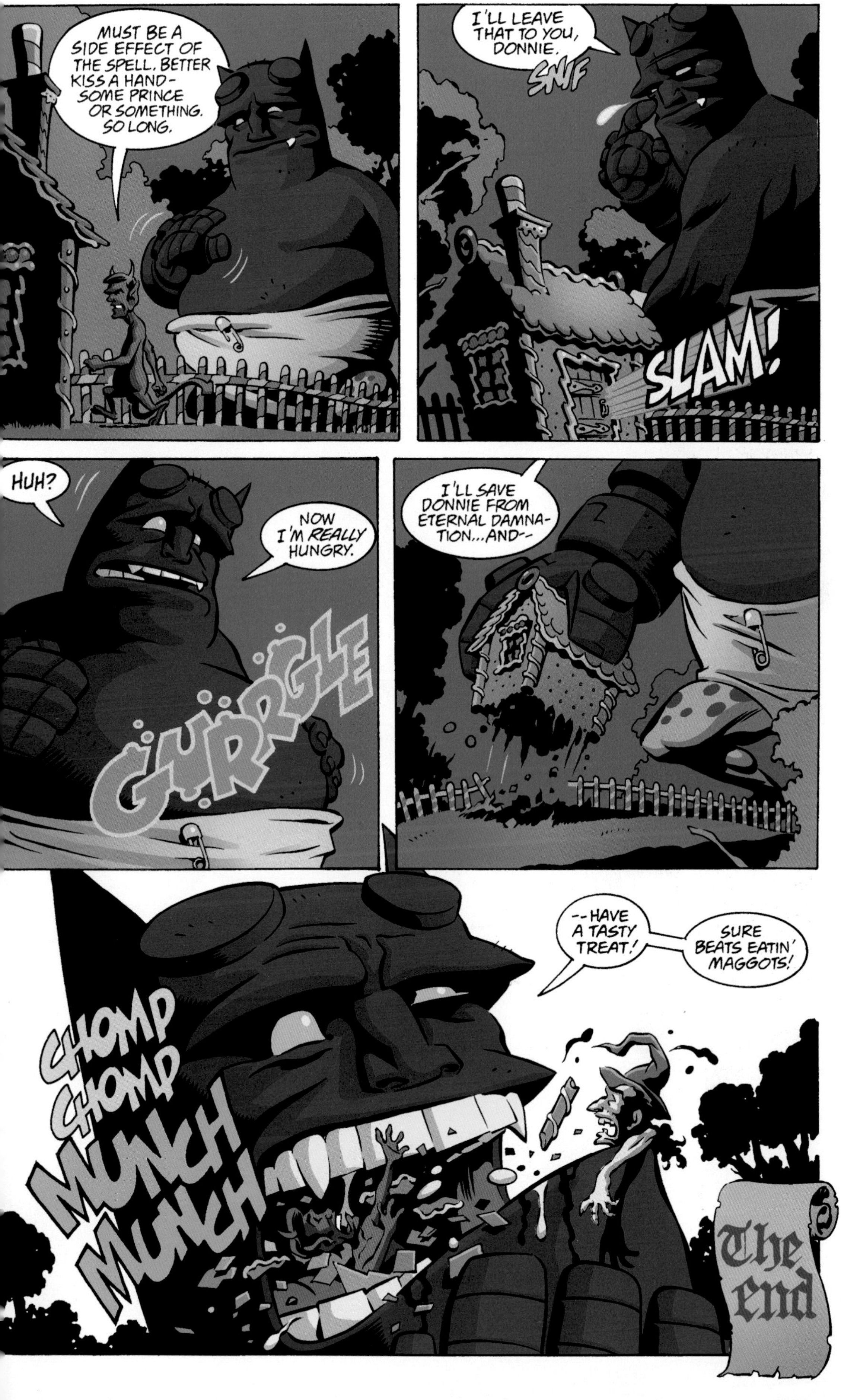

MUST BE A SIDE EFFECT OF THE SPELL. BETTER KISS A HAND-SOME PRINCE OR SOMETHING. SO LONG.
I'LL LEAVE THAT TO YOU, DONNIE.
SNIF
SLAM!
HUH?
NOW I'M *REALLY* HUNGRY.
GURRGLE
I'LL SAVE DONNIE FROM ETERNAL DAMNA-TION...AND--
--HAVE A TASTY TREAT!
SURE BEATS EATIN' MAGGOTS!
CHOMP CHOMP MUNCH MUNCH
The end

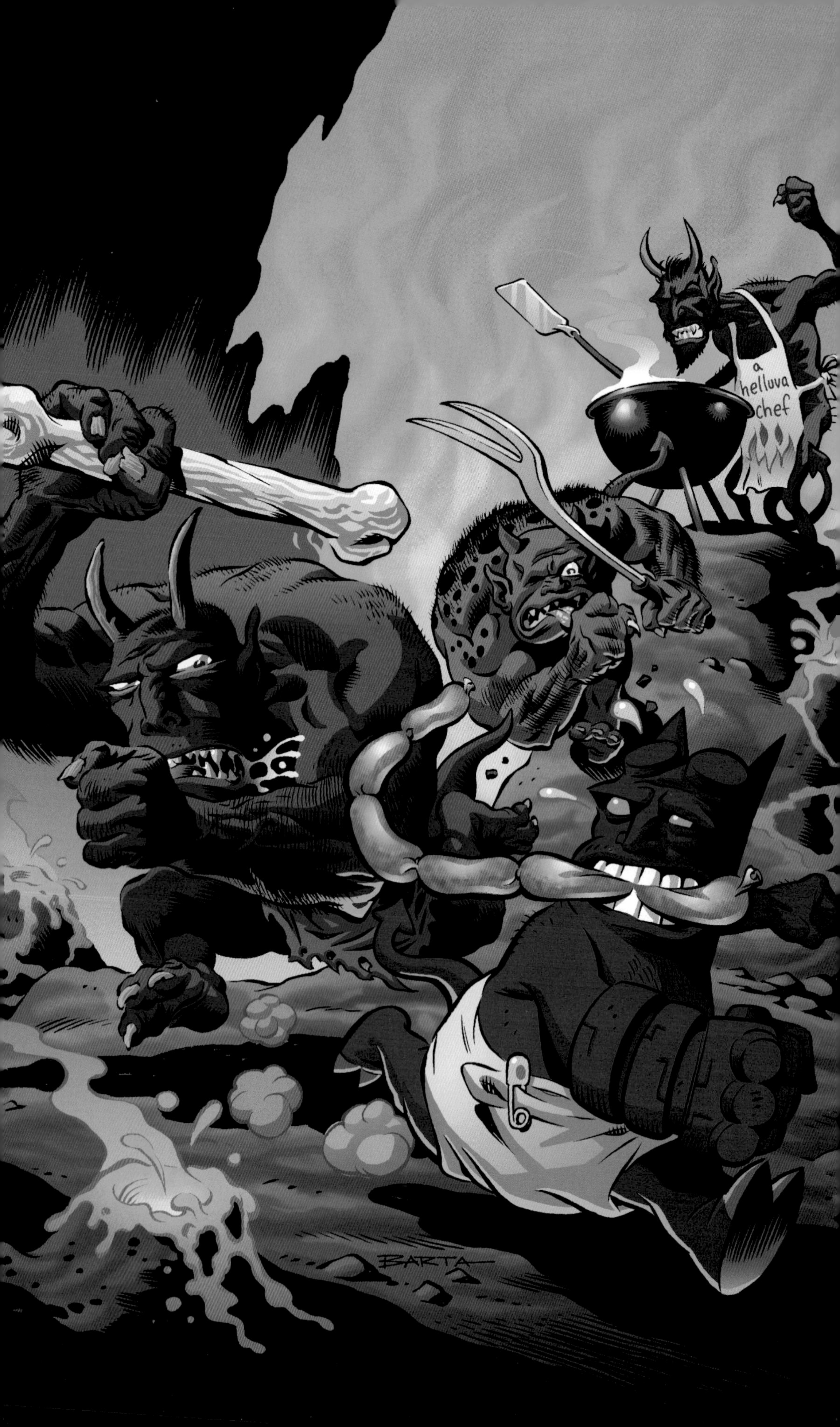
a helluva chef
BARTA

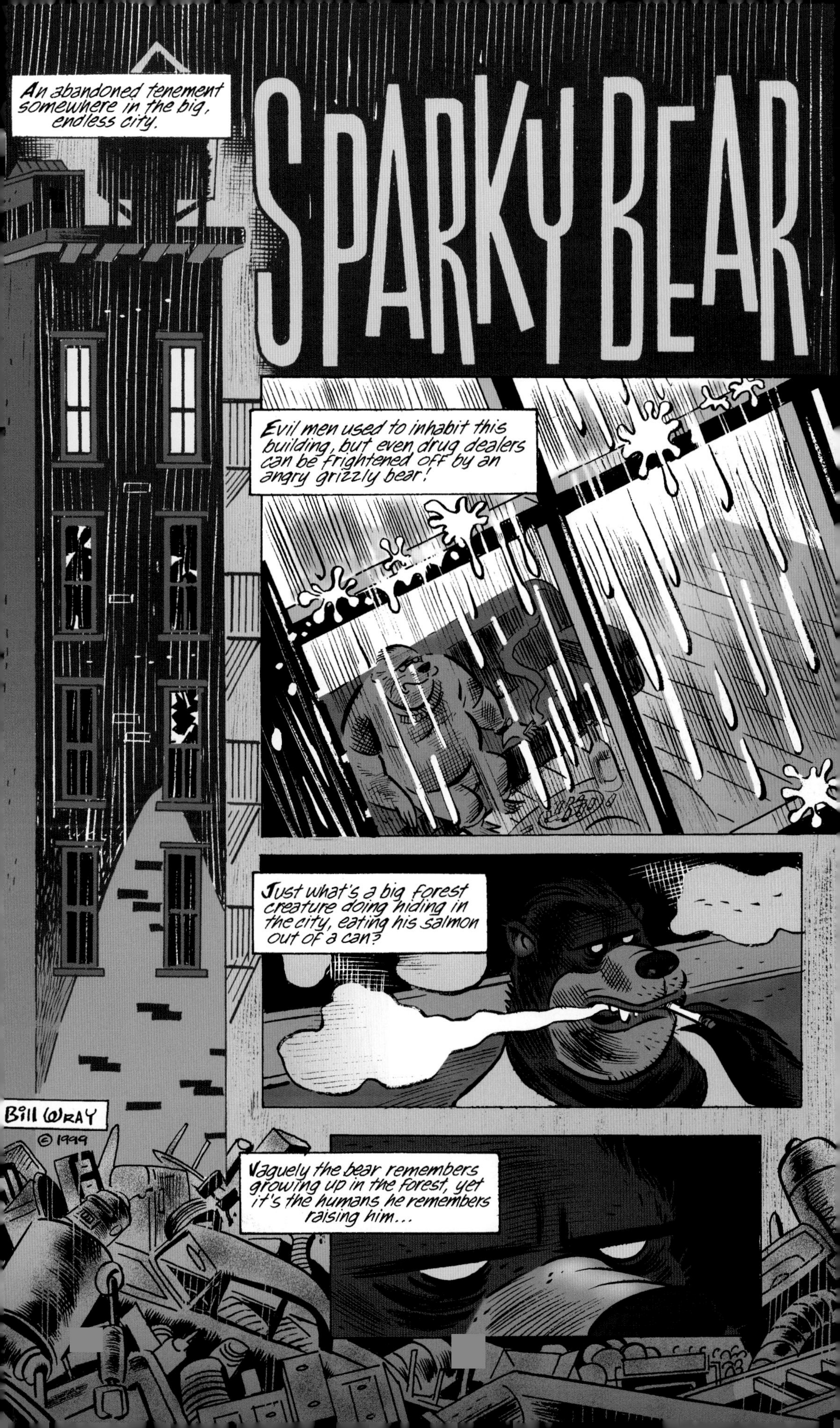
SPARKY BEAR
An abandoned tenement somewhere in the big, endless city.
Evil men used to inhabit this building, but even drug dealers can be frightened off by an angry grizzly bear!
Just what's a big forest creature doing hiding in the city, eating his salmon out of a can?
Vaguely the bear remembers growing up in the forest, yet it's the humans he remembers raising him...
Bill Wray
© 1999

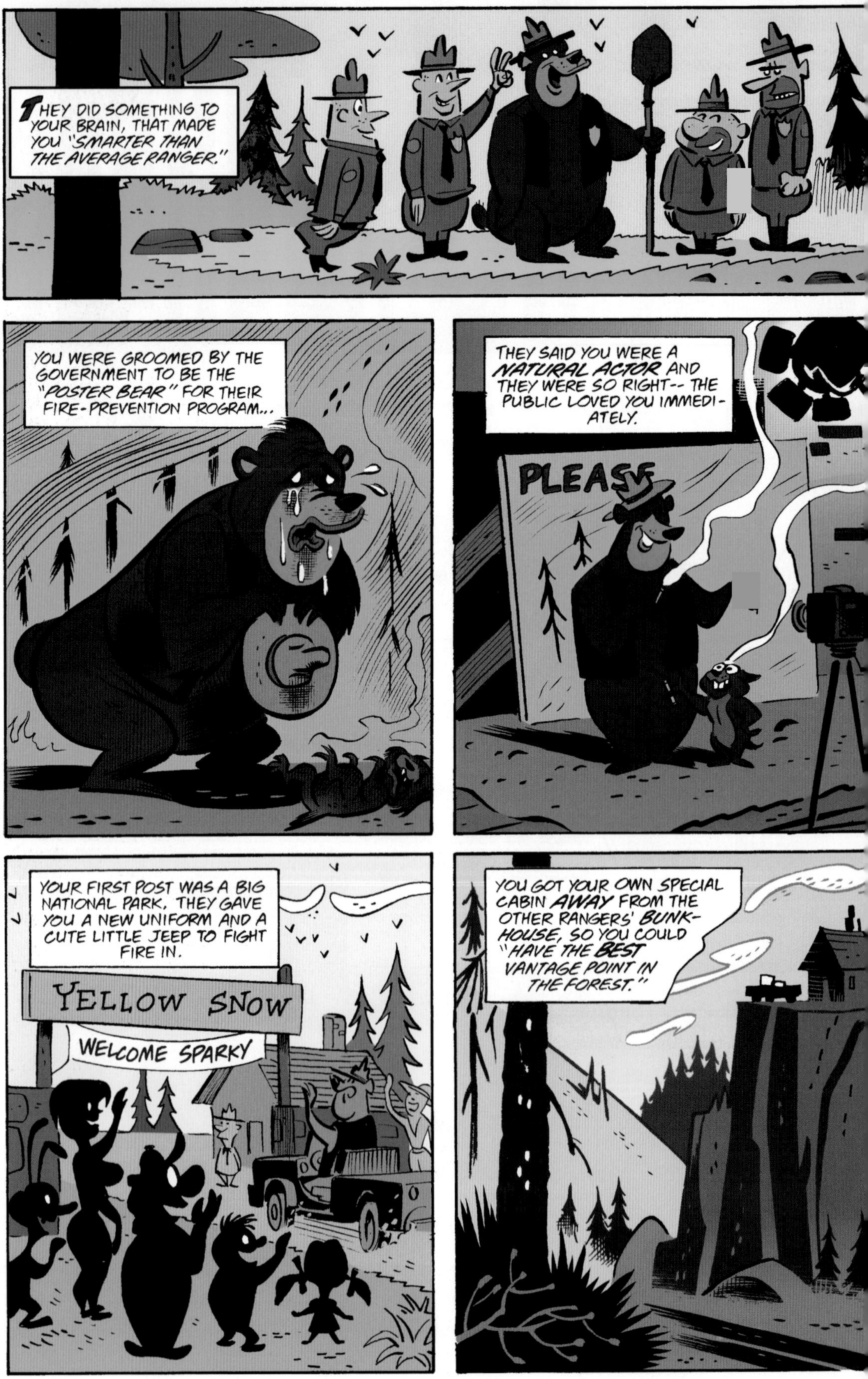
THEY DID SOMETHING TO YOUR BRAIN, THAT MADE YOU "SMARTER THAN THE AVERAGE RANGER."
YOU WERE GROOMED BY THE GOVERNMENT TO BE THE "POSTER BEAR" FOR THEIR FIRE-PREVENTION PROGRAM...
THEY SAID YOU WERE A NATURAL ACTOR AND THEY WERE SO RIGHT-- THE PUBLIC LOVED YOU IMMEDIATELY.
PLEASE
YOUR FIRST POST WAS A BIG NATIONAL PARK. THEY GAVE YOU A NEW UNIFORM AND A CUTE LITTLE JEEP TO FIGHT FIRE IN.
YELLOW SNOW
WELCOME SPARKY
YOU GOT YOUR OWN SPECIAL CABIN AWAY FROM THE OTHER RANGERS' BUNK-HOUSE, SO YOU COULD "HAVE THE BEST VANTAGE POINT IN THE FOREST."

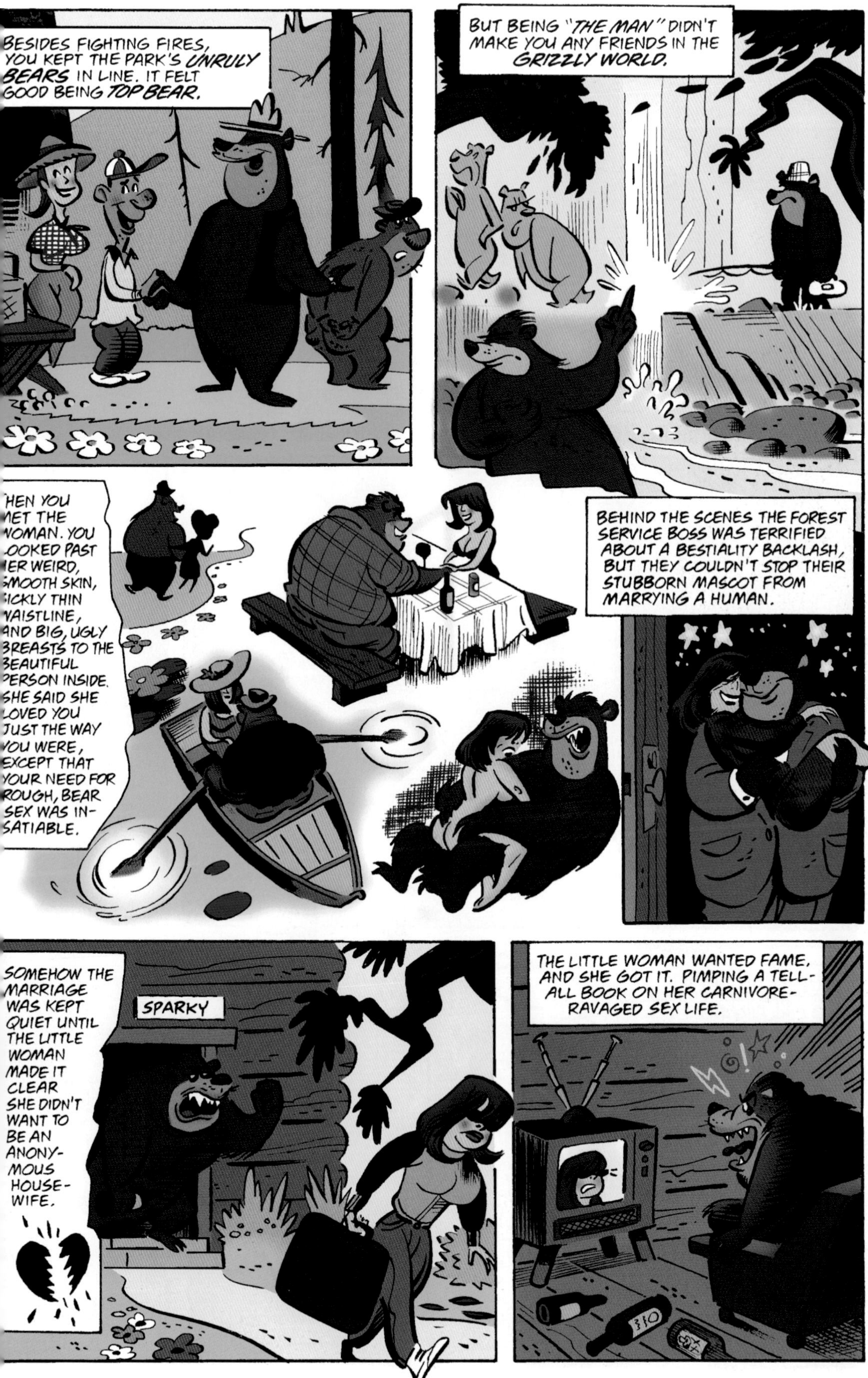
BESIDES FIGHTING FIRES, YOU KEPT THE PARK'S UNRULY BEARS IN LINE. IT FELT GOOD BEING TOP BEAR.
BUT BEING "THE MAN" DIDN'T MAKE YOU ANY FRIENDS IN THE GRIZZLY WORLD.
HEN YOU MET THE WOMAN. YOU OOKED PAST ER WEIRD, MOOTH SKIN, ICKLY THIN AISTLINE, AND BIG, UGLY BREASTS TO THE BEAUTIFUL PERSON INSIDE. SHE SAID SHE LOVED YOU JUST THE WAY YOU WERE, EXCEPT THAT YOUR NEED FOR ROUGH, BEAR SEX WAS IN-SATIABLE.
BEHIND THE SCENES THE FOREST SERVICE BOSS WAS TERRIFIED ABOUT A BESTIALITY BACKLASH, BUT THEY COULDN'T STOP THEIR STUBBORN MASCOT FROM MARRYING A HUMAN.
SOMEHOW THE MARRIAGE WAS KEPT QUIET UNTIL THE LITTLE WOMAN MADE IT CLEAR SHE DIDN'T WANT TO BE AN ANONY-MOUS HOUSE-WIFE.
SPARKY
THE LITTLE WOMAN WANTED FAME, AND SHE GOT IT. PIMPING A TELL-ALL BOOK ON HER CARNIVORE-RAVAGED SEX LIFE.

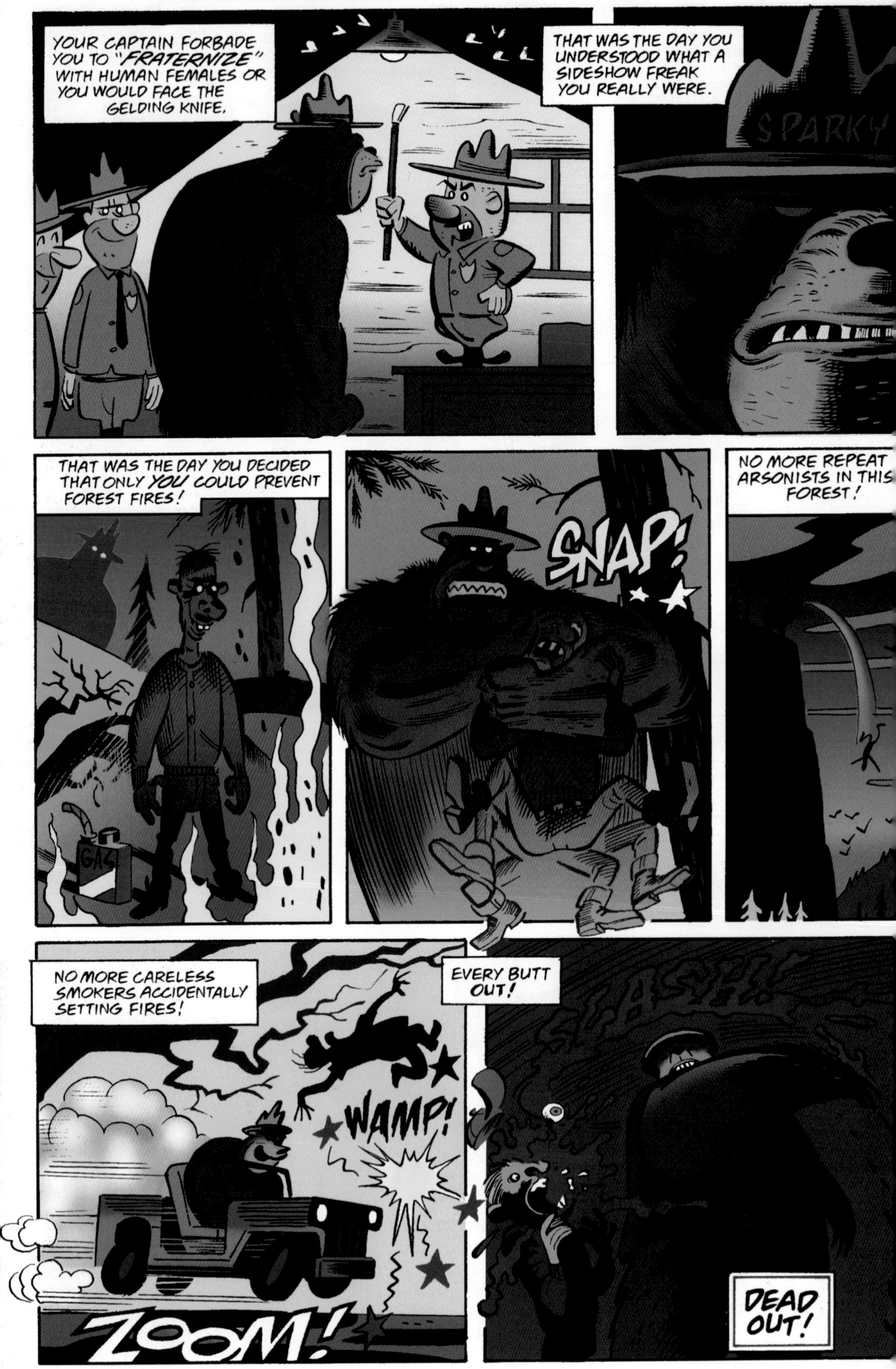
YOUR CAPTAIN FORBADE YOU TO "FRATERNIZE" WITH HUMAN FEMALES OR YOU WOULD FACE THE GELDING KNIFE.
THAT WAS THE DAY YOU UNDERSTOOD WHAT A SIDESHOW FREAK YOU REALLY WERE.
SPARKY
THAT WAS THE DAY YOU DECIDED THAT ONLY YOU COULD PREVENT FOREST FIRES!
GAS
SNAP!
NO MORE REPEAT ARSONISTS IN THIS FOREST!
NO MORE CARELESS SMOKERS ACCIDENTALLY SETTING FIRES!
EVERY BUTT OUT!
WAMP!
ZOOM!
DEAD OUT!

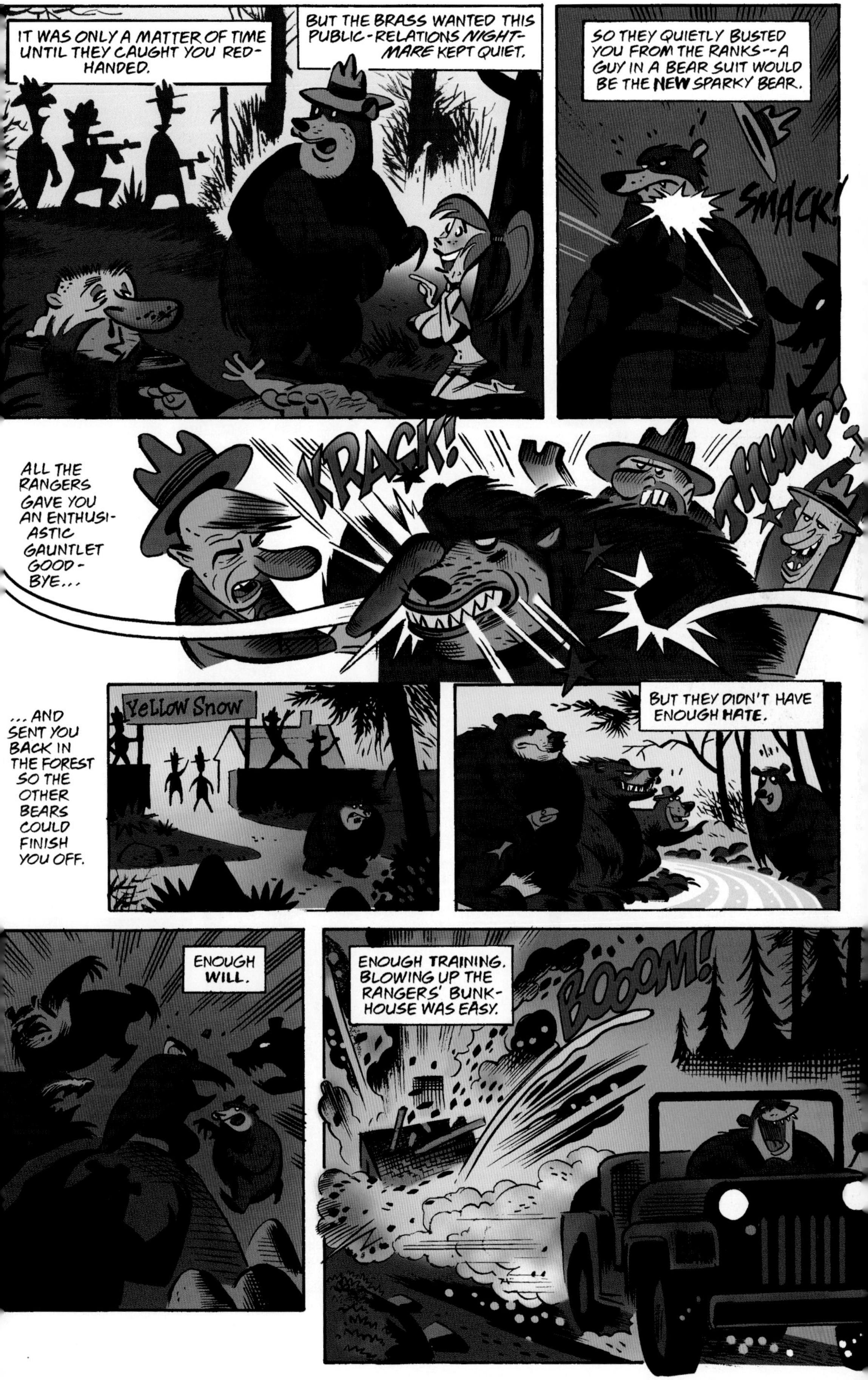
IT WAS ONLY A MATTER OF TIME UNTIL THEY CAUGHT YOU RED-HANDED.
BUT THE BRASS WANTED THIS PUBLIC-RELATIONS NIGHTMARE KEPT QUIET.
SO THEY QUIETLY BUSTED YOU FROM THE RANKS--A GUY IN A BEAR SUIT WOULD BE THE NEW SPARKY BEAR.
SMACK!
ALL THE RANGERS GAVE YOU AN ENTHUSIASTIC GAUNTLET GOOD-BYE...
KRACK!
THUMP!
...AND SENT YOU BACK IN THE FOREST SO THE OTHER BEARS COULD FINISH YOU OFF.
YeLLow Snow
BUT THEY DIDN'T HAVE ENOUGH HATE.
ENOUGH WILL.
ENOUGH TRAINING. BLOWING UP THE RANGERS' BUNKHOUSE WAS EASY.
BOOOM!

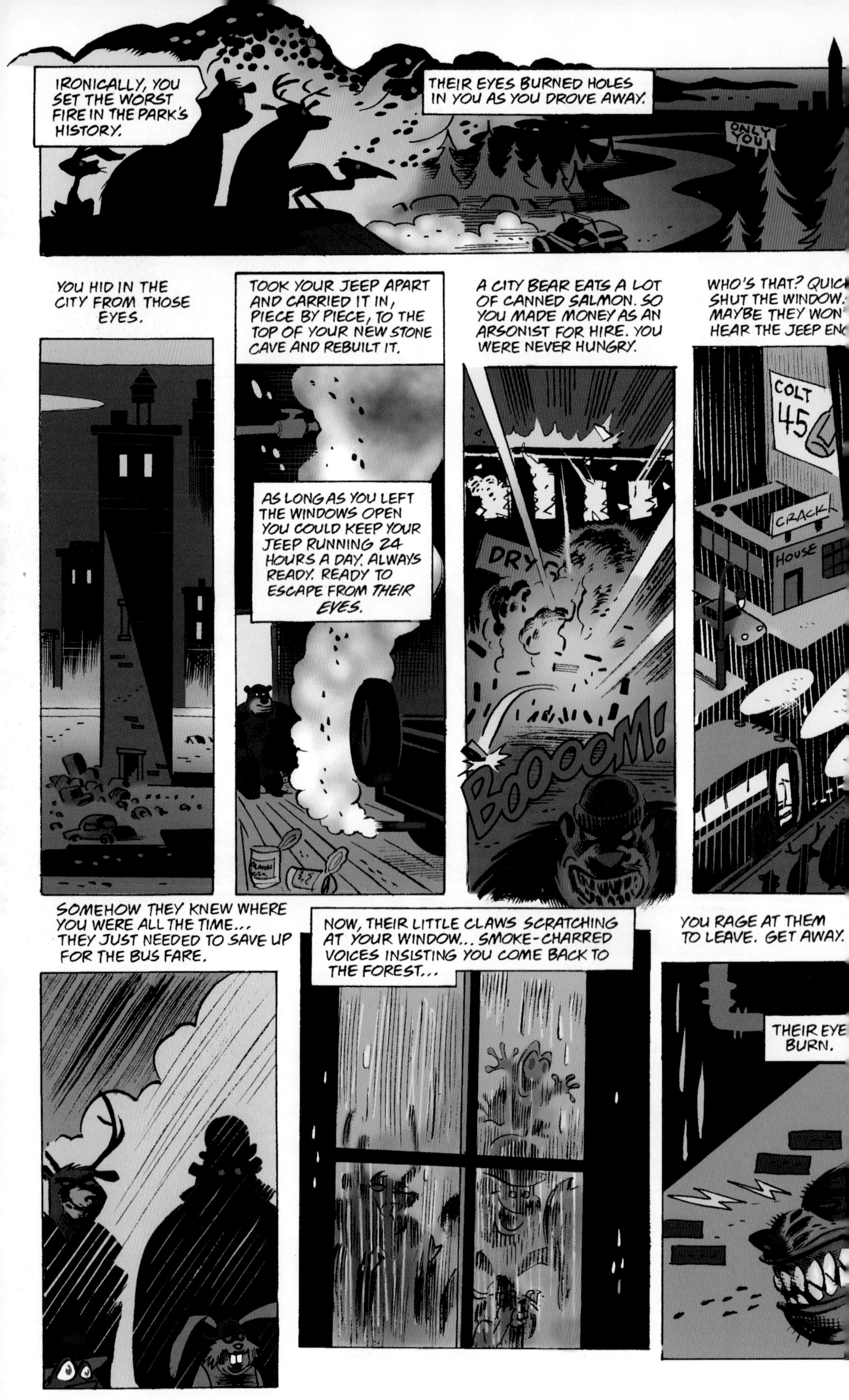
IRONICALLY, YOU SET THE WORST FIRE IN THE PARK'S HISTORY.
THEIR EYES BURNED HOLES IN YOU AS YOU DROVE AWAY.
ONLY YOU
YOU HID IN THE CITY FROM THOSE EYES.
TOOK YOUR JEEP APART AND CARRIED IT IN, PIECE BY PIECE, TO THE TOP OF YOUR NEW STONE CAVE AND REBUILT IT.
AS LONG AS YOU LEFT THE WINDOWS OPEN YOU COULD KEEP YOUR JEEP RUNNING 24 HOURS A DAY. ALWAYS READY. READY TO ESCAPE FROM THEIR EYES.
A CITY BEAR EATS A LOT OF CANNED SALMON. SO YOU MADE MONEY AS AN ARSONIST FOR HIRE. YOU WERE NEVER HUNGRY.
DRY
BOOOOM!
WHO'S THAT? QUIC
SHUT THE WINDOW.
MAYBE THEY WON
HEAR THE JEEP EN
COLT 45
CRACK
HOUSE
SOMEHOW THEY KNEW WHERE YOU WERE ALL THE TIME... THEY JUST NEEDED TO SAVE UP FOR THE BUS FARE.
NOW, THEIR LITTLE CLAWS SCRATCHING AT YOUR WINDOW... SMOKE-CHARRED VOICES INSISTING YOU COME BACK TO THE FOREST...
YOU RAGE AT THEM TO LEAVE. GET AWAY.
THEIR EYE BURN.

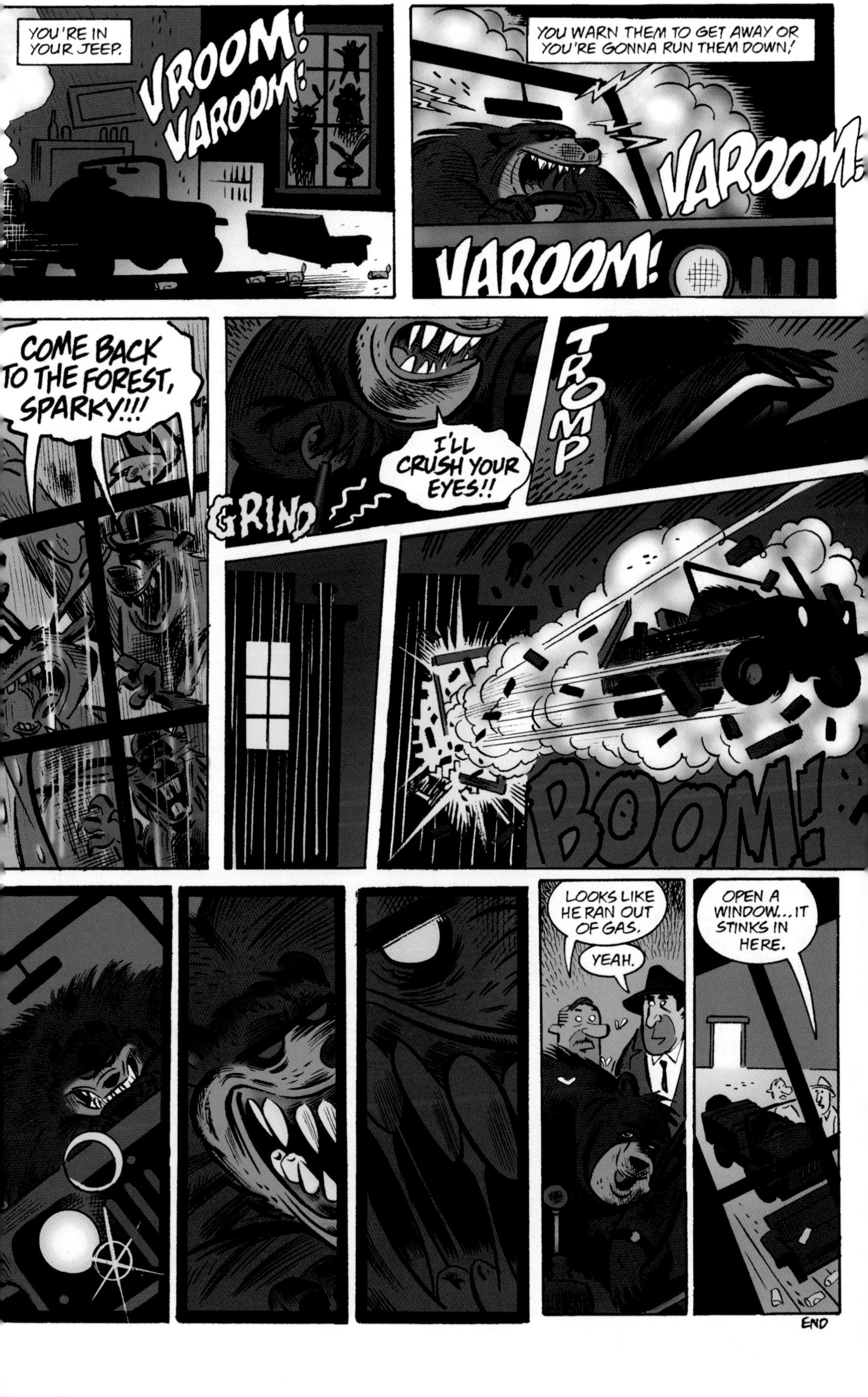
YOU'RE IN YOUR JEEP.
VROOM! VAROOM!
YOU WARN THEM TO GET AWAY OR YOU'RE GONNA RUN THEM DOWN!
VAROOM!
VAROOM!
COME BACK TO THE FOREST, SPARKY!!!
I'LL CRUSH YOUR EYES!!
GRIND
TROMP
BOOM!
LOOKS LIKE HE RAN OUT OF GAS.
YEAH.
OPEN A WINDOW... IT STINKS IN HERE.
END

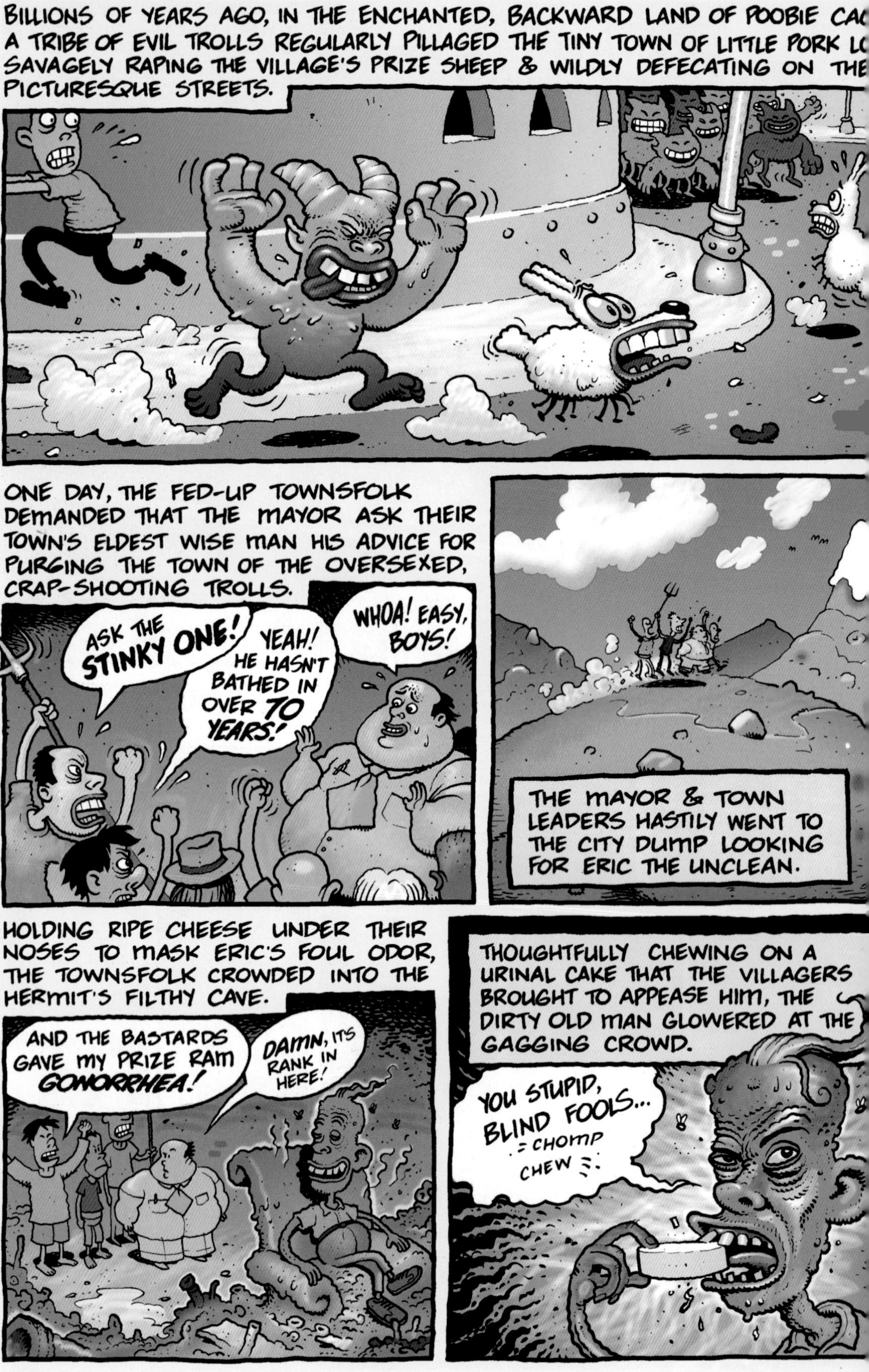
BILLIONS OF YEARS AGO, IN THE ENCHANTED, BACKWARD LAND OF POOBIE CA
A TRIBE OF EVIL TROLLS REGULARLY PILLAGED THE TINY TOWN OF LITTLE PORK L
SAVAGELY RAPING THE VILLAGE'S PRIZE SHEEP & WILDLY DEFECATING ON THE
PICTURESQUE STREETS.
ONE DAY, THE FED-UP TOWNSFOLK DEMANDED THAT THE MAYOR ASK THEIR TOWN'S ELDEST WISE MAN HIS ADVICE FOR PURGING THE TOWN OF THE OVERSEXED, CRAP-SHOOTING TROLLS.
ASK THE STINKY ONE!
YEAH! HE HASN'T BATHED IN OVER 70 YEARS!
WHOA! EASY, BOYS!
THE MAYOR & TOWN LEADERS HASTILY WENT TO THE CITY DUMP LOOKING FOR ERIC THE UNCLEAN.
HOLDING RIPE CHEESE UNDER THEIR NOSES TO MASK ERIC'S FOUL ODOR, THE TOWNSFOLK CROWDED INTO THE HERMIT'S FILTHY CAVE.
AND THE BASTARDS GAVE MY PRIZE RAM GONORRHEA!
DAMN, IT'S RANK IN HERE!
THOUGHTFULLY CHEWING ON A URINAL CAKE THAT THE VILLAGERS BROUGHT TO APPEASE HIM, THE DIRTY OLD MAN GLOWERED AT THE GAGGING CROWD.
YOU STUPID, BLIND FOOLS...
CHOMP
CHEW

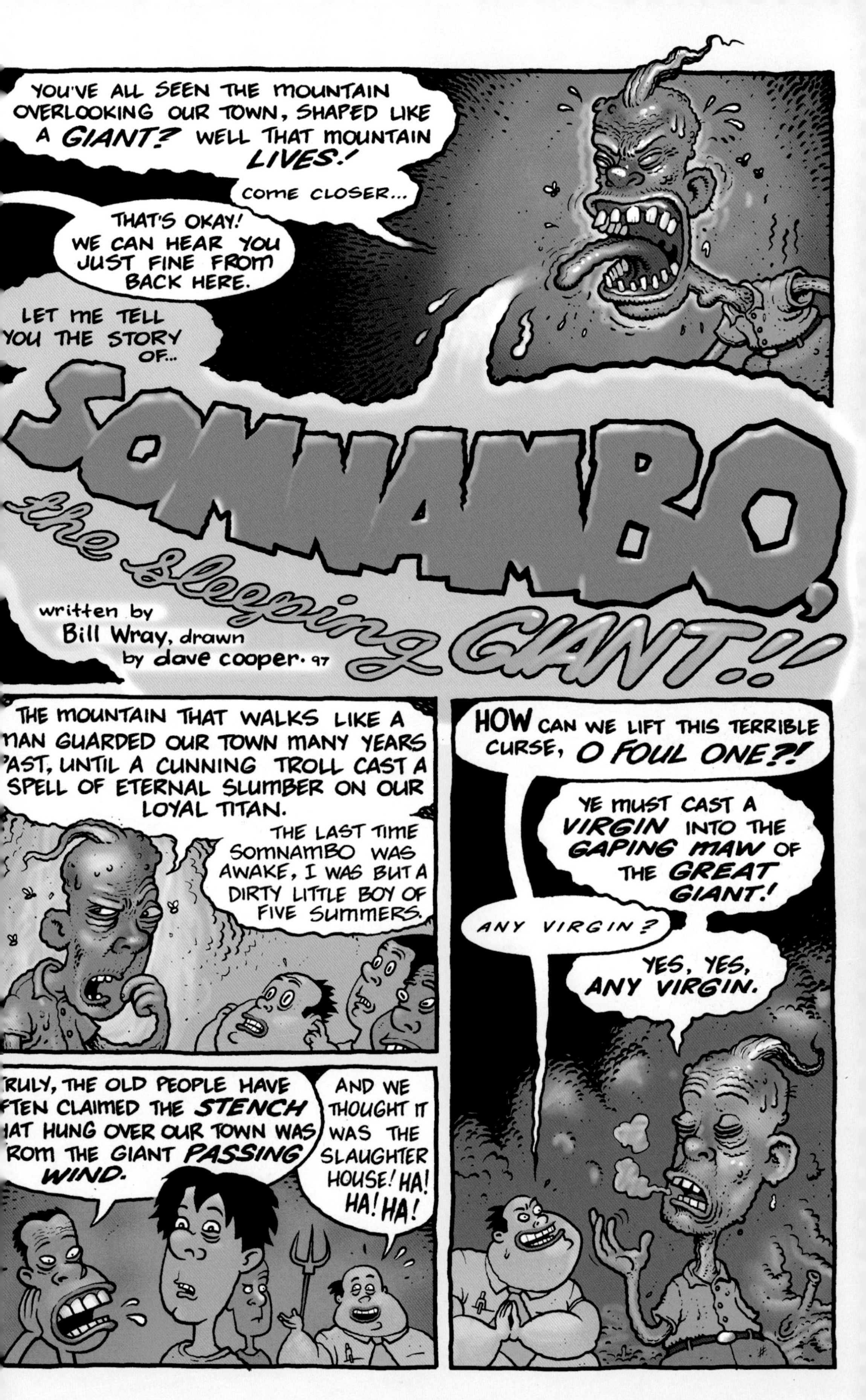
YOU'VE ALL SEEN THE MOUNTAIN OVERLOOKING OUR TOWN, SHAPED LIKE A GIANT? WELL THAT MOUNTAIN LIVES!
COME CLOSER...
THAT'S OKAY! WE CAN HEAR YOU JUST FINE FROM BACK HERE.
LET ME TELL YOU THE STORY OF...
SOMNAMBO, the sleeping GIANT!!
written by Bill Wray, drawn by dave cooper. 97
THE MOUNTAIN THAT WALKS LIKE A MAN GUARDED OUR TOWN MANY YEARS PAST, UNTIL A CUNNING TROLL CAST A SPELL OF ETERNAL SLUMBER ON OUR LOYAL TITAN.
THE LAST TIME SOMNAMBO WAS AWAKE, I WAS BUT A DIRTY LITTLE BOY OF FIVE SUMMERS.
RULY, THE OLD PEOPLE HAVE FTEN CLAIMED THE STENCH HAT HUNG OVER OUR TOWN WAS ROM THE GIANT PASSING WIND.
AND WE THOUGHT IT WAS THE SLAUGHTER HOUSE! HA! HA! HA!
HOW CAN WE LIFT THIS TERRIBLE CURSE, O FOUL ONE?!
YE MUST CAST A VIRGIN INTO THE GAPING MAW OF THE GREAT GIANT!
ANY VIRGIN?
YES, YES, ANY VIRGIN.

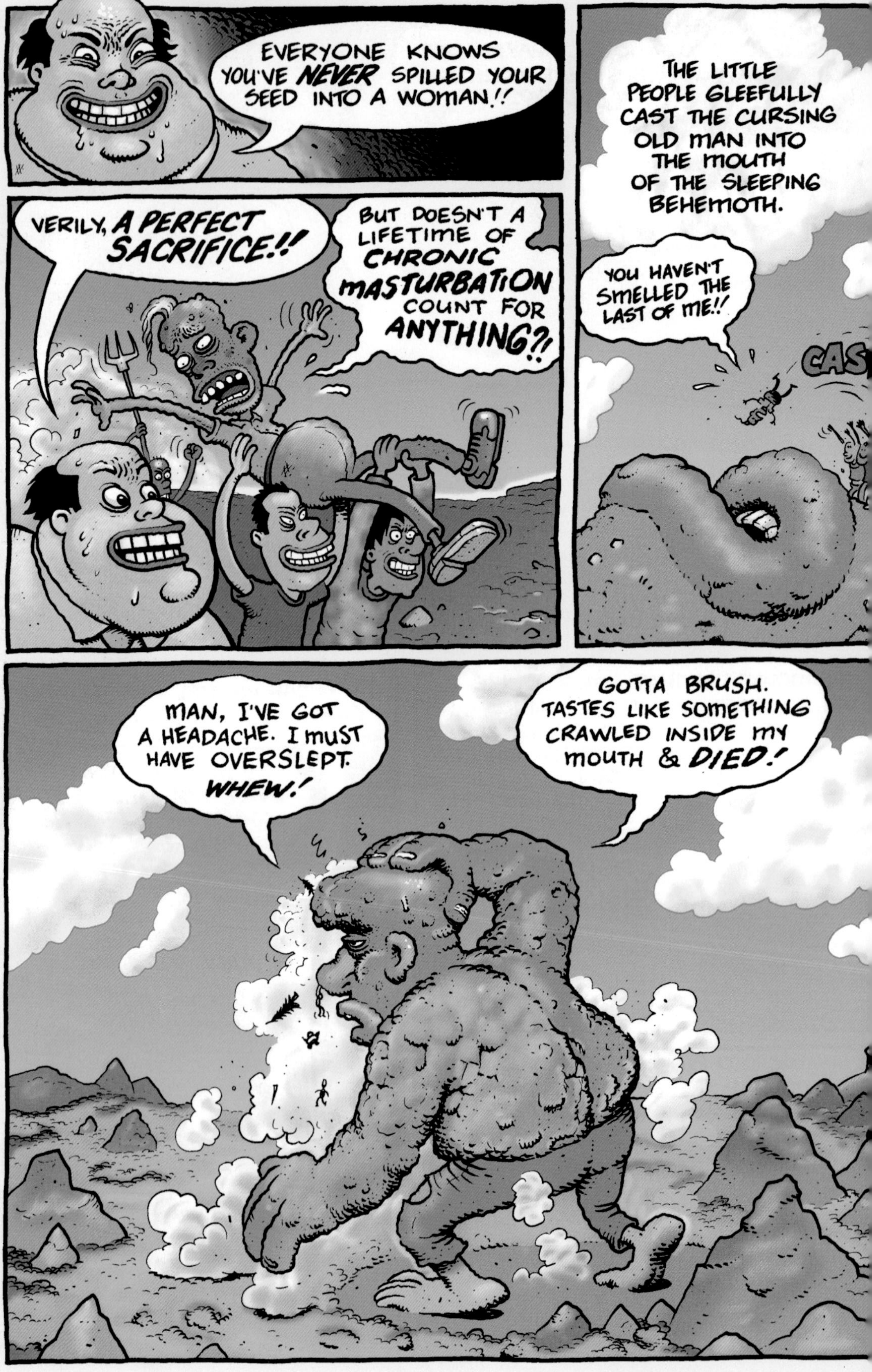
EVERYONE KNOWS YOU'VE NEVER SPILLED YOUR SEED INTO A WOMAN!!
VERILY, A PERFECT SACRIFICE!!
BUT DOESN'T A LIFETIME OF CHRONIC MASTURBATION COUNT FOR ANYTHING?!
THE LITTLE PEOPLE GLEEFULLY CAST THE CURSING OLD MAN INTO THE MOUTH OF THE SLEEPING BEHEMOTH.
YOU HAVEN'T SMELLED THE LAST OF ME!!
MAN, I'VE GOT A HEADACHE. I MUST HAVE OVERSLEPT. WHEW!
GOTTA BRUSH. TASTES LIKE SOMETHING CRAWLED INSIDE MY MOUTH & DIED!

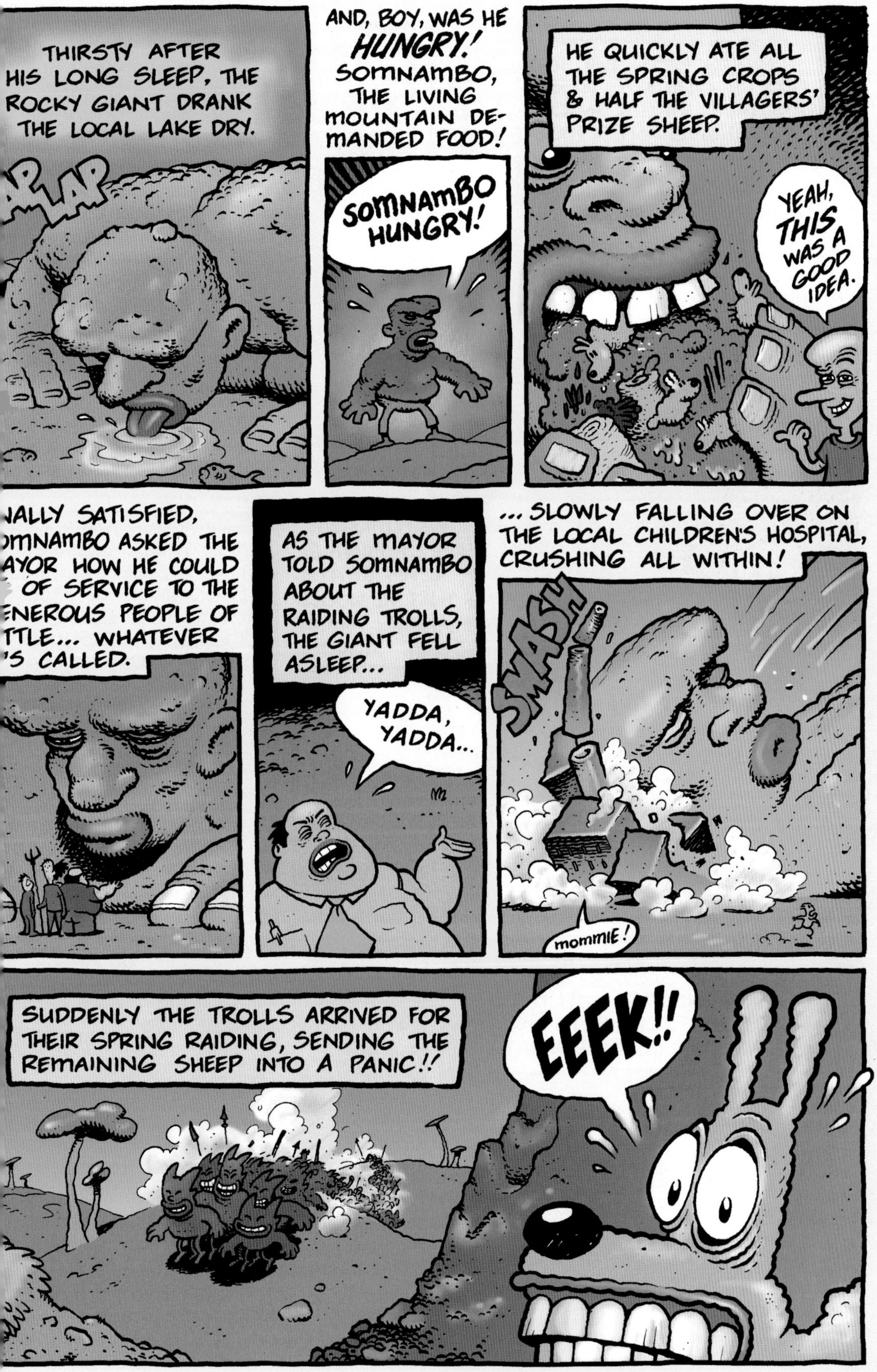
THIRSTY AFTER HIS LONG SLEEP, THE ROCKY GIANT DRANK THE LOCAL LAKE DRY.
AP LAP
AND, BOY, WAS HE HUNGRY! SOMNAMBO, THE LIVING MOUNTAIN DE-MANDED FOOD!
SOMNAMBO HUNGRY!
HE QUICKLY ATE ALL THE SPRING CROPS & HALF THE VILLAGERS' PRIZE SHEEP.
YEAH, THIS WAS A GOOD IDEA.
NALLY SATISFIED, OMNAMBO ASKED THE AYOR HOW HE COULD OF SERVICE TO THE ENEROUS PEOPLE OF TTLE... WHATEVER 'S CALLED.
AS THE MAYOR TOLD SOMNAMBO ABOUT THE RAIDING TROLLS, THE GIANT FELL ASLEEP...
YADDA, YADDA...
...SLOWLY FALLING OVER ON THE LOCAL CHILDREN'S HOSPITAL, CRUSHING ALL WITHIN!
SMASH
mommIE!
SUDDENLY THE TROLLS ARRIVED FOR THEIR SPRING RAIDING, SENDING THE REMAINING SHEEP INTO A PANIC!!
EEEK!!

THINKING FAST, THE TOWNS-PEOPLE QUICKLY TOSSED ANOTHER VIRGIN INTO THE SLEEPING GIANT'S MOUTH.

TOSS

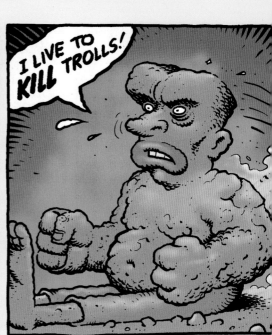

I LIVE TO **KILL** TROLLS!

DIE, YOU LITTLE FREAKS!

AIFEE!

A BRAVE KAMIKAZE TROLL HAPPILY FLUNG HIMSELF TO HIS DEATH, KNOWING THAT HE WOULD PUT THE ANGRY GIANT BACK TO SLEEP AGAIN.

BONZAI!

THE TROLL WORKED LIKE A SLEEPING PILL & SOMNAMBO FELL ONTO THE LOCAL CHURCH, CRUSHING ONLY THOSE MOST DEVOTED TO GOD.

JESUS!

A HORRIBLE BACK-&-FORTH CONTEST ENSUED WITH MANY SACRIFICES FROM BOTH SIDES LASTING LONG INTO THE NIGHT...

GO AHEAD, YOU BIG BASTARD, EAT ME!!

WAIT!! I'M MARRIED TO **JESUS**!!

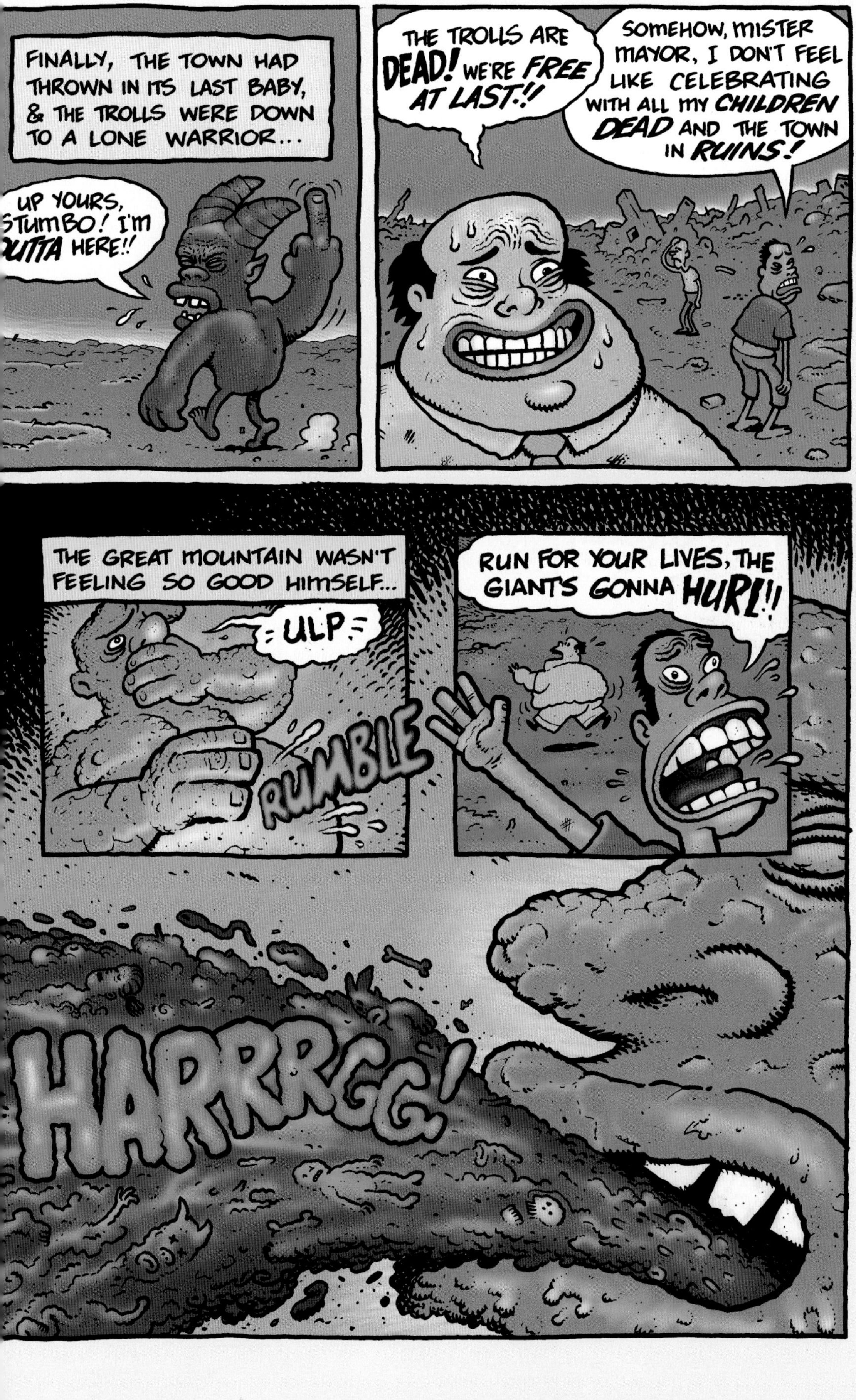
FINALLY, THE TOWN HAD THROWN IN ITS LAST BABY, & THE TROLLS WERE DOWN TO A LONE WARRIOR...
UP YOURS, STUMBO! I'M OUTTA HERE!!
THE TROLLS ARE DEAD! WE'RE FREE AT LAST!!
SOMEHOW, MISTER MAYOR, I DON'T FEEL LIKE CELEBRATING WITH ALL MY CHILDREN DEAD AND THE TOWN IN RUINS!
THE GREAT MOUNTAIN WASN'T FEELING SO GOOD HIMSELF...
ULP
RUMBLE
RUN FOR YOUR LIVES, THE GIANT'S GONNA HURL!!
HARRRGG!

LIKE A LIVING VOLCANO, THE GIANT SPEWED HUGE QUANTITIES OF MOLTEN LAVA AND FLAMING CORPSES INTO THE CITY STREETS...

...IMMEDIATELY SETTING THE TOWN *AFLAME!* WITH NO LAKE WAT TO FIGHT THE FIRE, THE LITTLE TOW BURNED TO THE GROUND.

YOU DESTROYED OUR VILLAGE, YOU... YOU... *MONSTER!*

WHAT'RE YOU GONNA DO *NOW?*

I... I... I'm SORRY... ≳CHOKE≲

I DIDN'T MEAN ANY HAR BOO, HOO, HOO, *BAWHAA*

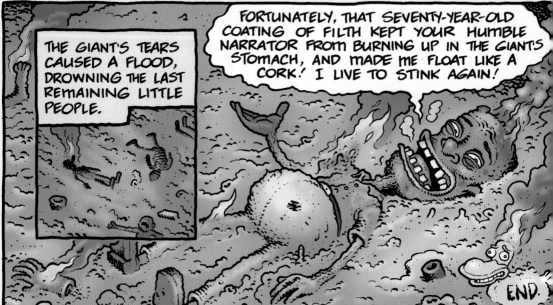

THE GIANT'S TEARS CAUSED A FLOOD, DROWNING THE LAST REMAINING LITTLE PEOPLE.

FORTUNATELY, THAT SEVENTY-YEAR-OLD COATING OF FILTH KEPT YOUR HUMBLE NARRATOR FROM BURNING UP IN THE GIANT'S STOMACH, AND MADE ME FLOAT LIKE A CORK! I LIVE TO STINK AGAIN!

END.

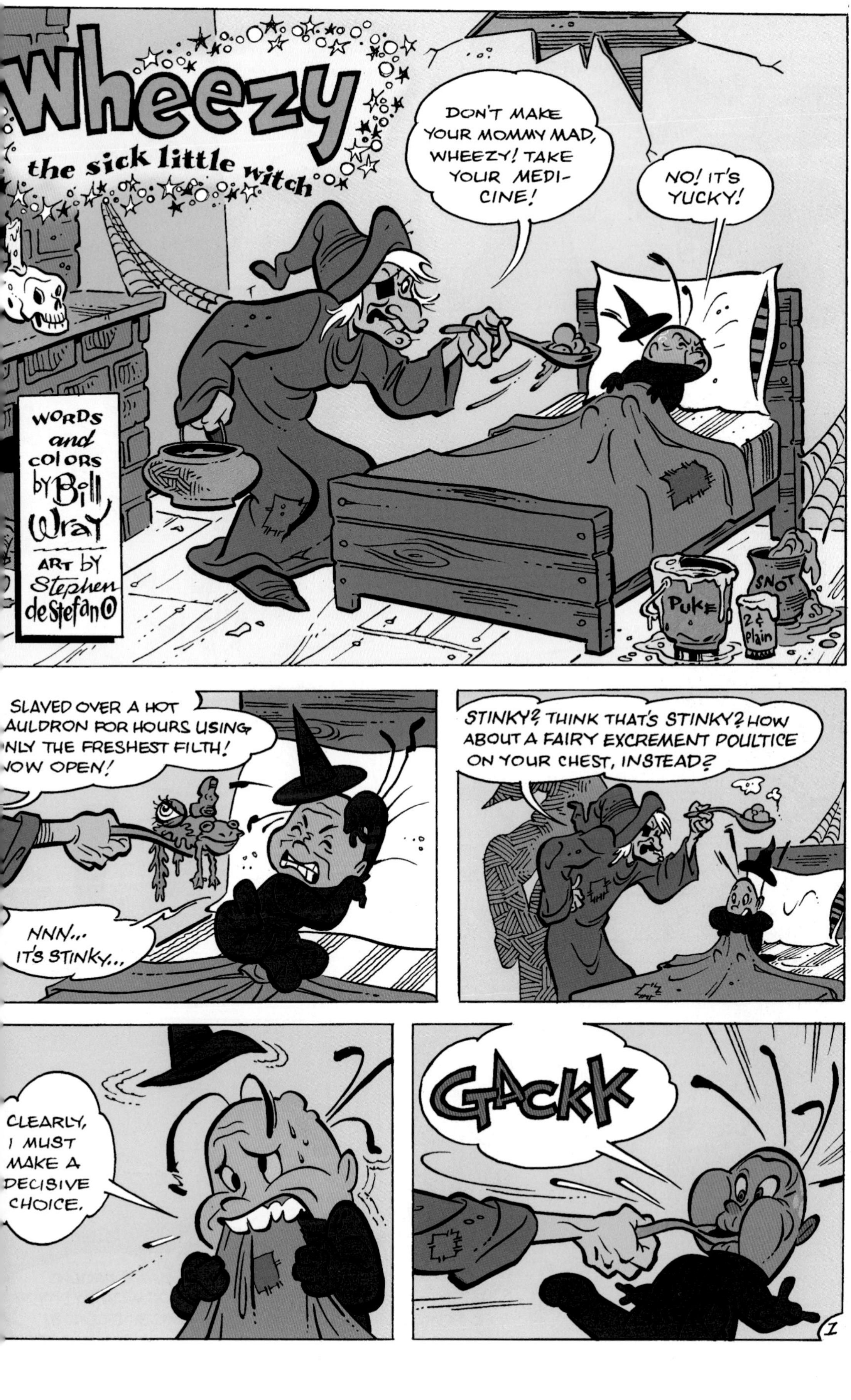
Wheezy
the sick little witch
WORDS and COLORS by Bill Wray
ART BY Stephen deStefano
DON'T MAKE YOUR MOMMY MAD, WHEEZY! TAKE YOUR MEDI- CINE!
NO! IT'S YUCKY!
PUKE
SNOT
2¢ plain
SLAVED OVER A HOT
AULDRON FOR HOURS USING
NLY THE FRESHEST FILTH!
OW OPEN!
NNN... IT'S STINKY...
STINKY? THINK THAT'S STINKY? HOW ABOUT A FAIRY EXCREMENT POULTICE ON YOUR CHEST, INSTEAD?
CLEARLY, I MUST MAKE A DECISIVE CHOICE.
GACKK

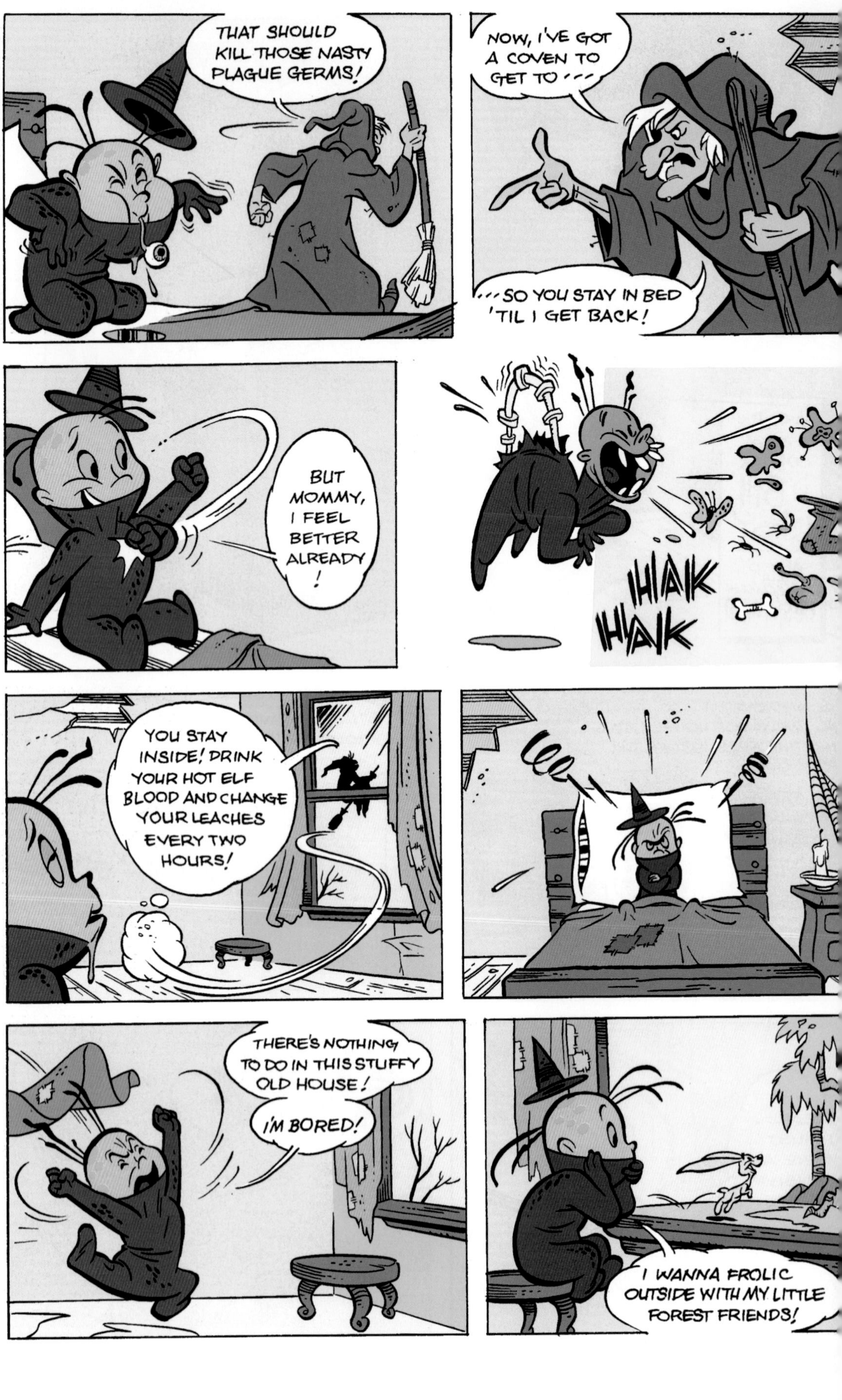
THAT SHOULD KILL THOSE NASTY PLAGUE GERMS!
NOW, I'VE GOT A COVEN TO GET TO ...
...SO YOU STAY IN BED 'TIL I GET BACK!
BUT MOMMY, I FEEL BETTER ALREADY!
HAK HAK
YOU STAY INSIDE! DRINK YOUR HOT ELF BLOOD AND CHANGE YOUR LEACHES EVERY TWO HOURS!
THERE'S NOTHING TO DO IN THIS STUFFY OLD HOUSE!
I'M BORED!
I WANNA FROLIC OUTSIDE WITH MY LITTLE FOREST FRIENDS!

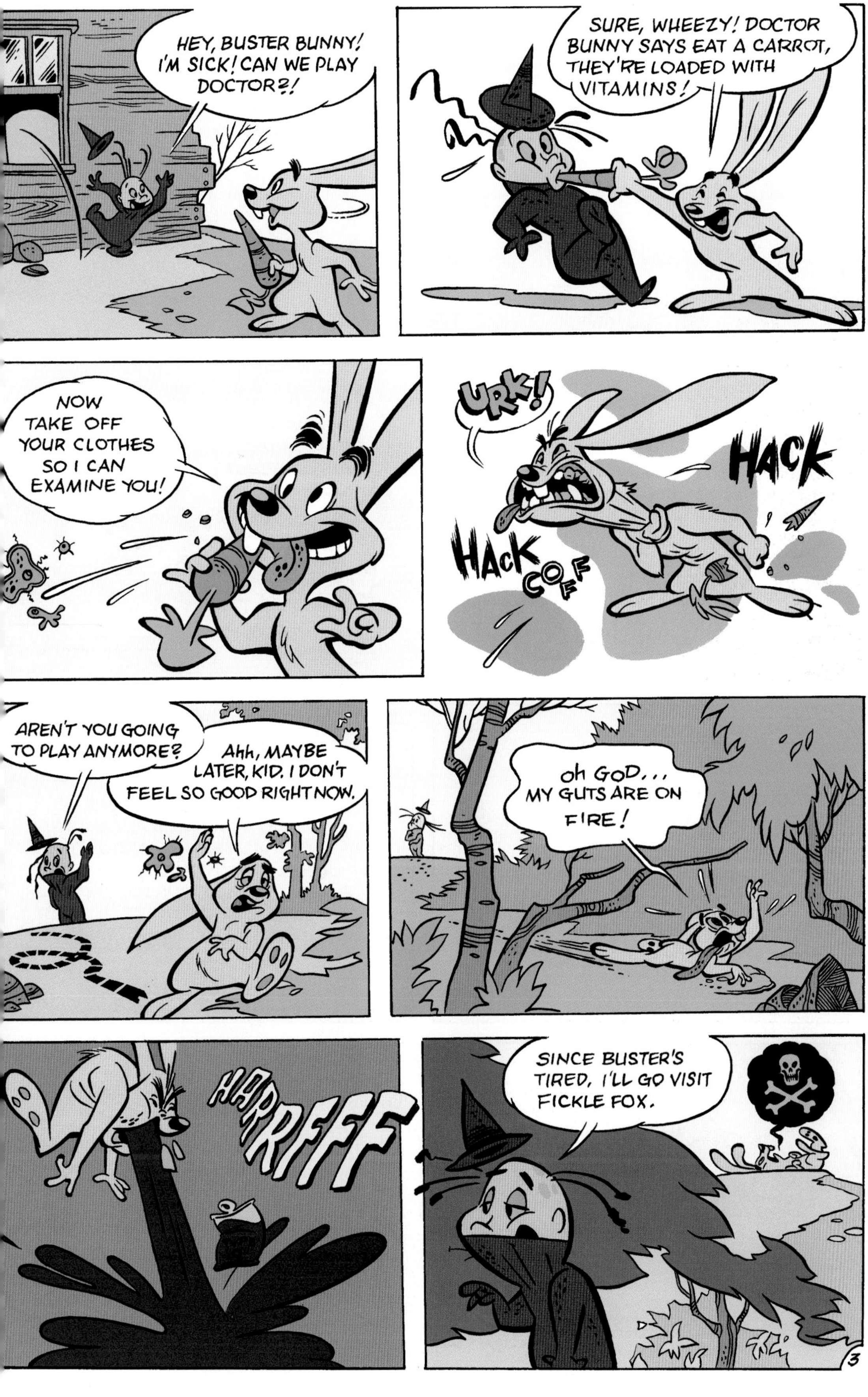

HEY, BUSTER BUNNY! I'M SICK! CAN WE PLAY DOCTOR?!
SURE, WHEEZY! DOCTOR BUNNY SAYS EAT A CARROT, THEY'RE LOADED WITH VITAMINS!
NOW TAKE OFF YOUR CLOTHES SO I CAN EXAMINE YOU!
URK!
HACK
HACK
COFF
AREN'T YOU GOING TO PLAY ANYMORE?
Ahh, MAYBE LATER, KID. I DON'T FEEL SO GOOD RIGHT NOW.
oh GOD... MY GUTS ARE ON FIRE!
HARRFFF
SINCE BUSTER'S TIRED, I'LL GO VISIT FICKLE FOX.

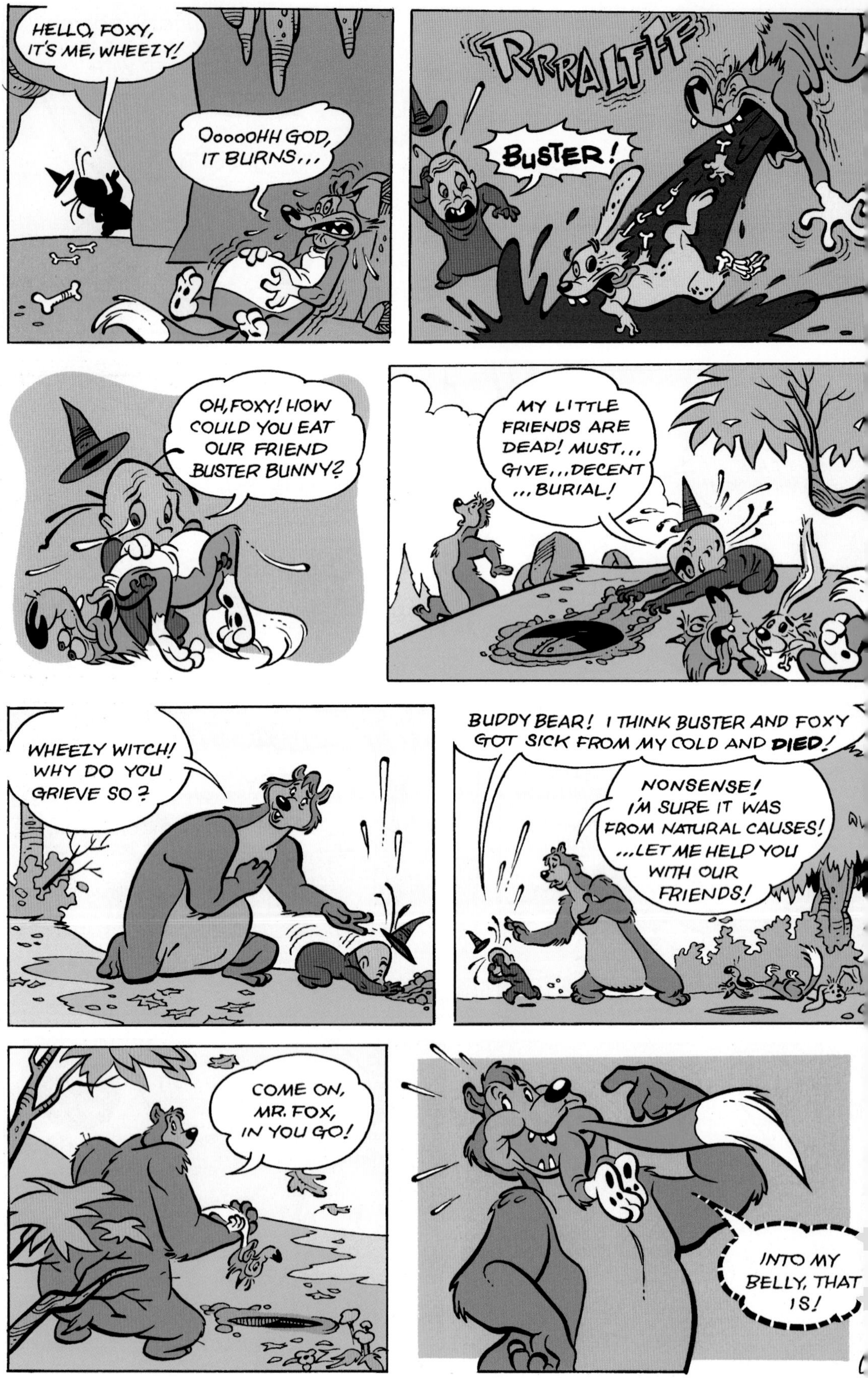
HELLO, FOXY, IT'S ME, WHEEZY!
OooooHH GOD, IT BURNS,,,
RRRALTFFF
BUSTER!
OH, FOXY! HOW COULD YOU EAT OUR FRIEND BUSTER BUNNY?
MY LITTLE FRIENDS ARE DEAD! MUST,,, GIVE,,,DECENT ,,,BURIAL!
WHEEZY WITCH! WHY DO YOU GRIEVE SO?
BUDDY BEAR! I THINK BUSTER AND FOXY GOT SICK FROM MY COLD AND DIED!
NONSENSE! I'M SURE IT WAS FROM NATURAL CAUSES! ...LET ME HELP YOU WITH OUR FRIENDS!
COME ON, MR. FOX, IN YOU GO!
INTO MY BELLY, THAT IS!

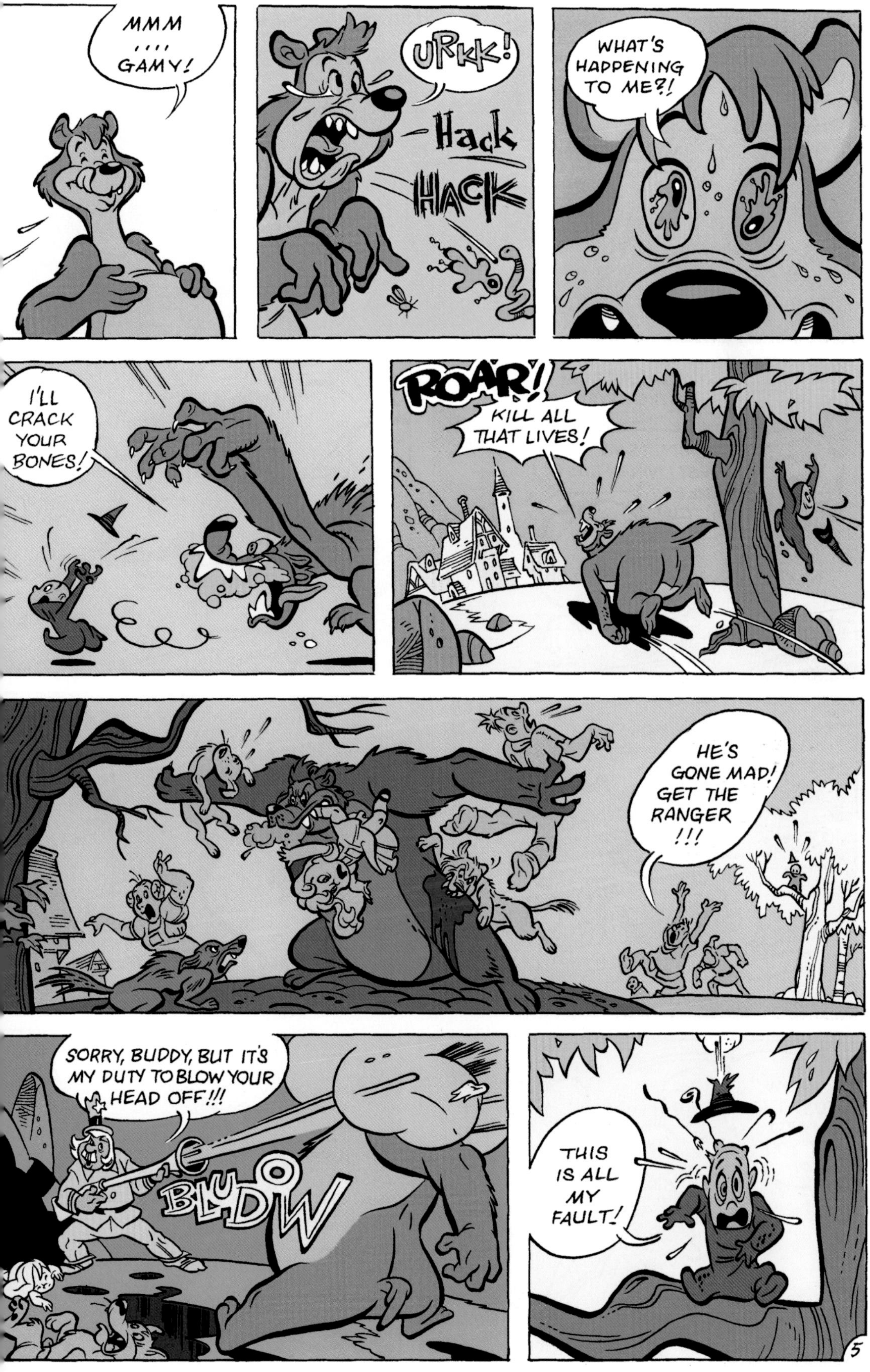
MMM .... GAMY!
URKK!
Hack
HACK
WHAT'S HAPPENING TO ME?!
I'LL CRACK YOUR BONES!
ROAR!
KILL ALL THAT LIVES!
HE'S GONE MAD! GET THE RANGER !!!
SORRY, BUDDY, BUT IT'S MY DUTY TO BLOW YOUR HEAD OFF!!!
BLUDOW
THIS IS ALL MY FAULT!

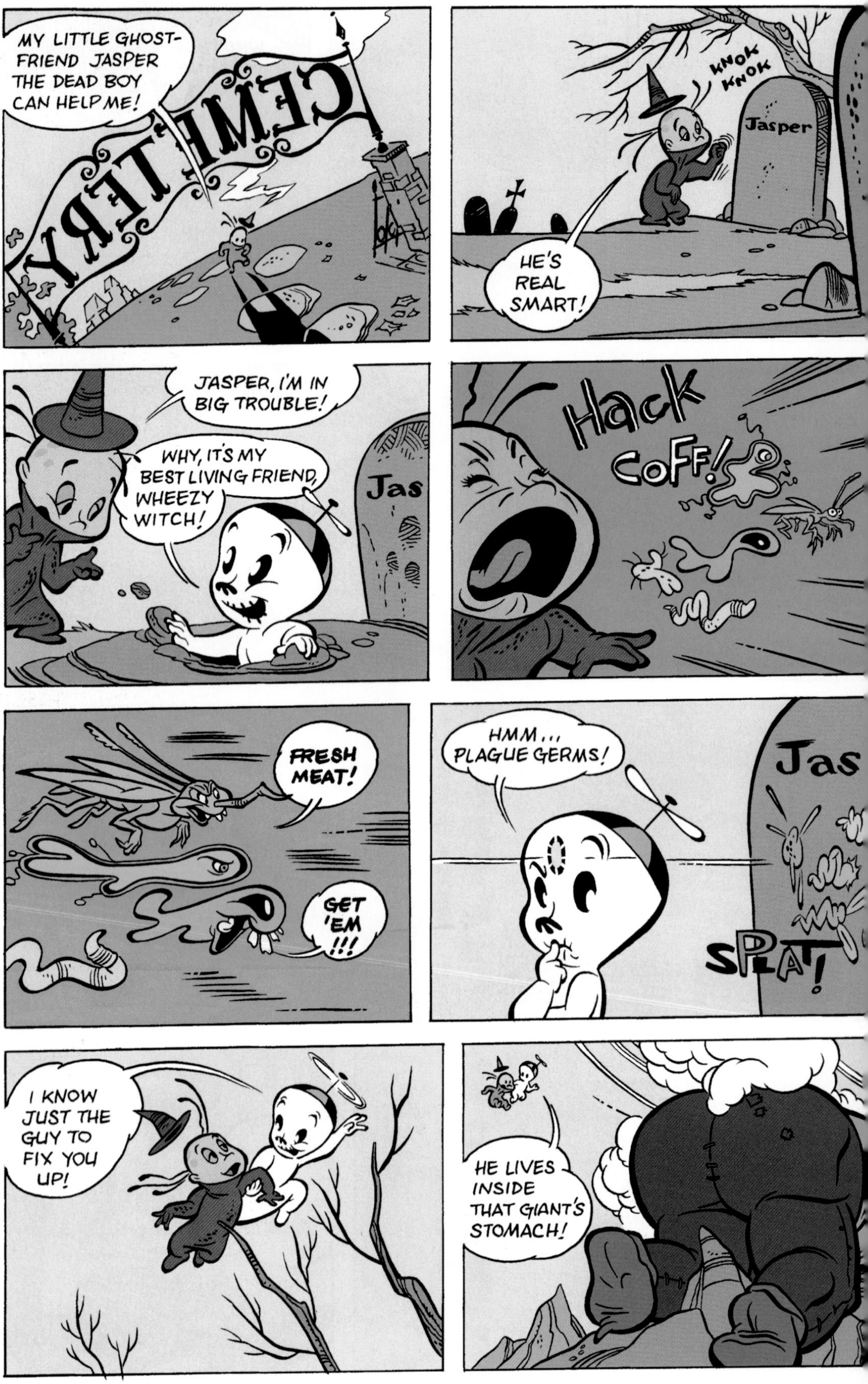
MY LITTLE GHOST-FRIEND JASPER THE DEAD BOY CAN HELP ME!
CEMETERY
KNOK KNOK
Jasper
HE'S REAL SMART!
JASPER, I'M IN BIG TROUBLE!
WHY, IT'S MY BEST LIVING FRIEND, WHEEZY WITCH!
Jas
Hack
CoFF!
FRESH MEAT!
GET 'EM !!!
HMM... PLAGUE GERMS!
Jas
SPLAT!
I KNOW JUST THE GUY TO FIX YOU UP!
HE LIVES INSIDE THAT GIANT'S STOMACH!

GREETINGS, O GREAT MEDICINE TROLL! GOT ANOTHER PLAGUE VICTIM FOR YA!

OKAY, WITCHIE, BUT I MUST WARN THEE, MY CURE IS VERY PAINFUL AND THE FEE IS GOING TO COST YOU AN ARM AND A LEG!

ANYTHING YOU SAY, DOC!

FIRST, WE CAREFULLY REACH INSIDE THE PATIENT.

THEN, WE PULL OUT THE SICKLY ENTRAILS...

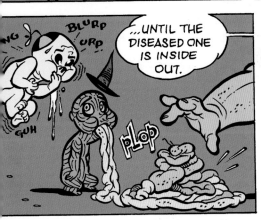

...UNTIL THE DISEASED ONE IS INSIDE OUT.

BLURP URP

GUH

PLOP

WOMP WOMP WOMP

NOW, BEAT VIGOROUSLY WITH A FLAMING 2 X 4 'TIL THE GERMS ARE DEAD.

HEY, IT WORKED! I FEEL GREAT!

EXCELLENT! NOW, ABOUT MY FEE... LET'S HAVE THAT ARM AND LEG!

7

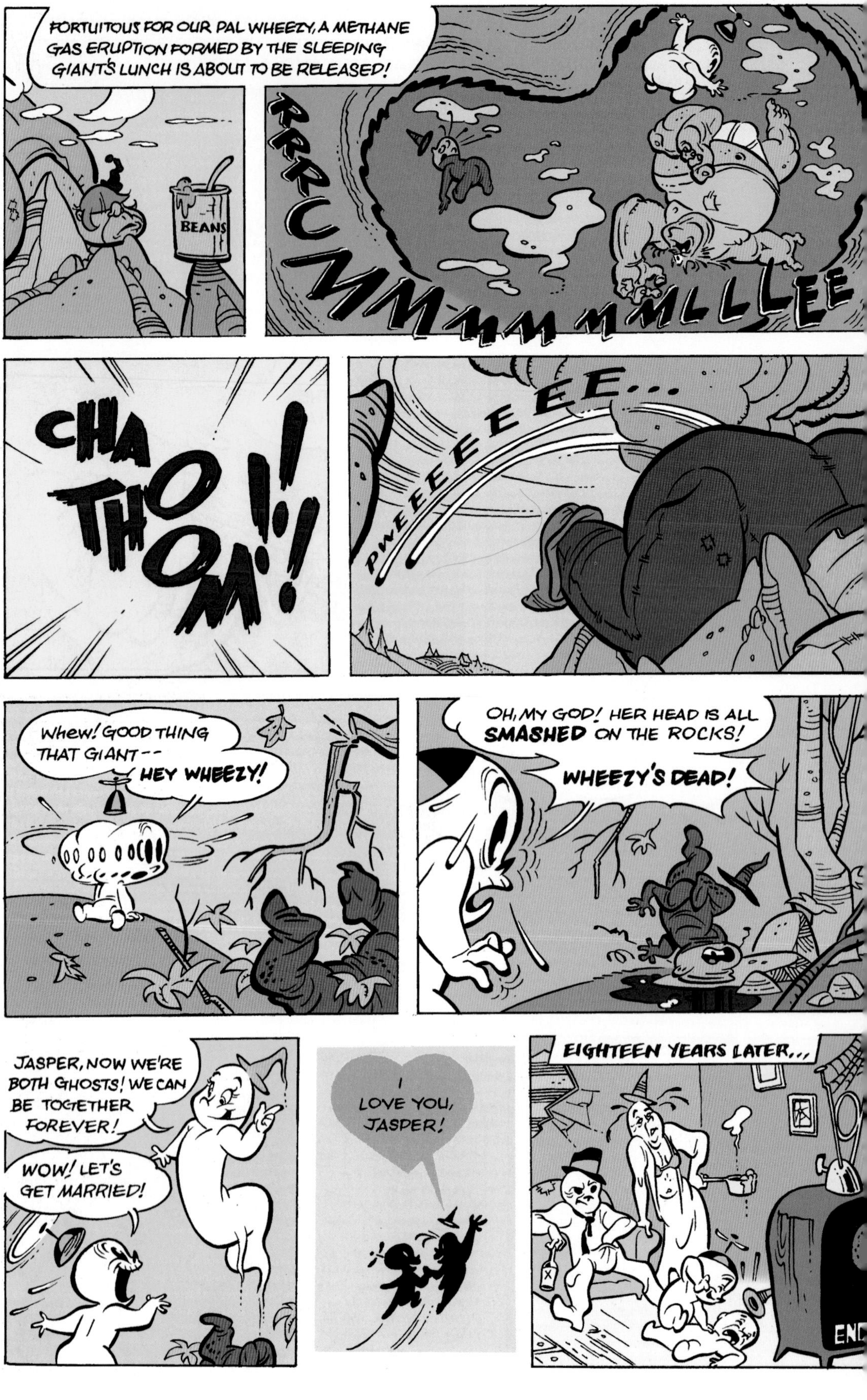
FORTUITOUS FOR OUR PAL WHEEZY, A METHANE GAS ERUPTION FORMED BY THE SLEEPING GIANT'S LUNCH IS ABOUT TO BE RELEASED!
BEANS
RRRRUMMMMMMMLLLEE
CHA THOOM!!!
PWEEEEEEEEEE...
Whew! GOOD THING THAT GIANT--
HEY WHEEZY!
OH, MY GOD! HER HEAD IS ALL SMASHED ON THE ROCKS!
WHEEZY'S DEAD!
JASPER, NOW WE'RE BOTH GHOSTS! WE CAN BE TOGETHER FOREVER!
WOW! LET'S GET MARRIED!
I LOVE YOU, JASPER!
EIGHTEEN YEARS LATER...

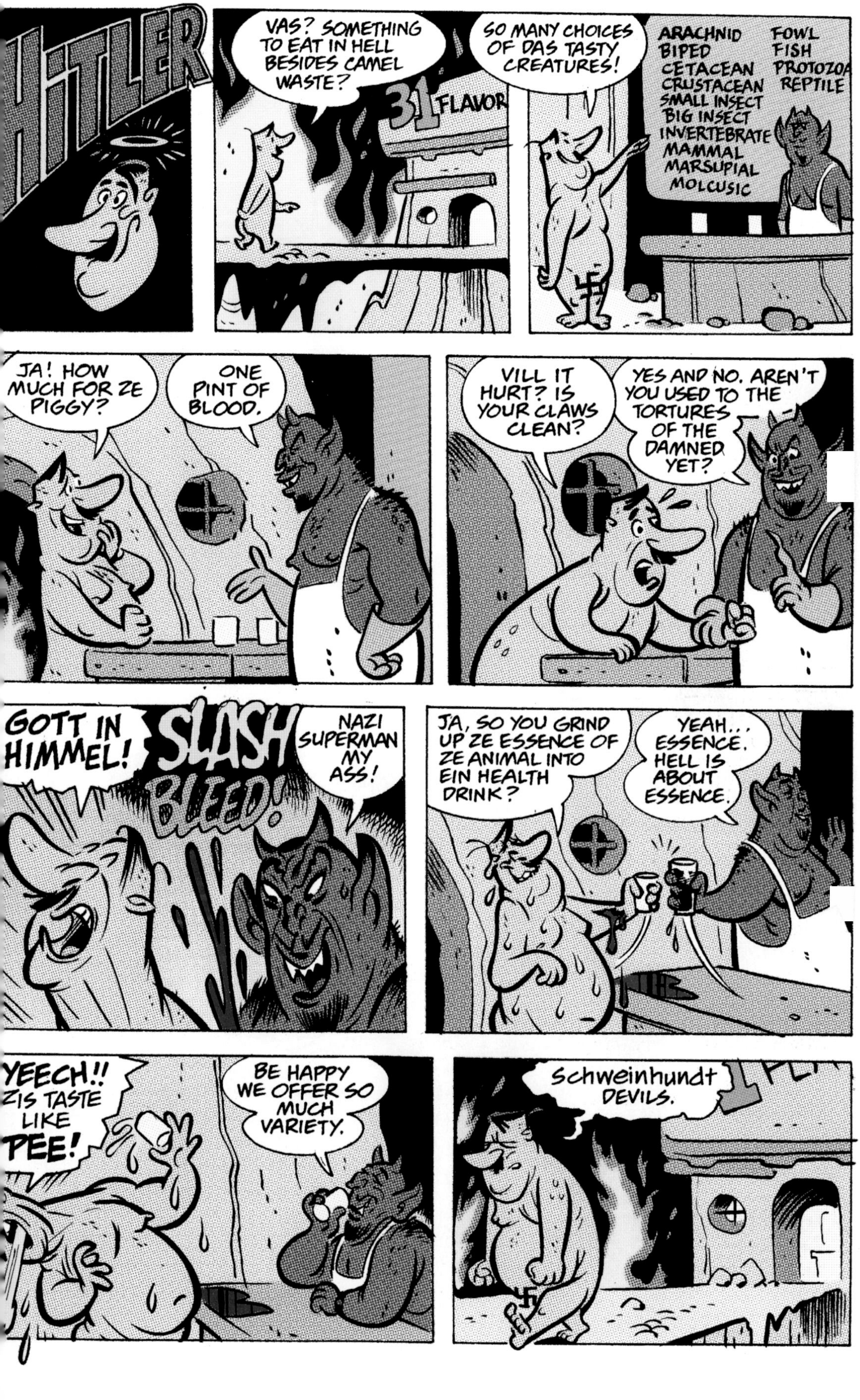
HITLER
VAS? SOMETHING TO EAT IN HELL BESIDES CAMEL WASTE?
31 FLAVOR
SO MANY CHOICES OF DAS TASTY CREATURES!
ARACHNID
BIPED
CETACEAN
CRUSTACEAN
SMALL INSECT
BIG INSECT
INVERTEBRATE
MAMMAL
MARSUPIAL
MOLCUSIC
FOWL
FISH
PROTOZOA
REPTILE
JA! HOW MUCH FOR ZE PIGGY?
ONE PINT OF BLOOD.
VILL IT HURT? IS YOUR CLAWS CLEAN?
YES AND NO. AREN'T YOU USED TO THE TORTURES OF THE DAMNED YET?
GOTT IN HIMMEL!
SLASH
BLEED!
NAZI SUPERMAN MY ASS!
JA, SO YOU GRIND UP ZE ESSENCE OF ZE ANIMAL INTO EIN HEALTH DRINK?
YEAH... ESSENCE. HELL IS ABOUT ESSENCE.
YEECH!! ZIS TASTE LIKE PEE!
BE HAPPY WE OFFER SO MUCH VARIETY.
Schweinhundt DEVILS.

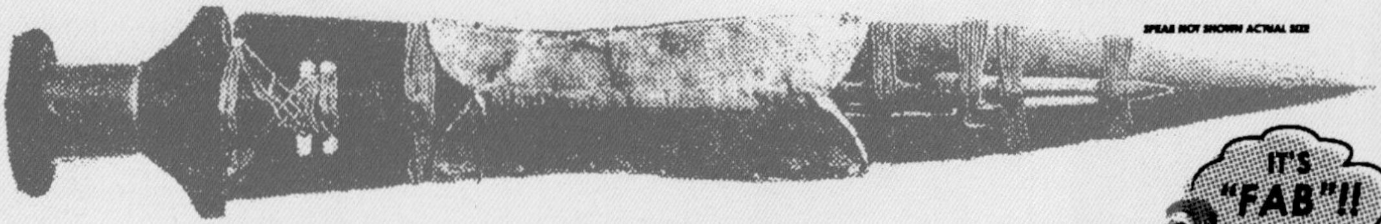

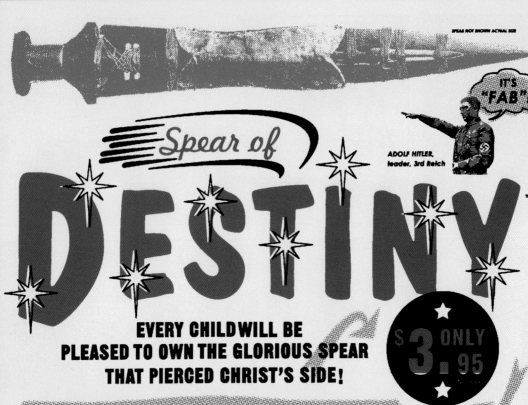

SPEAR NOT SHOWN ACTUAL SIZE

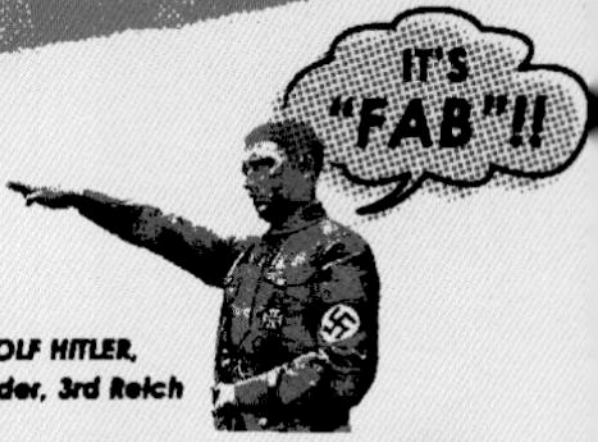
IT'S "FAB"!!

ADOLF HITLER,
leader, 3rd Reich

Spear of DESTINY™

EVERY CHILDWILL BE PLEASED TO OWN THE GLORIOUS SPEAR THAT PIERCED CHRIST'S SIDE!

$3.95 ONLY

- Great for Easter Celebrations
- Fulfill YOUR Destiny
- Make martyrs of your parents (They act that way anyway)
- Help revive Crucifixion
- Inspire your friends to win battles, even when hopelessly outnumbered
- Rule the World

ARTIST'S IMPRESSION

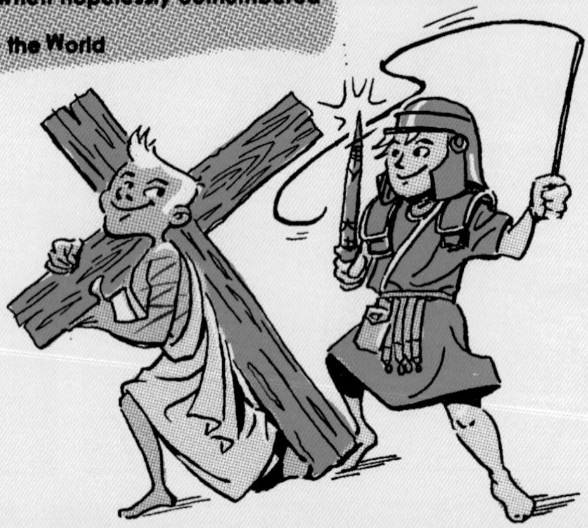

SEE WHAT THESE GREAT POSSESSORS OF THE SPEAR HAVE TO SAY:

Dynasty founder Charlemagne

"I enslaved millions with it; the damn thing made me a frigging prophet."

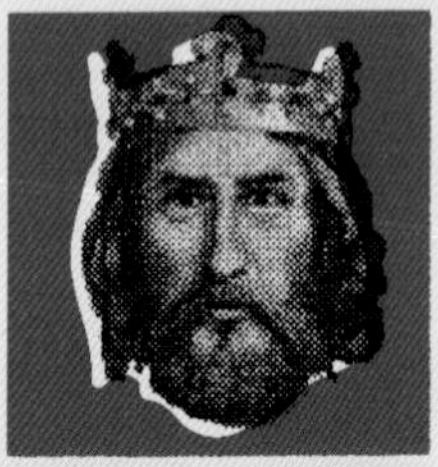

Roman Soldier Gaius Cassius

"I couldn't have killed Christ without it!"

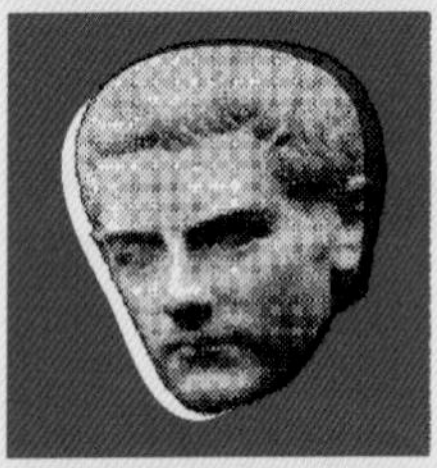

Aryan Opera Composer Richard Wagner

"It helped awaken me to the grandeur of the superior quality of my German blood"

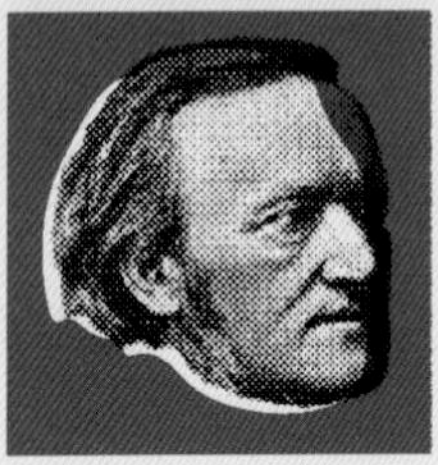

SEND NOW!

MONEY-BACK GUARANTEE!

Full refund if you do not rule the world in 14 days.

Send to: S.O.D. PRODUCTS, DEPT HB, PO BOX 399, OH.

Please rush me ___ Spear(s) of Destiny at $3.95each, inc. P+P.

NAME ________________

ADDRESS ________________

**Crucifixion Nail extra.*
Warning: dropping spear in heat of battle can result in agonizing death.

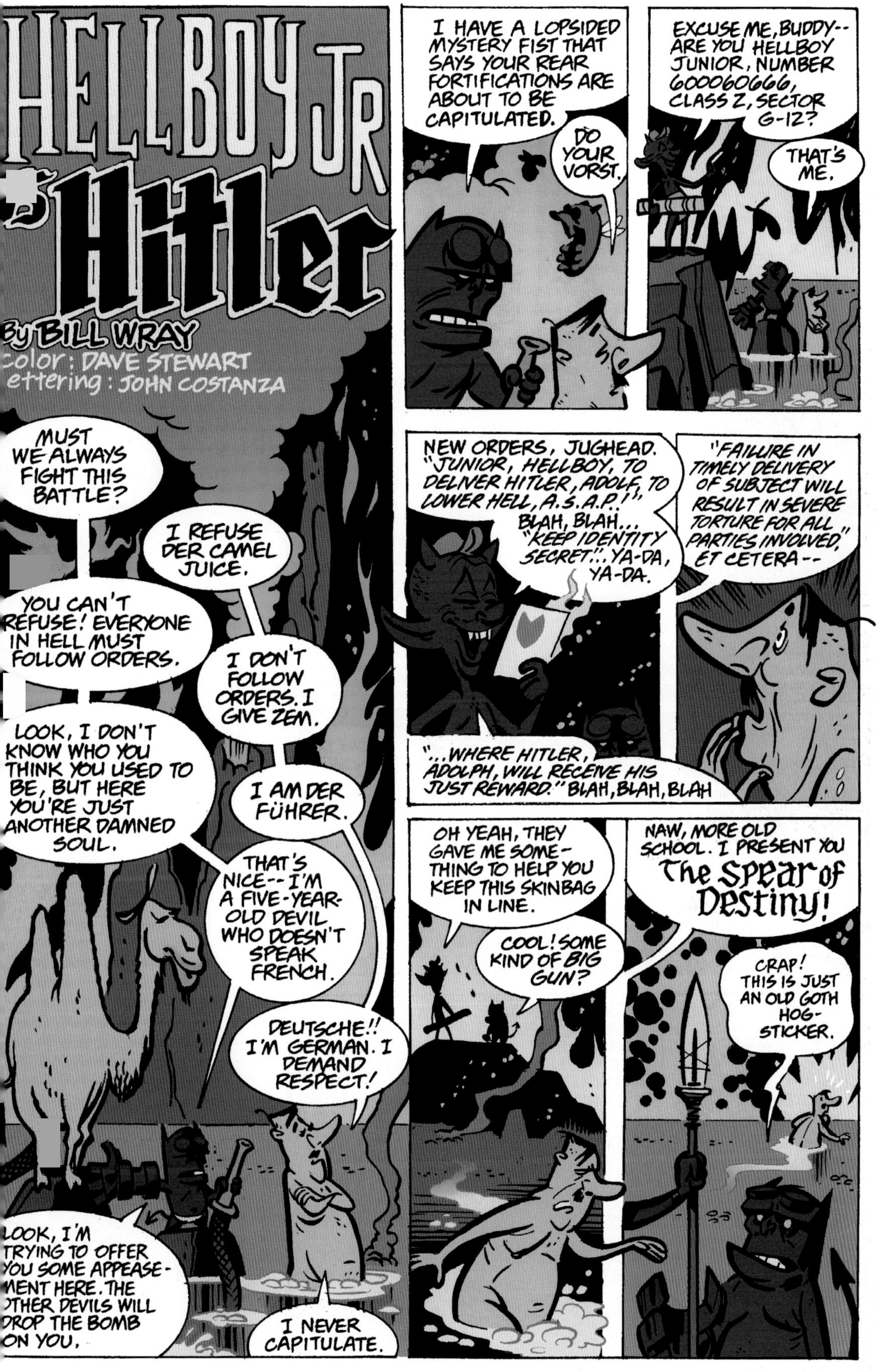

HELLBOY JR
Hitler
By BILL WRAY
color : DAVE STEWART
ettering : JOHN COSTANZA
MUST WE ALWAYS FIGHT THIS BATTLE?
I REFUSE DER CAMEL JUICE.
YOU CAN'T REFUSE! EVERYONE IN HELL MUST FOLLOW ORDERS.
I DON'T FOLLOW ORDERS. I GIVE ZEM.
LOOK, I DON'T KNOW WHO YOU THINK YOU USED TO BE, BUT HERE YOU'RE JUST ANOTHER DAMNED SOUL.
I AM DER FÜHRER.
THAT'S NICE-- I'M A FIVE-YEAR-OLD DEVIL WHO DOESN'T SPEAK FRENCH.
DEUTSCHE!! I'M GERMAN. I DEMAND RESPECT!
LOOK, I'M TRYING TO OFFER YOU SOME APPEASE-MENT HERE. THE OTHER DEVILS WILL DROP THE BOMB ON YOU.
I NEVER CAPITULATE.
I HAVE A LOPSIDED MYSTERY FIST THAT SAYS YOUR REAR FORTIFICATIONS ARE ABOUT TO BE CAPITULATED.
DO YOUR VORST.
EXCUSE ME, BUDDY-- ARE YOU HELLBOY JUNIOR, NUMBER 600060666, CLASS Z, SECTOR G-12?
THAT'S ME.
NEW ORDERS, JUGHEAD. "JUNIOR, HELLBOY, TO DELIVER HITLER, ADOLF, TO LOWER HELL, A.S.A.P.!" BLAH, BLAH... "KEEP IDENTITY SECRET!"... YA-DA, YA-DA.
"FAILURE IN TIMELY DELIVERY OF SUBJECT WILL RESULT IN SEVERE TORTURE FOR ALL PARTIES INVOLVED," ET CETERA--
"...WHERE HITLER, ADOLPH, WILL RECEIVE HIS JUST REWARD." BLAH, BLAH, BLAH
OH YEAH, THEY GAVE ME SOME-THING TO HELP YOU KEEP THIS SKINBAG IN LINE.
COOL! SOME KIND OF BIG GUN?
NAW, MORE OLD SCHOOL. I PRESENT YOU The Spear of Destiny!
CRAP! THIS IS JUST AN OLD GOTH HOG-STICKER.

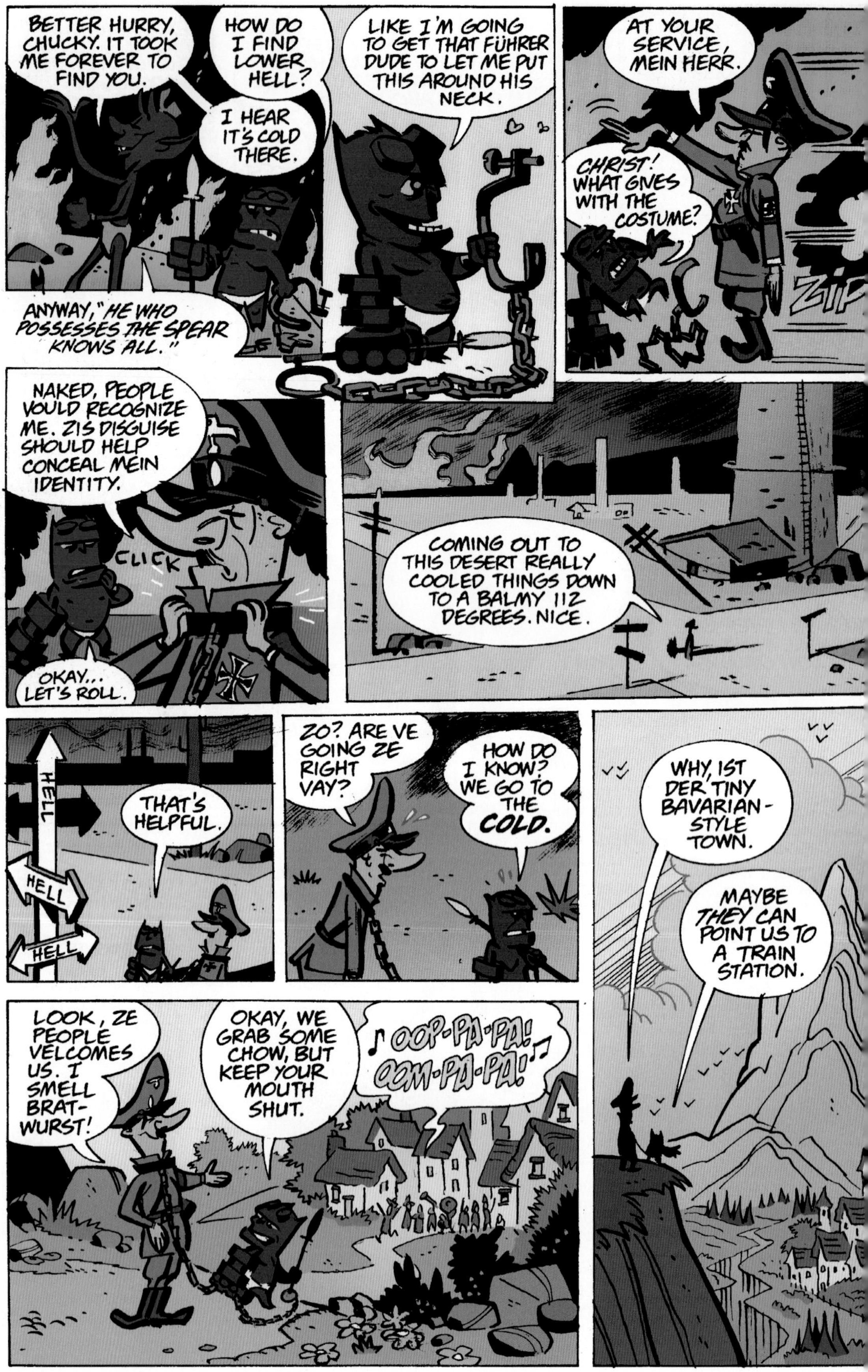
BETTER HURRY, CHUCKY. IT TOOK ME FOREVER TO FIND YOU.
HOW DO I FIND LOWER HELL?
I HEAR IT'S COLD THERE.
ANYWAY, "HE WHO POSSESSES THE SPEAR KNOWS ALL."
LIKE I'M GOING TO GET THAT FÜHRER DUDE TO LET ME PUT THIS AROUND HIS NECK.
AT YOUR SERVICE, MEIN HERR.
CHRIST! WHAT GIVES WITH THE COSTUME?
ZIP
NAKED, PEOPLE VOULD RECOGNIZE ME. ZIS DISGUISE SHOULD HELP CONCEAL MEIN IDENTITY.
CLICK
OKAY... LET'S ROLL.
COMING OUT TO THIS DESERT REALLY COOLED THINGS DOWN TO A BALMY 112 DEGREES. NICE.
HELL
HELL
HELL
THAT'S HELPFUL.
ZO? ARE VE GOING ZE RIGHT VAY?
HOW DO I KNOW? WE GO TO THE COLD.
WHY, IST DER TINY BAVARIAN-STYLE TOWN.
MAYBE THEY CAN POINT US TO A TRAIN STATION.
LOOK, ZE PEOPLE VELCOMES US. I SMELL BRATWURST!
OKAY, WE GRAB SOME CHOW, BUT KEEP YOUR MOUTH SHUT.
OOP-PA-PA! OOM-PA-PA!

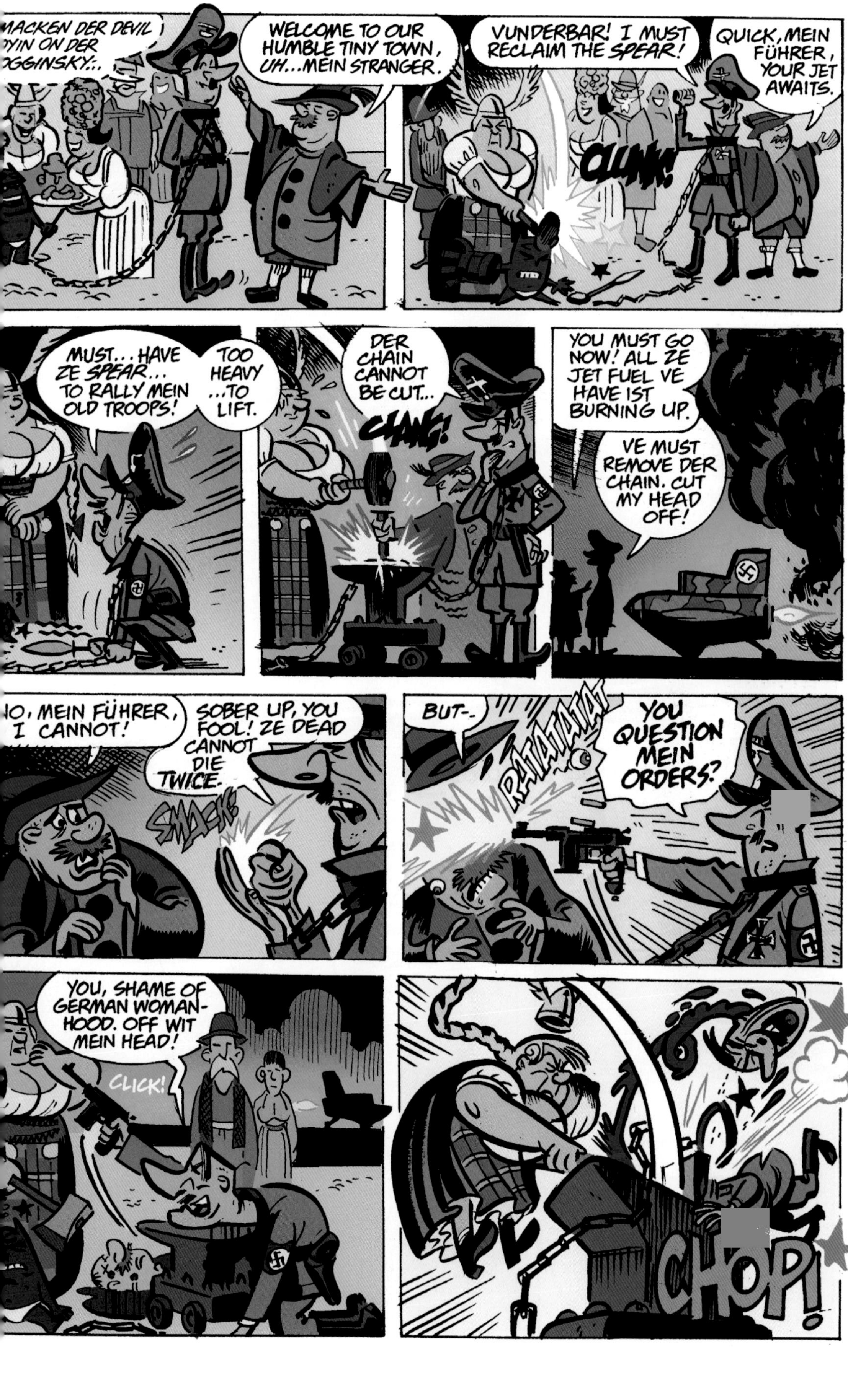
MACKEN DER DEVIL
YIN ON DER
GGINSKY:..
WELCOME TO OUR HUMBLE TINY TOWN, UH... MEIN STRANGER.
VUNDERBAR! I MUST RECLAIM THE SPEAR!
QUICK, MEIN FÜHRER, YOUR JET AWAITS.
CLUNK!
MUST... HAVE ZE SPEAR... TO RALLY MEIN OLD TROOPS!
TOO HEAVY ...TO LIFT.
DER CHAIN CANNOT BE CUT...
CHANG!
YOU MUST GO NOW! ALL ZE JET FUEL VE HAVE IST BURNING UP.
VE MUST REMOVE DER CHAIN. CUT MY HEAD OFF!
NO, MEIN FÜHRER, I CANNOT!
SOBER UP, YOU FOOL! ZE DEAD CANNOT DIE TWICE.
SMACK!
BUT-.
RATATATAT
YOU QUESTION MEIN ORDERS?
YOU, SHAME OF GERMAN WOMAN-HOOD. OFF WIT MEIN HEAD!
CLICK!
CHOP!

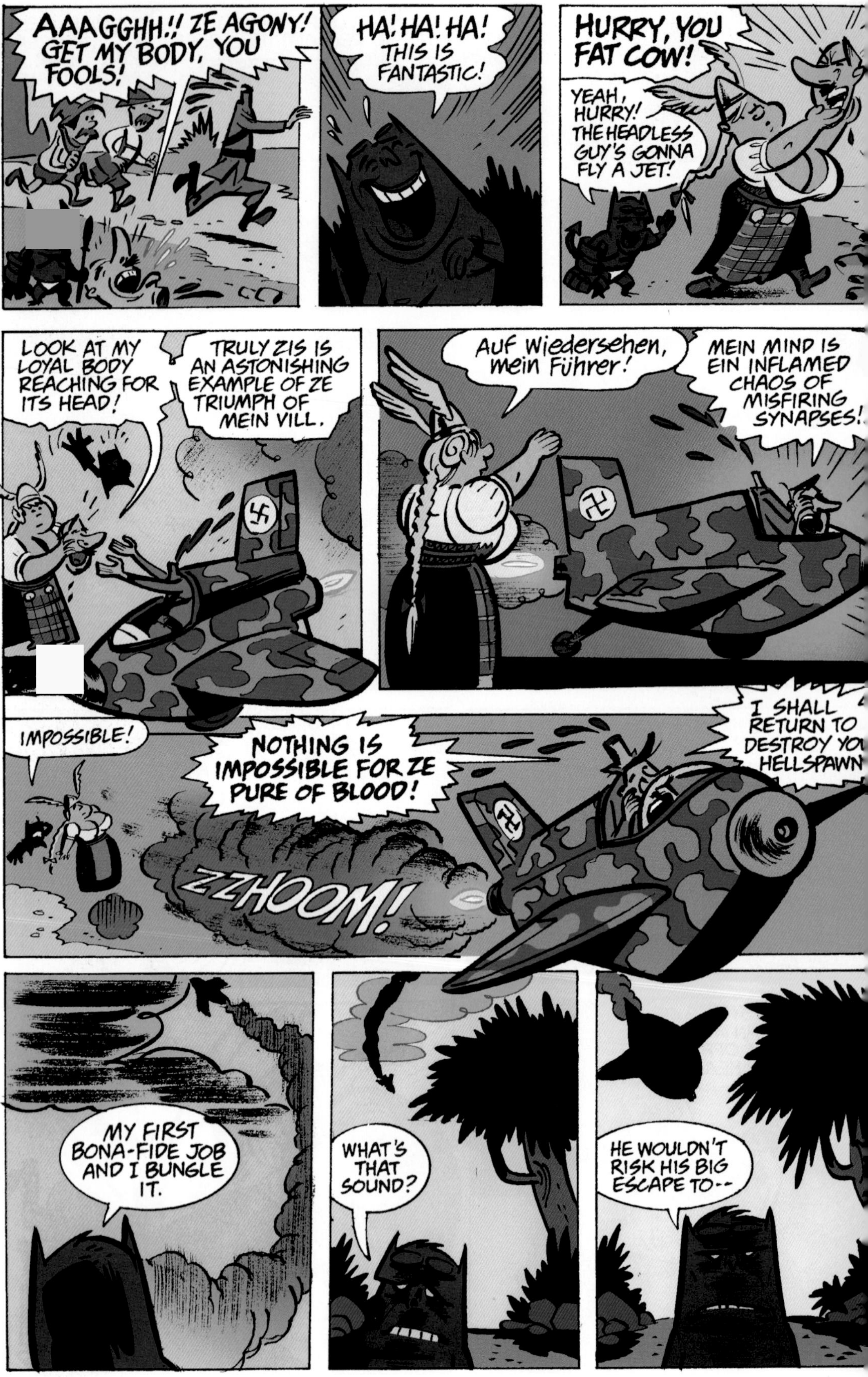
AAAGGHH!! ZE AGONY! GET MY BODY, YOU FOOLS!
HA! HA! HA! THIS IS FANTASTIC!
HURRY, YOU FAT COW!
YEAH, HURRY! THE HEADLESS GUY'S GONNA FLY A JET!
LOOK AT MY LOYAL BODY REACHING FOR ITS HEAD!
TRULY ZIS IS AN ASTONISHING EXAMPLE OF ZE TRIUMPH OF MEIN VILL.
Auf Wiedersehen, mein Führer!
MEIN MIND IS EIN INFLAMED CHAOS OF MISFIRING SYNAPSES!
IMPOSSIBLE!
NOTHING IS IMPOSSIBLE FOR ZE PURE OF BLOOD!
I SHALL RETURN TO DESTROY YOU HELLSPAWN
ZZHOOM!
MY FIRST BONA-FIDE JOB AND I BUNGLE IT.
WHAT'S THAT SOUND?
HE WOULDN'T RISK HIS BIG ESCAPE TO--

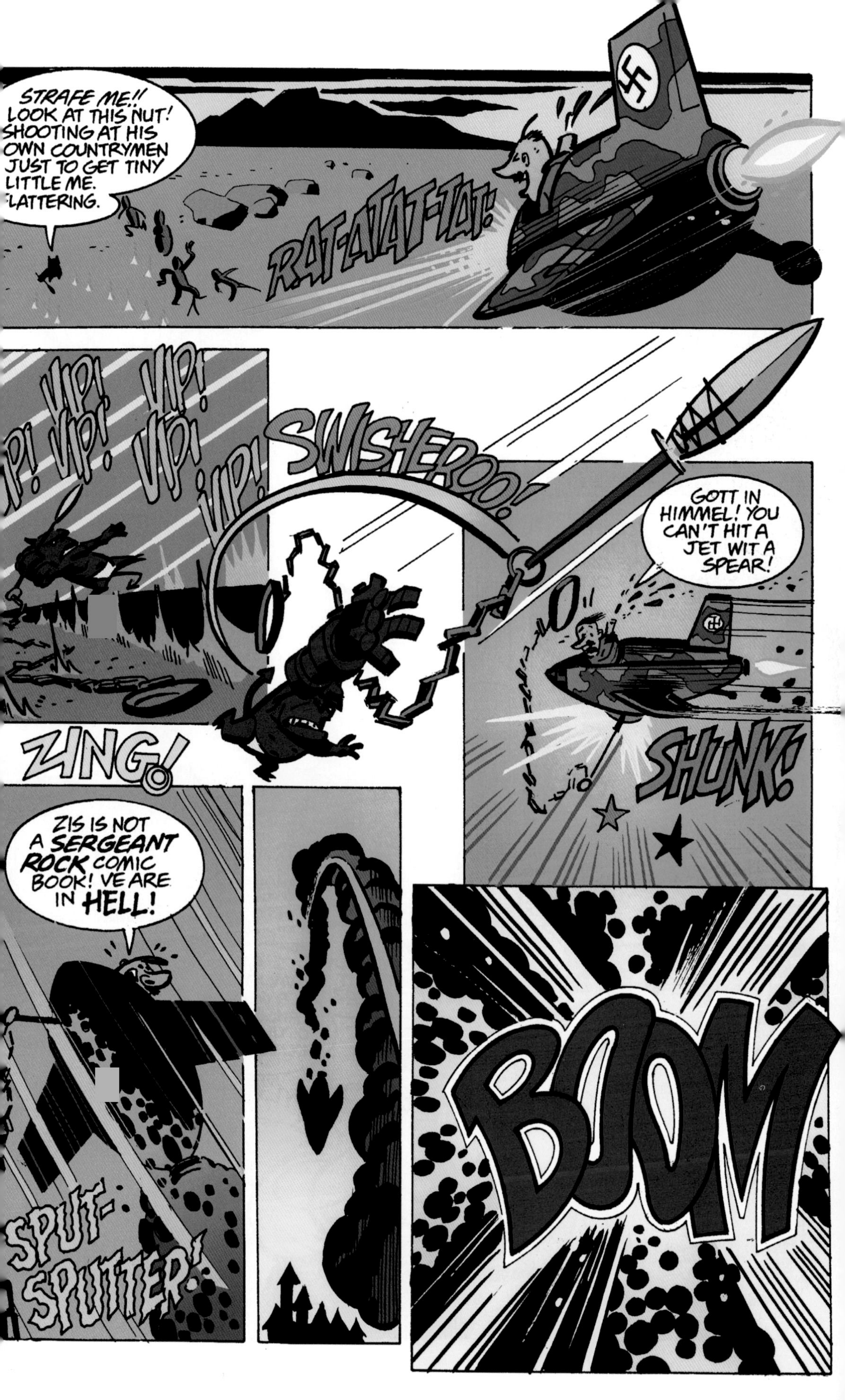
STRAFE ME!! LOOK AT THIS NUT! SHOOTING AT HIS OWN COUNTRYMEN JUST TO GET TINY LITTLE ME. FLATTERING.
RAT-A-TAT-TAT!
VIP! VIP! VIP! VIP! VIP! VIP!
SWISHEROO!
GOTT IN HIMMEL! YOU CAN'T HIT A JET WIT A SPEAR!
SHUNK!
ZING!
ZIS IS NOT A SERGEANT ROCK COMIC BOOK! VE ARE IN HELL!
SPUT-SPUTTER!
BOOM

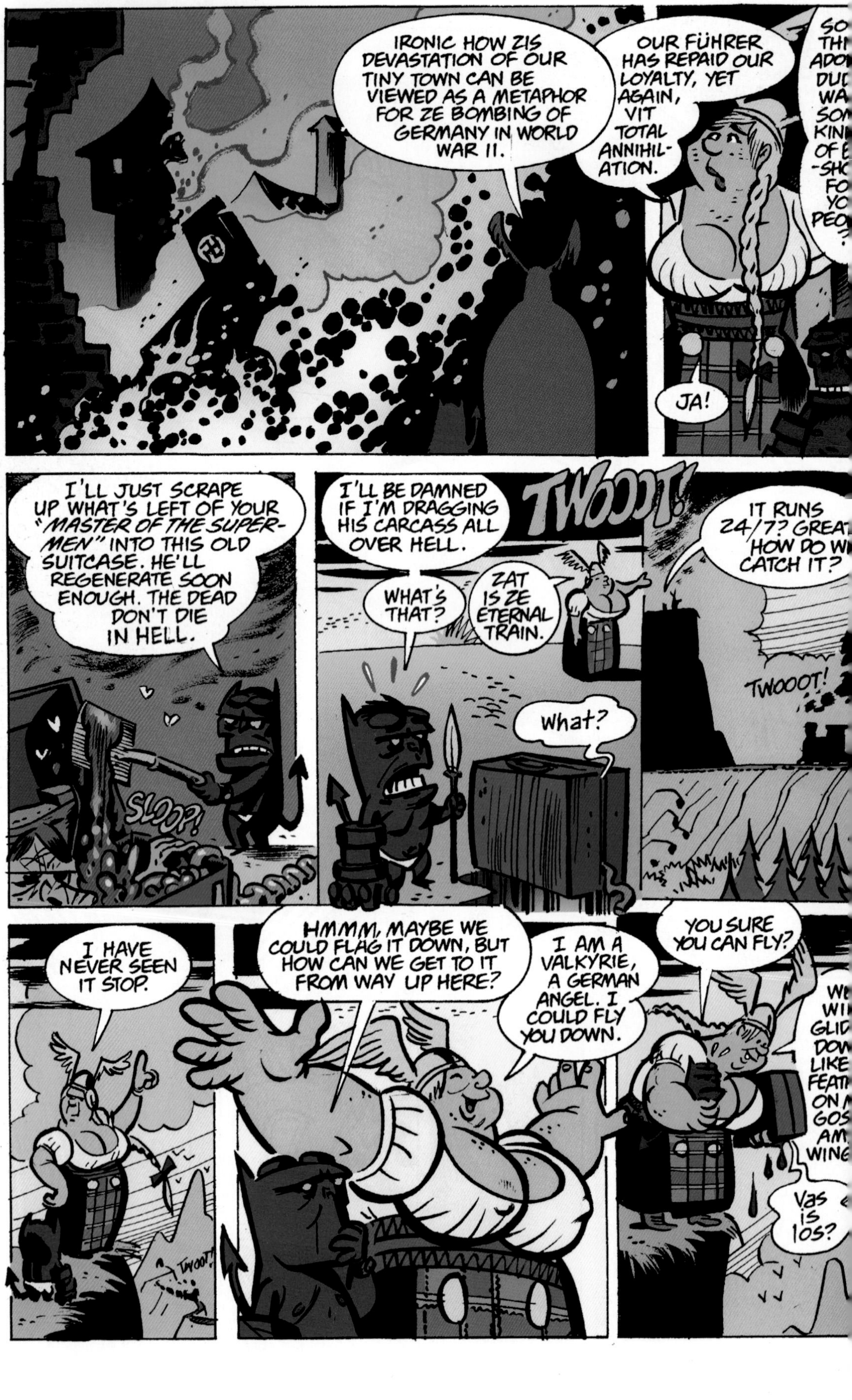
IRONIC HOW ZIS DEVASTATION OF OUR TINY TOWN CAN BE VIEWED AS A METAPHOR FOR ZE BOMBING OF GERMANY IN WORLD WAR II.
OUR FÜHRER HAS REPAID OUR LOYALTY, YET AGAIN, VIT TOTAL ANNIHIL-ATION.
JA!
I'LL JUST SCRAPE UP WHAT'S LEFT OF YOUR "MASTER OF THE SUPER-MEN" INTO THIS OLD SUITCASE. HE'LL REGENERATE SOON ENOUGH. THE DEAD DON'T DIE IN HELL.
SLOOP!
I'LL BE DAMNED IF I'M DRAGGING HIS CARCASS ALL OVER HELL.
TWOOOT!
WHAT'S THAT?
ZAT IS ZE ETERNAL TRAIN.
What?
IT RUNS 24/7?
TWOOOT!
I HAVE NEVER SEEN IT STOP.
HMMM, MAYBE WE COULD FLAG IT DOWN, BUT HOW CAN WE GET TO IT FROM WAY UP HERE?
I AM A VALKYRIE, A GERMAN ANGEL. I COULD FLY YOU DOWN.
YOU SURE YOU CAN FLY?
Vas is los?

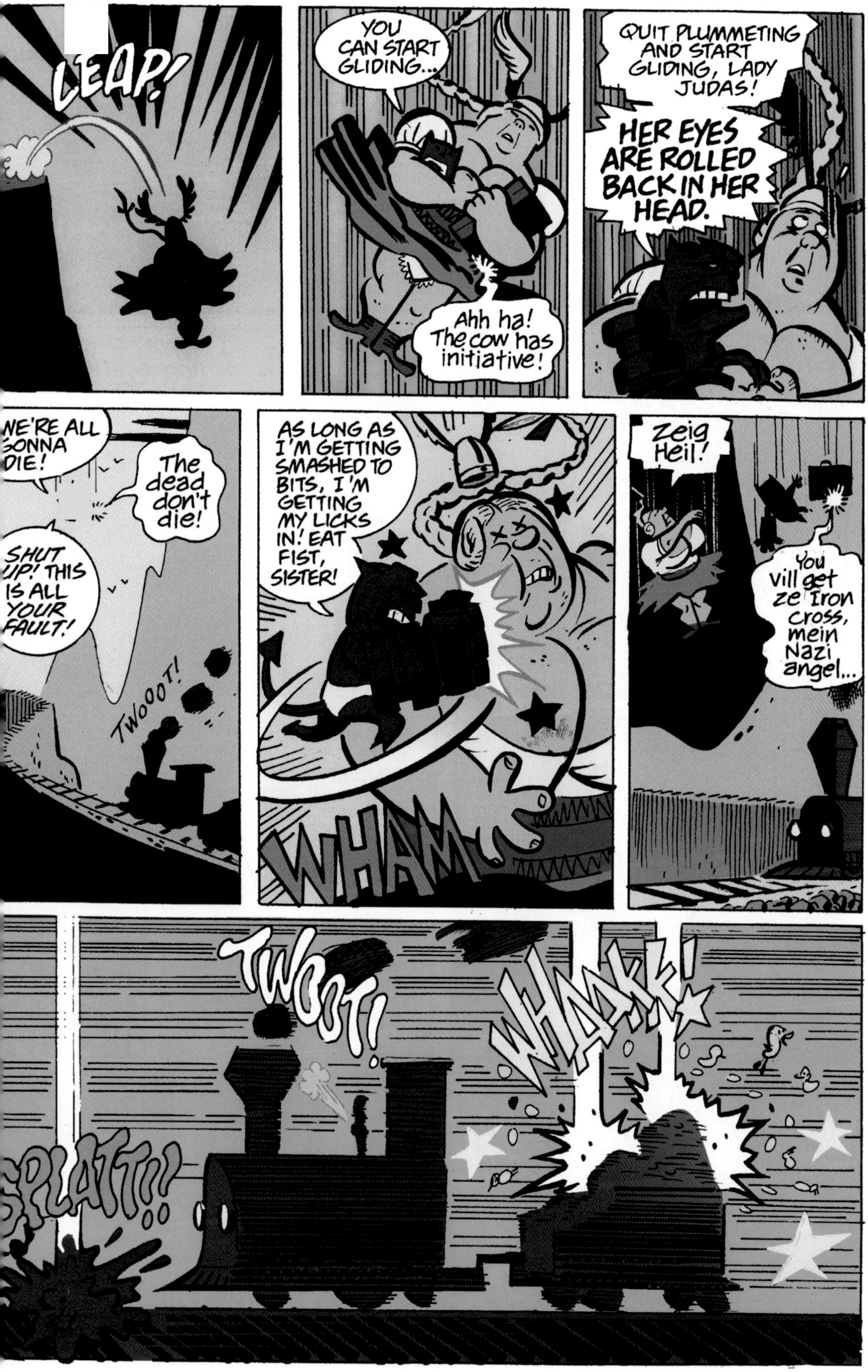
LEAP!
YOU CAN START GLIDING...
Ahh ha! The cow has initiative!
QUIT PLUMMETING AND START GLIDING, LADY JUDAS!
HER EYES ARE ROLLED BACK IN HER HEAD.
WE'RE ALL GONNA DIE!
The dead don't die!
SHUT UP! THIS IS ALL YOUR FAULT!
TWOOOT!
AS LONG AS I'M GETTING SMASHED TO BITS, I'M GETTING MY LICKS IN! EAT FIST, SISTER!
WHAM
Zeig Heil!
You vill get ze Iron cross, mein Nazi angel...
TWOOT!
WHAKK!
SPLATT!!

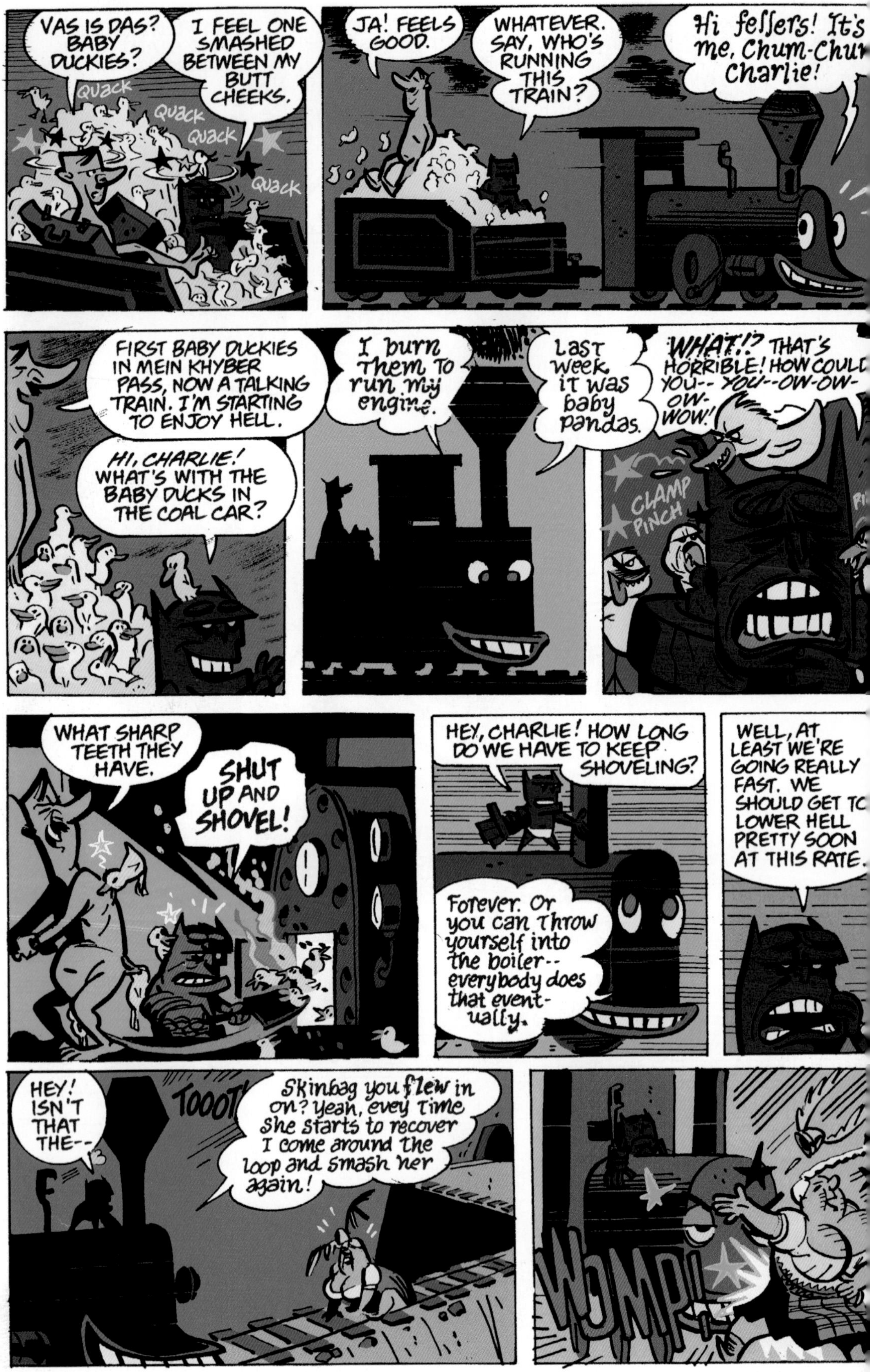
VAS IS DAS? BABY DUCKIES?
I FEEL ONE SMASHED BETWEEN MY BUTT CHEEKS.
QUACK
QUACK
QUACK
QUACK
JA! FEELS GOOD.
WHATEVER. SAY, WHO'S RUNNING THIS TRAIN?
Hi fellers! It's me, Chum-Chum Charlie!
FIRST BABY DUCKIES IN MEIN KHYBER PASS, NOW A TALKING TRAIN. I'M STARTING TO ENJOY HELL.
HI, CHARLIE! WHAT'S WITH THE BABY DUCKS IN THE COAL CAR?
I burn them to run my engine.
Last week it was baby pandas.
WHAT!? THAT'S HORRIBLE! HOW COULD YOU-- YOU--OW-OW-OW-WOW!
CLAMP
PINCH
WHAT SHARP TEETH THEY HAVE.
SHUT UP AND SHOVEL!
HEY, CHARLIE! HOW LONG DO WE HAVE TO KEEP SHOVELING?
Forever. Or you can throw yourself into the boiler-- everybody does that eventually.
WELL, AT LEAST WE'RE GOING REALLY FAST. WE SHOULD GET TO LOWER HELL PRETTY SOON AT THIS RATE.
HEY! ISN'T THAT THE--
TOOOT!
Skinbag you flew in on? Yeah, evey time she starts to recover I come around the loop and smash her again!
WOMP!

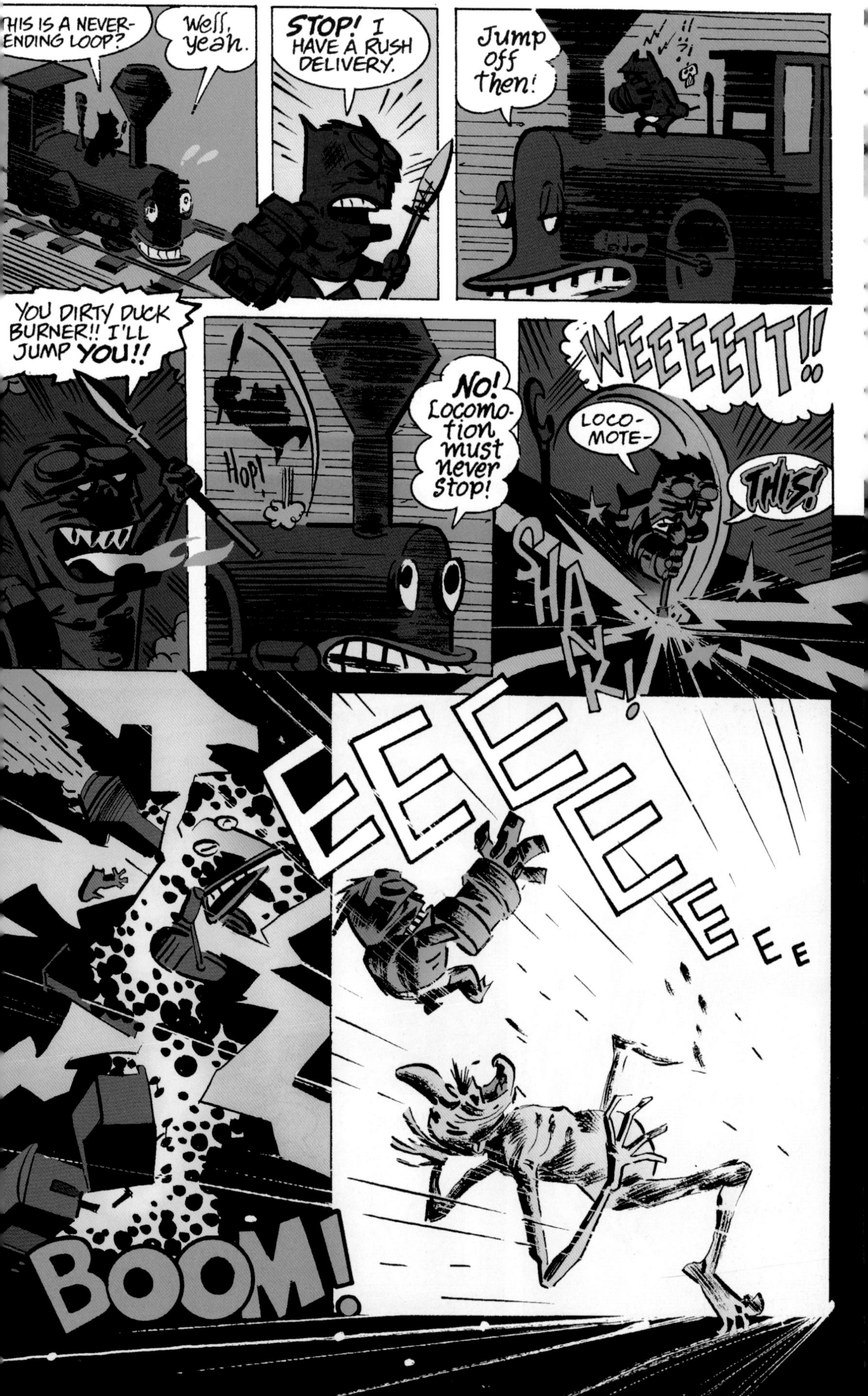
THIS IS A NEVER-ENDING LOOP?
Well, yeah.
STOP! I HAVE A RUSH DELIVERY.
Jump off then!
YOU DIRTY DUCK BURNER!! I'LL JUMP YOU!!
HOP!
NO! Locomotion must never stop!
WEEEETT!!
LOCO-MOTE-
THIS!
SHANK!
EEEEEEEE
BOOM!

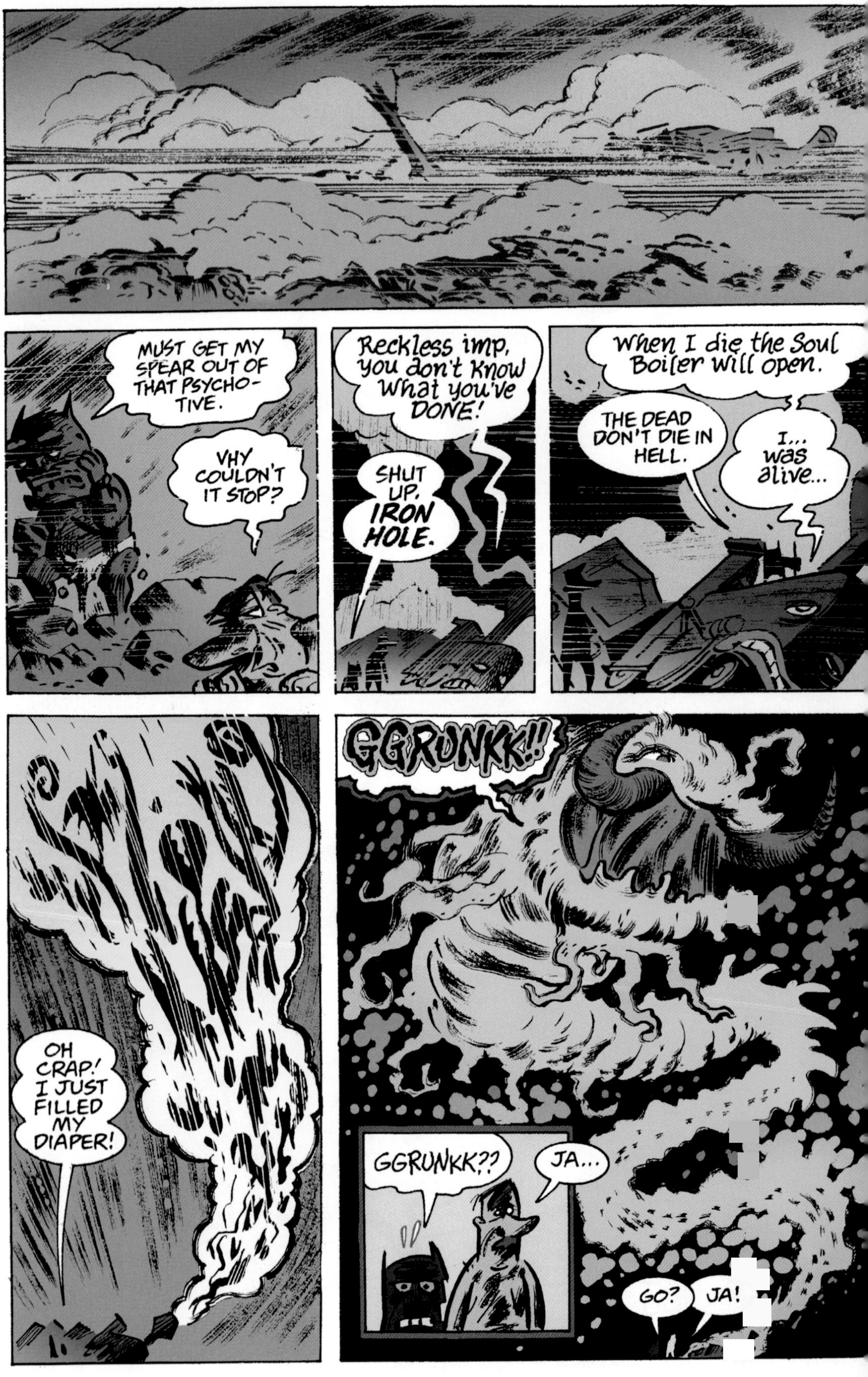
MUST GET MY SPEAR OUT OF THAT PSYCHO-TIVE.
VHY COULDN'T IT STOP?
Reckless imp, you don't know what you've DONE!
SHUT UP, IRON HOLE.
When I die the Soul Boiler will open.
THE DEAD DON'T DIE IN HELL.
I... was alive...
OH CRAP! I JUST FILLED MY DIAPER!
GGRUNKK!!
GGRUNKK??
JA...
GO?
JA!

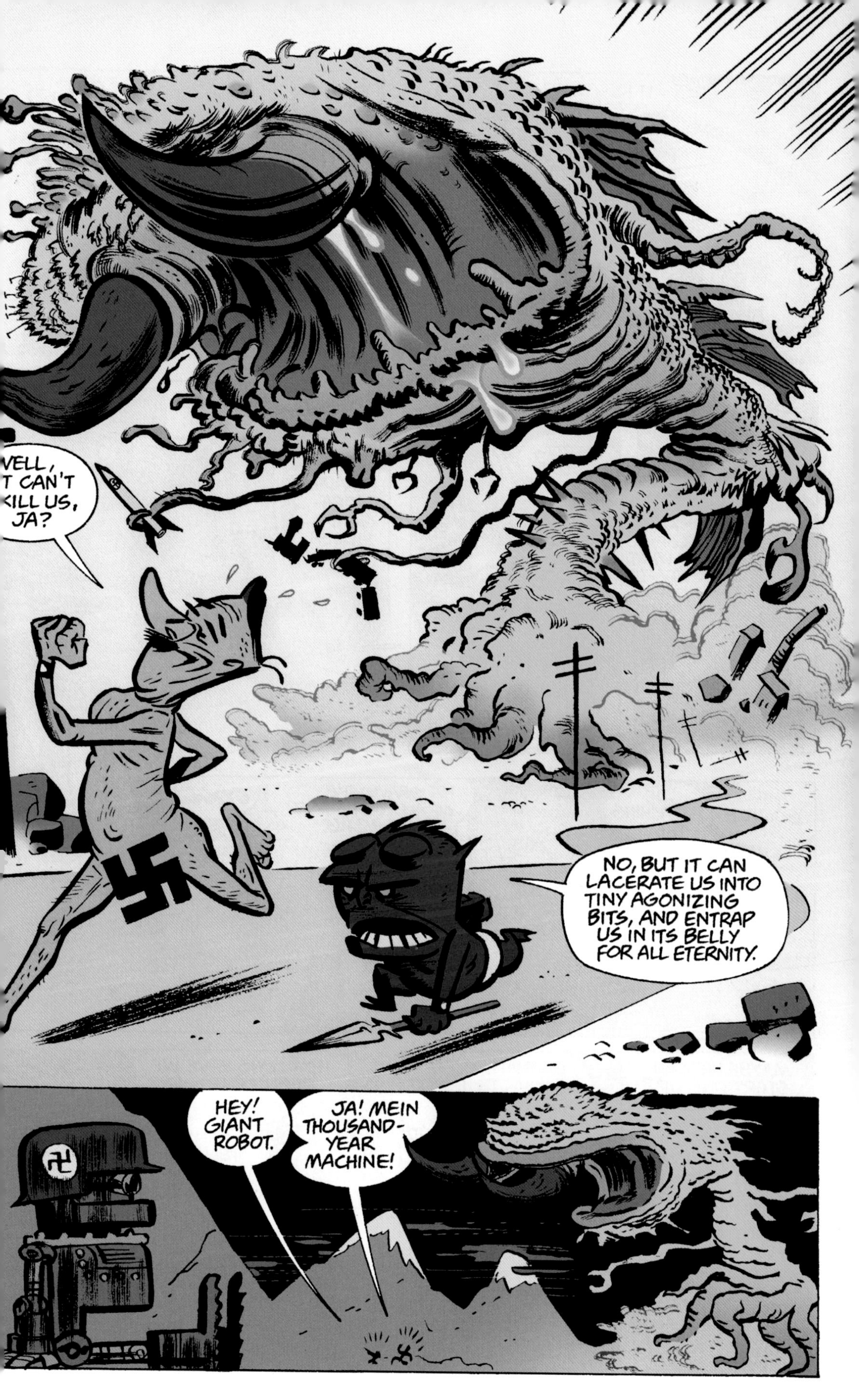
VELL, T CAN'T KILL US, JA?
NO, BUT IT CAN LACERATE US INTO TINY AGONIZING BITS, AND ENTRAP US IN ITS BELLY FOR ALL ETERNITY.
HEY! GIANT ROBOT.
JA! MEIN THOUSAND-YEAR MACHINE!

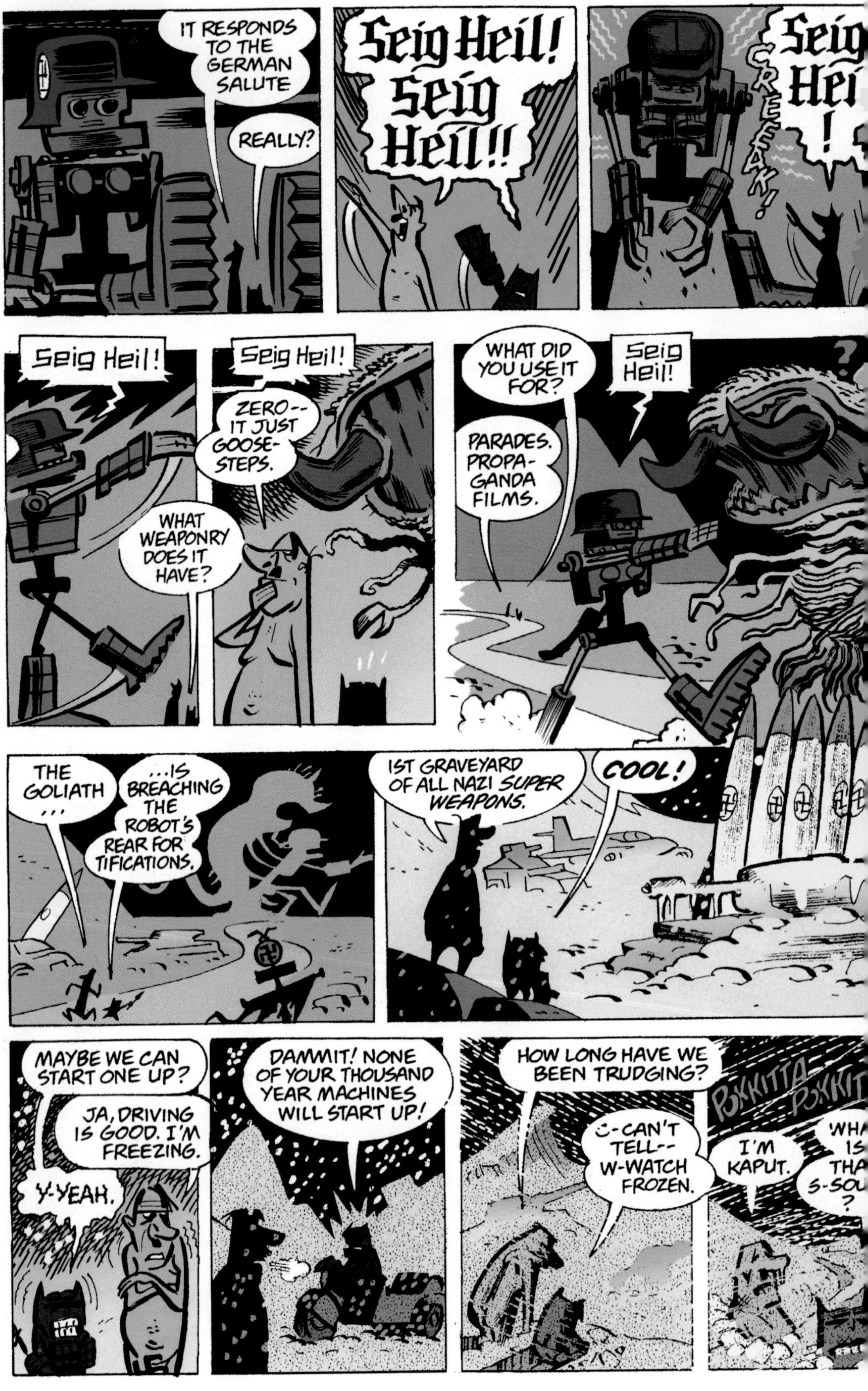
IT RESPONDS TO THE GERMAN SALUTE
REALLY?
Seig Heil! Seig Heil!!
CREEAK!
Seig
Seig Heil!
Seig Heil!
ZERO-- IT JUST GOOSE-STEPS.
WHAT WEAPONRY DOES IT HAVE?
WHAT DID YOU USE IT FOR?
Seig Heil!
PARADES. PROPA-GANDA FILMS.
?
THE GOLIATH ...
...IS BREACHING THE ROBOT'S REAR FOR TIFICATIONS.
IST GRAVEYARD OF ALL NAZI SUPER WEAPONS.
COOL!
MAYBE WE CAN START ONE UP?
JA, DRIVING IS GOOD. I'M FREEZING.
Y-YEAH.
DAMMIT! NONE OF YOUR THOUSAND YEAR MACHINES WILL START UP!
HOW LONG HAVE WE BEEN TRUDGING?
C-CAN'T TELL-- W-WATCH FROZEN.
I'M KAPUT.

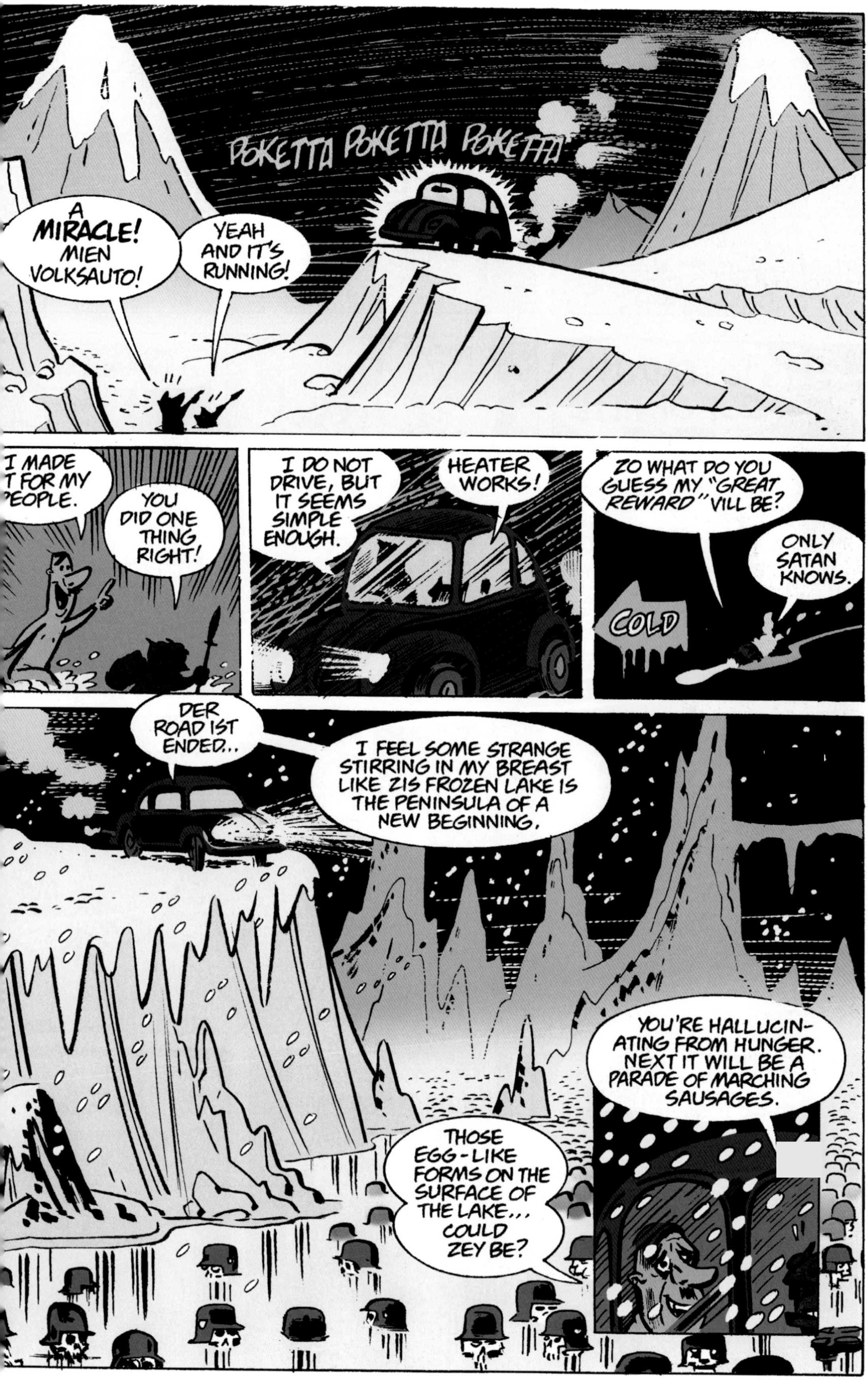
POKETTA POKETTA POKETTA
A MIRACLE! MIEN VOLKSAUTO!
YEAH AND IT'S RUNNING!
I MADE T FOR MY PEOPLE.
YOU DID ONE THING RIGHT!
I DO NOT DRIVE, BUT IT SEEMS SIMPLE ENOUGH.
HEATER WORKS!
ZO WHAT DO YOU GUESS MY "GREAT REWARD" VILL BE?
ONLY SATAN KNOWS.
COLD
DER ROAD IST ENDED...
I FEEL SOME STRANGE STIRRING IN MY BREAST LIKE ZIS FROZEN LAKE IS THE PENINSULA OF A NEW BEGINNING.
YOU'RE HALLUCINATING FROM HUNGER. NEXT IT WILL BE A PARADE OF MARCHING SAUSAGES.
THOSE EGG-LIKE FORMS ON THE SURFACE OF THE LAKE... COULD ZEY BE?

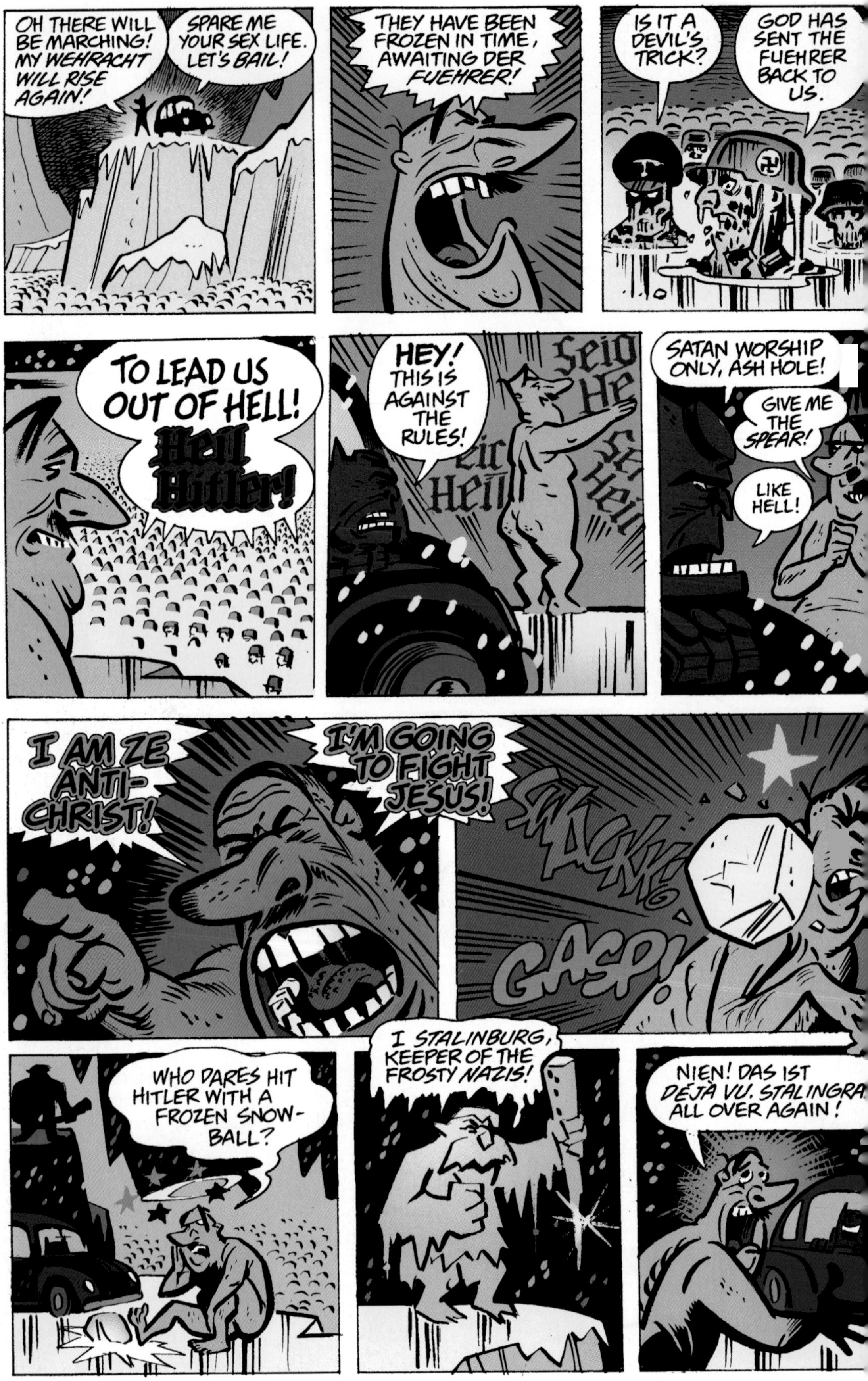
OH THERE WILL BE MARCHING! MY WEHRACHT WILL RISE AGAIN!
SPARE ME YOUR SEX LIFE. LET'S BAIL!
THEY HAVE BEEN FROZEN IN TIME, AWAITING DER FUEHRER!
IS IT A DEVIL'S TRICK?
GOD HAS SENT THE FUEHRER BACK TO US.
TO LEAD US OUT OF HELL!
Heil Hitler!
HEY! THIS IS AGAINST THE RULES!
Seig Heil
Seig Heil
Seig Heil
SATAN WORSHIP ONLY, ASH HOLE!
GIVE ME THE SPEAR!
LIKE HELL!
I AM ZE ANTI-CHRIST!
I'M GOING TO FIGHT JESUS!
GASP!
WHO DARES HIT HITLER WITH A FROZEN SNOW-BALL?
I STALINBURG, KEEPER OF THE FROSTY NAZIS!
NIEN! DAS IST DÉJÀ VU. STALINGRA ALL OVER AGAIN!

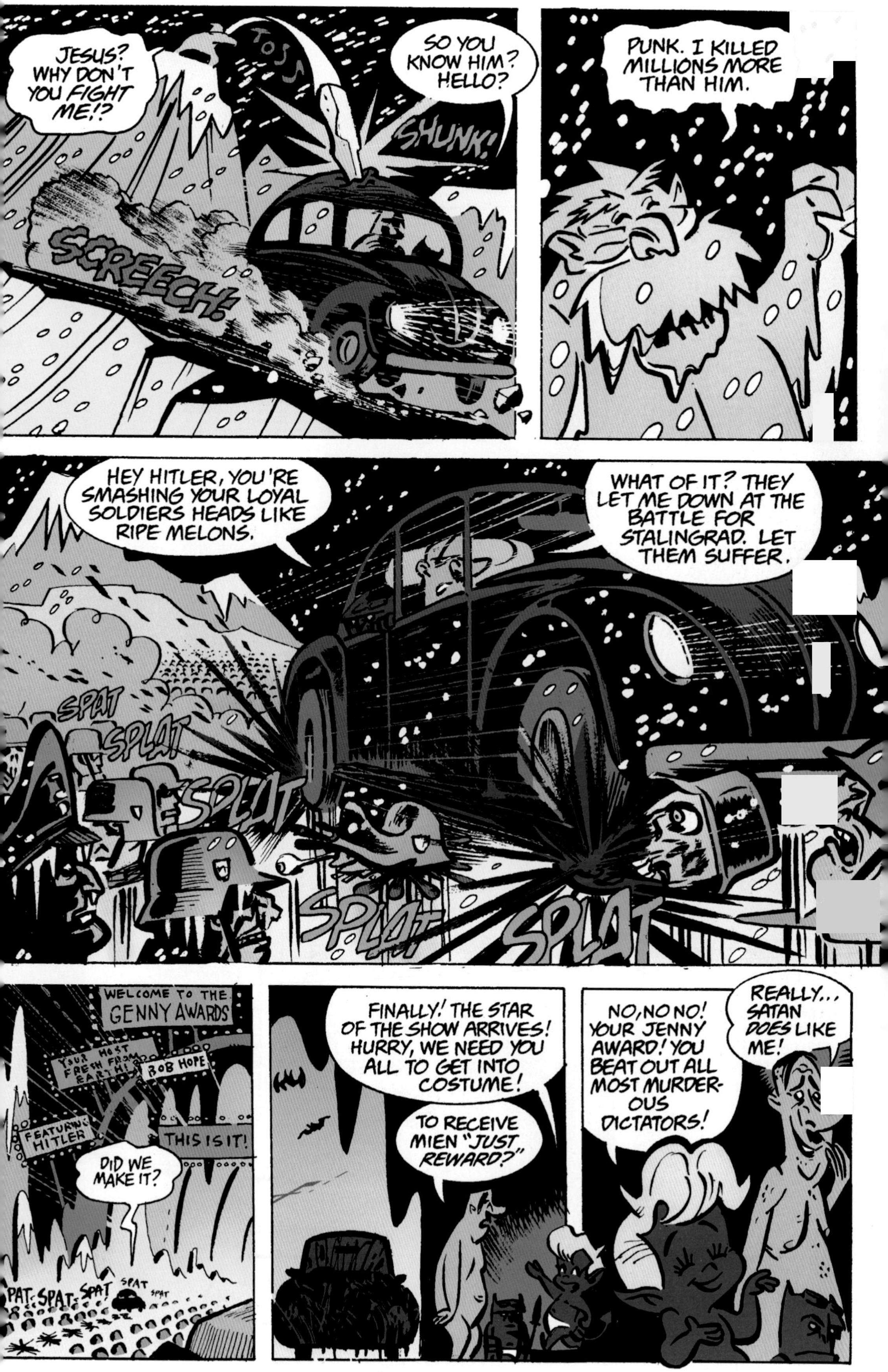
JESUS? WHY DON'T YOU FIGHT ME!?
TOSS
SO YOU KNOW HIM? HELLO?
SHUNK!
SCREEECH!
PUNK. I KILLED MILLIONS MORE THAN HIM.
HEY HITLER, YOU'RE SMASHING YOUR LOYAL SOLDIERS HEADS LIKE RIPE MELONS.
WHAT OF IT? THEY LET ME DOWN AT THE BATTLE FOR STALINGRAD. LET THEM SUFFER.
SPAT
SPLAT
SPLAT
SPLAT
SPLAT
WELCOME TO THE GENNY AWARDS
YOUR HOST FRESH FROM EARTH
BOB HOPE
FEATURING HITLER
THIS IS IT!
DID WE MAKE IT?
PAT SPAT SPAT SPAT SPAT
FINALLY! THE STAR OF THE SHOW ARRIVES! HURRY, WE NEED YOU ALL TO GET INTO COSTUME!
TO RECEIVE MIEN "JUST REWARD?"
NO, NO NO! YOUR JENNY AWARD! YOU BEAT OUT ALL MOST MURDER-OUS DICTATORS!
REALLY... SATAN DOES LIKE ME!

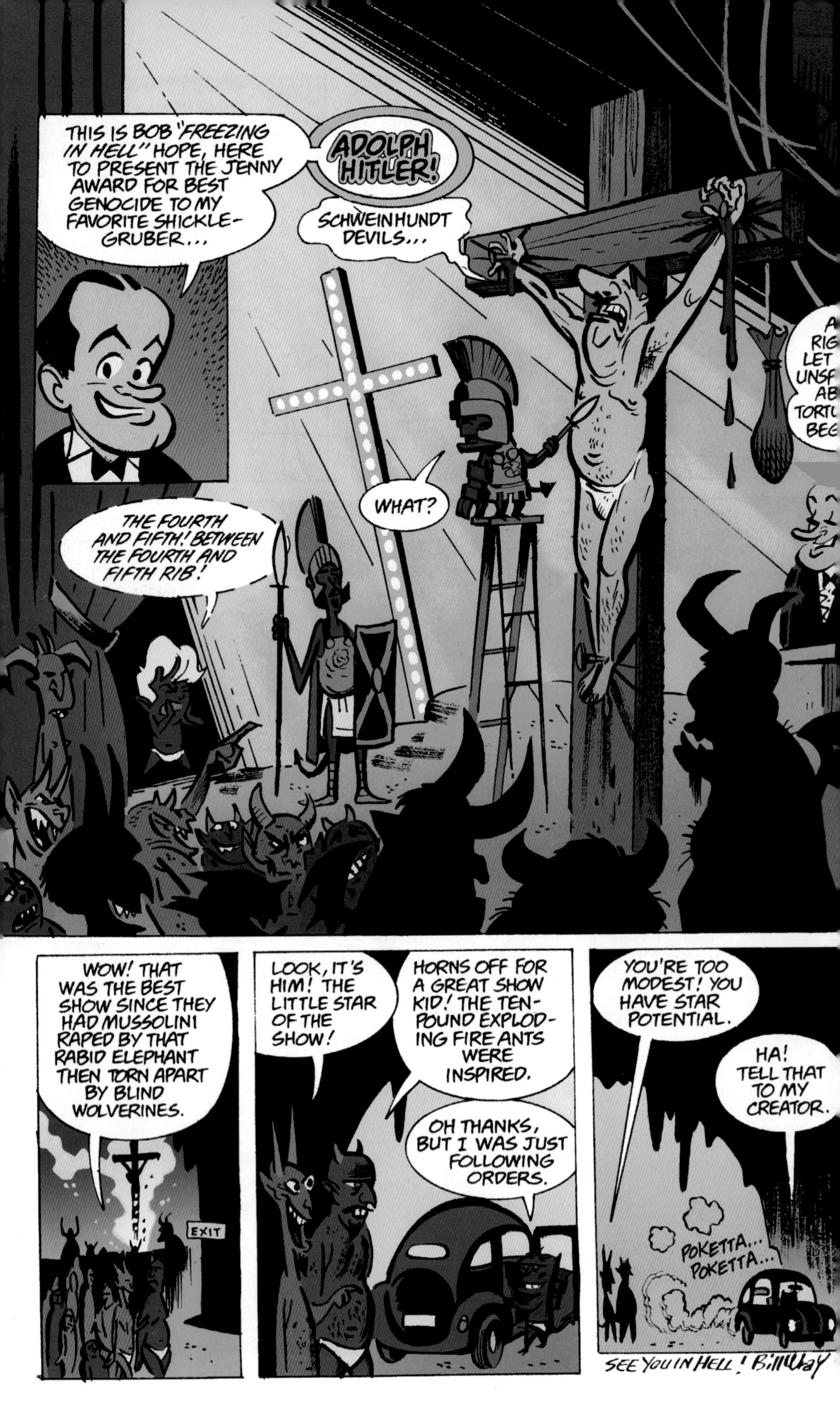
THIS IS BOB "FREEZING IN HELL" HOPE, HERE TO PRESENT THE JENNY AWARD FOR BEST GENOCIDE TO MY FAVORITE SHICKLE-GRUBER...
ADOLPH HITLER!
SCHWEINHUNDT DEVILS...
WHAT?
THE FOURTH AND FIFTH! BETWEEN THE FOURTH AND FIFTH RIB!
WOW! THAT WAS THE BEST SHOW SINCE THEY HAD MUSSOLINI RAPED BY THAT RABID ELEPHANT THEN TORN APART BY BLIND WOLVERINES.
EXIT
LOOK, IT'S HIM! THE LITTLE STAR OF THE SHOW!
HORNS OFF FOR A GREAT SHOW KID! THE TEN-POUND EXPLODING FIRE ANTS WERE INSPIRED.
OH THANKS, BUT I WAS JUST FOLLOWING ORDERS.
YOU'RE TOO MODEST! YOU HAVE STAR POTENTIAL.
HA! TELL THAT TO MY CREATOR.
POKETTA... POKETTA...

SEE YOU IN HELL! Bill Wray

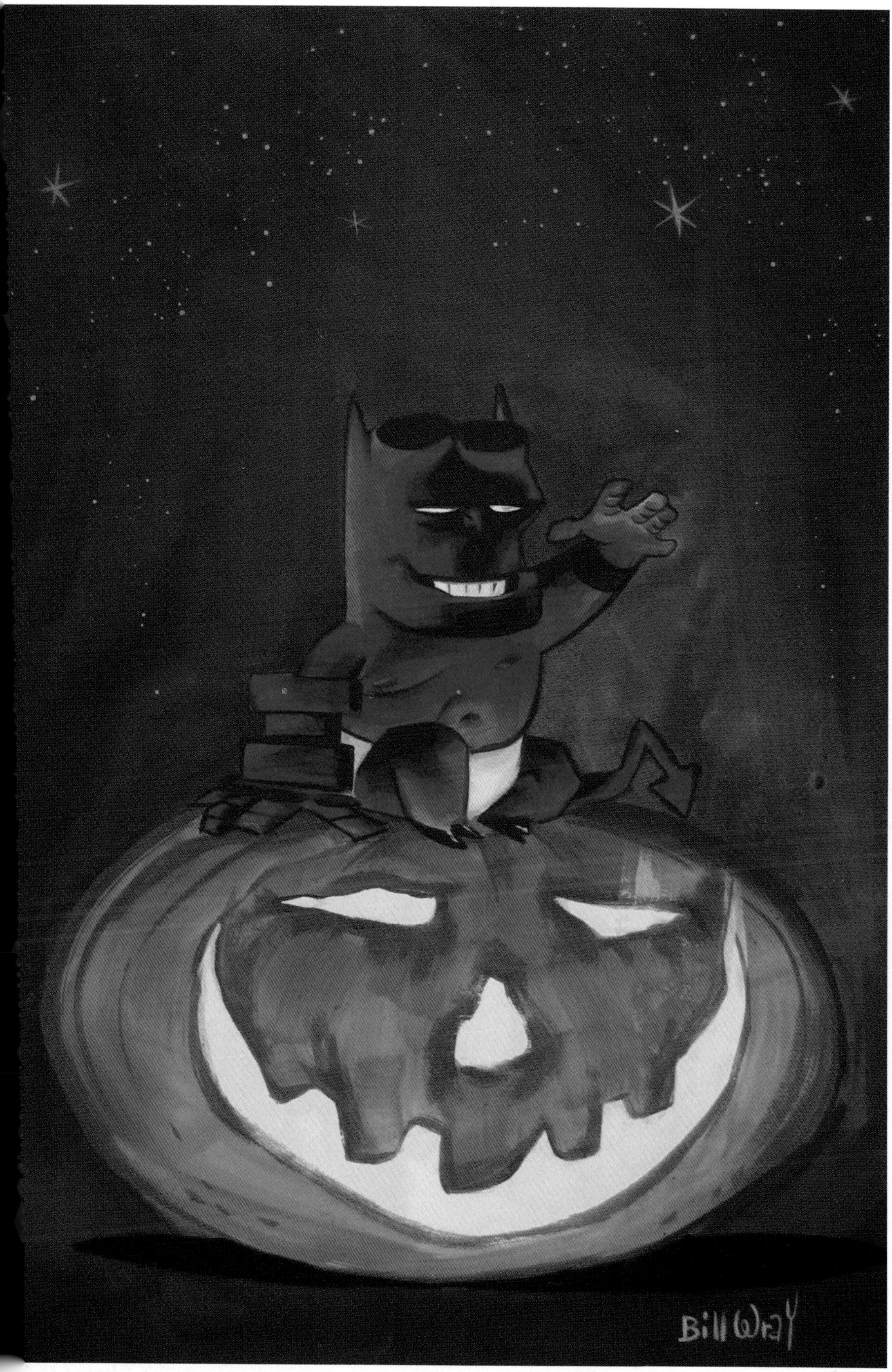
Bill Wray

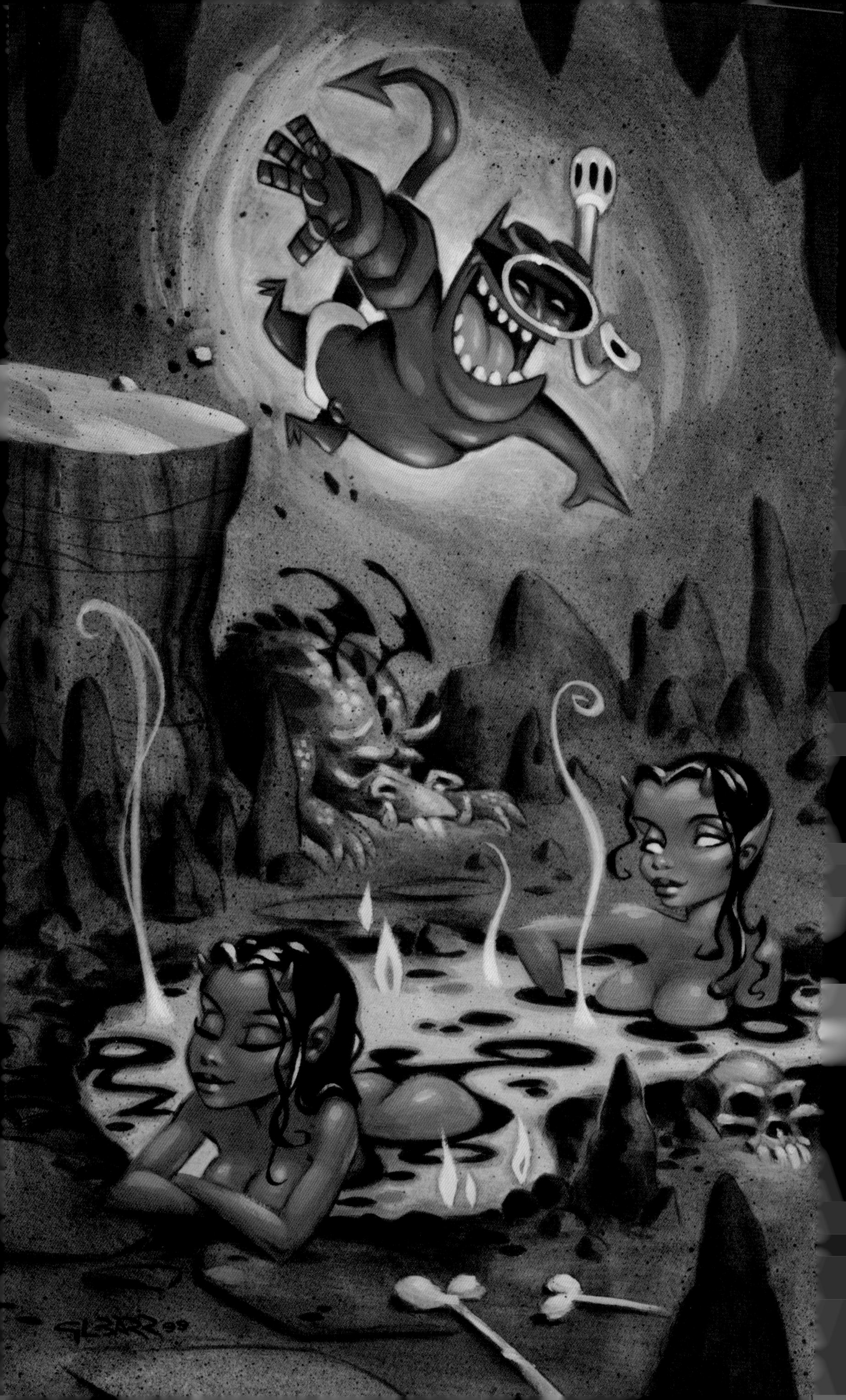

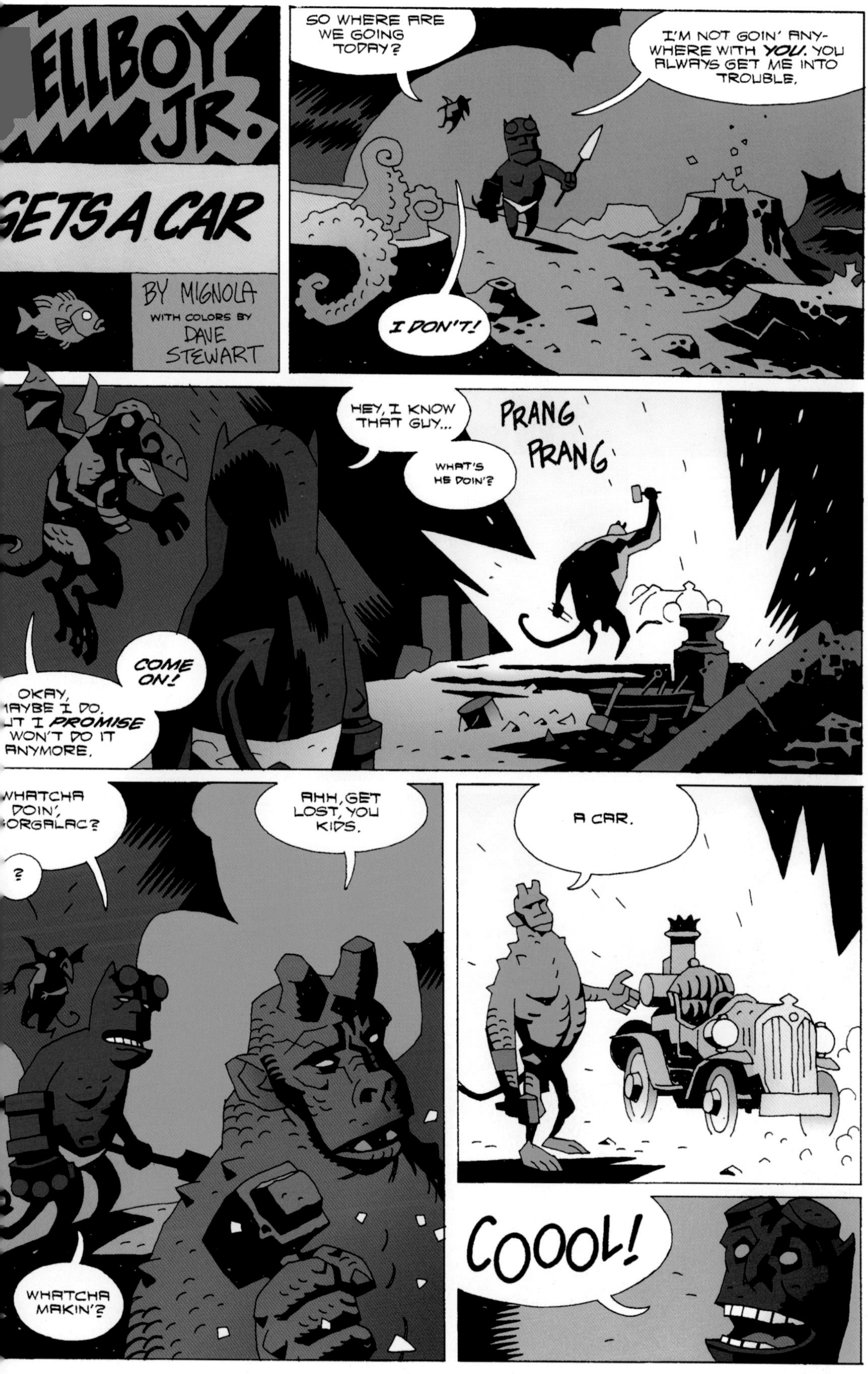
ELLBOY JR.
GETS A CAR
BY MIGNOLA
WITH COLORS BY DAVE STEWART
SO WHERE ARE WE GOING TODAY?
I'M NOT GOIN' ANY-WHERE WITH YOU. YOU ALWAYS GET ME INTO TROUBLE.
I DON'T!
HEY, I KNOW THAT GUY...
WHAT'S HE DOIN'?
PRANG
PRANG
COME ON!
OKAY, MAYBE I DO. UT I PROMISE WON'T DO IT ANYMORE.
WHATCHA DOIN', GORGALAC?
?
AHH, GET LOST, YOU KIDS.
WHATCHA MAKIN'?
A CAR.
COOOL!

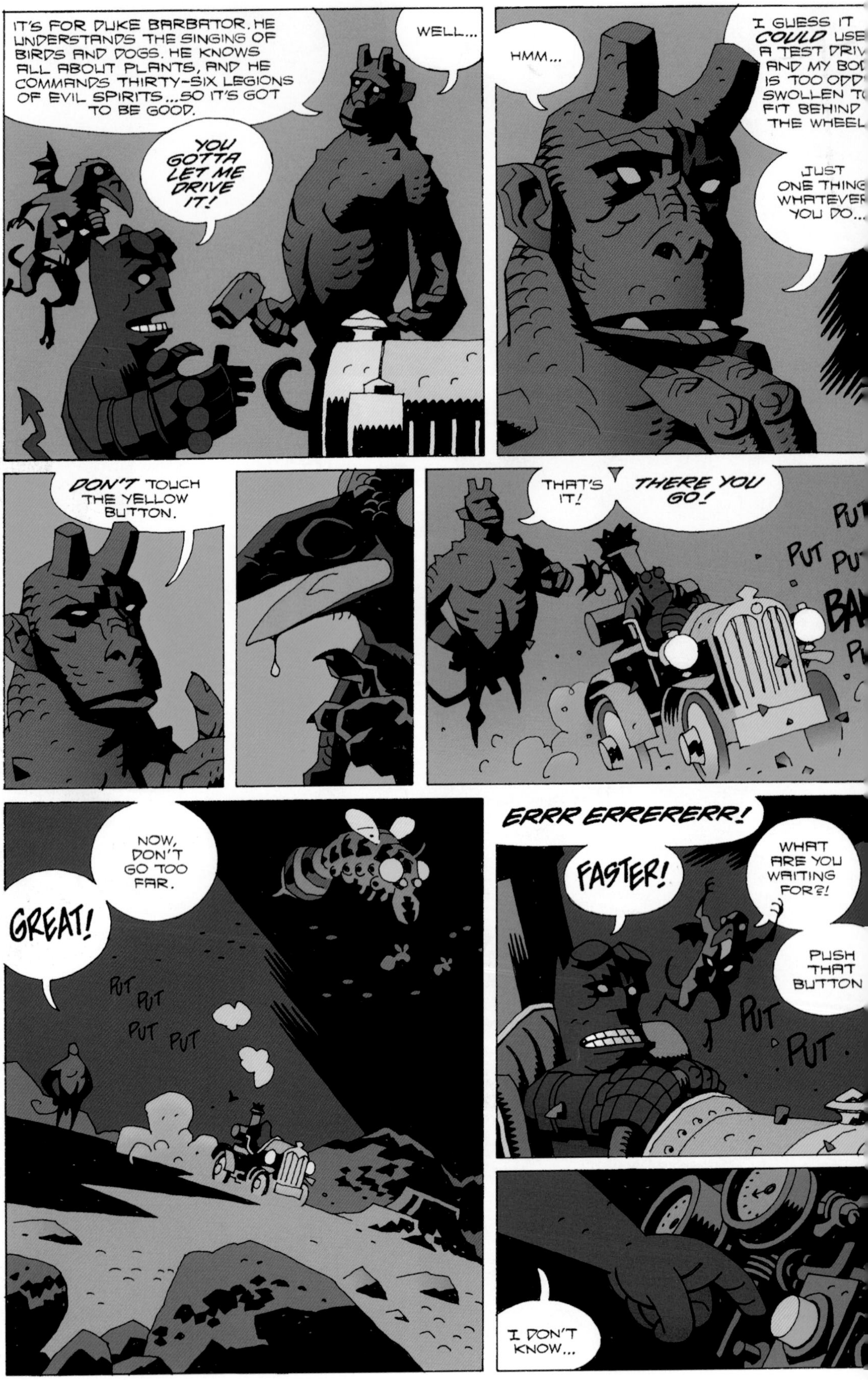
IT'S FOR DUKE BARBATOR. HE UNDERSTANDS THE SINGING OF BIRDS AND DOGS. HE KNOWS ALL ABOUT PLANTS, AND HE COMMANDS THIRTY-SIX LEGIONS OF EVIL SPIRITS... SO IT'S GOT TO BE GOOD.
WELL...
YOU GOTTA LET ME DRIVE IT!
HMM...
I GUESS IT COULD USE A TEST DRIV AND MY BOD IS TOO ODD SWOLLEN T FIT BEHIND THE WHEEL
JUST ONE THING WHATEVER YOU DO...
DON'T TOUCH THE YELLOW BUTTON.
THAT'S IT!
THERE YOU GO!
PUT PUT PUT
NOW, DON'T GO TOO FAR.
GREAT!
PUT PUT PUT PUT
ERRR ERRERERR!
FASTER!
WHAT ARE YOU WAITING FOR?!
PUSH THAT BUTTON
PUT PUT
I DON'T KNOW...

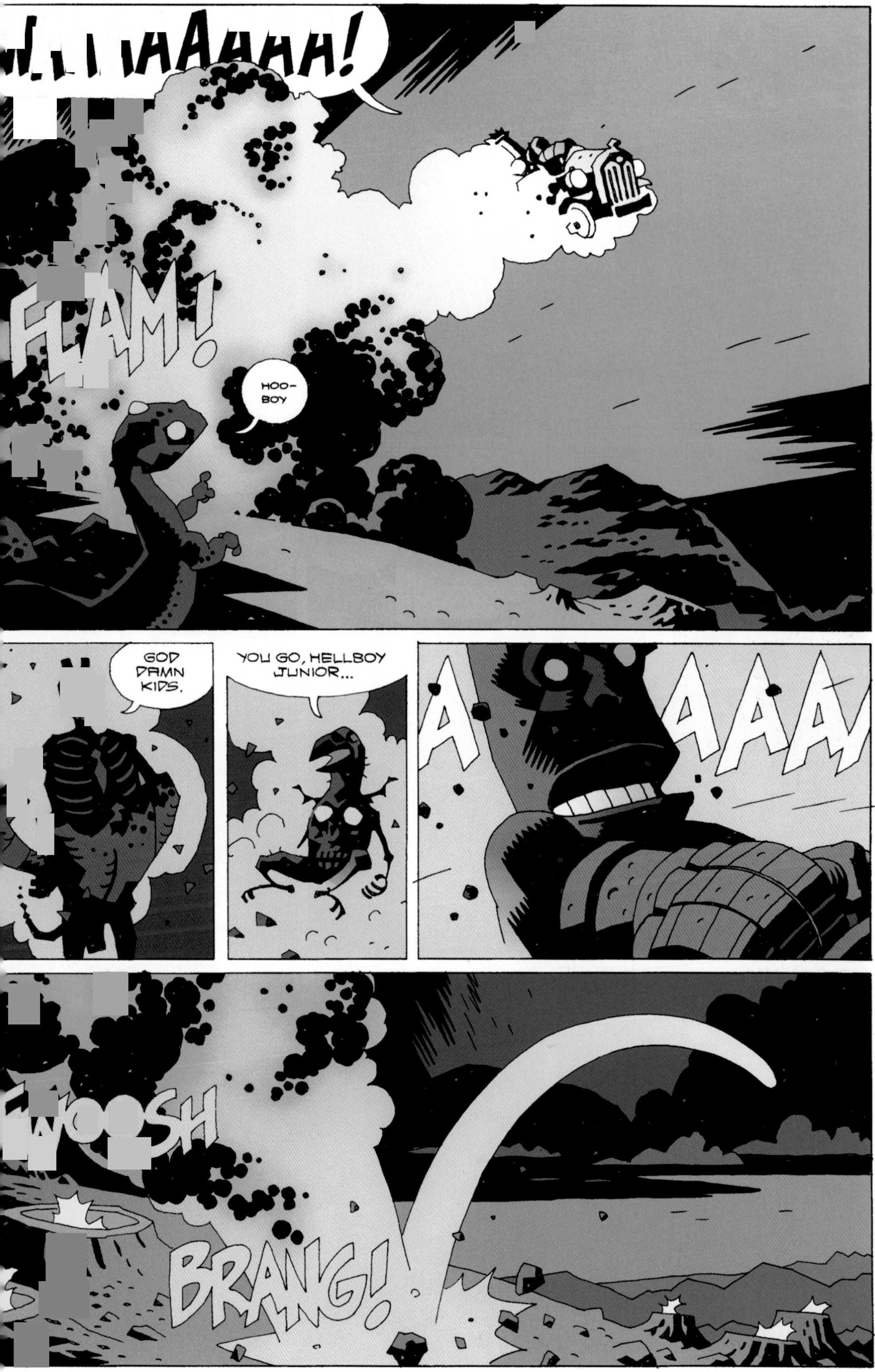
AAAAH!
FLAM!
HOO-BOY
GOD DAMN KIDS.
YOU GO, HELLBOY JUNIOR...
AAAA
WOOSH
BRANG!

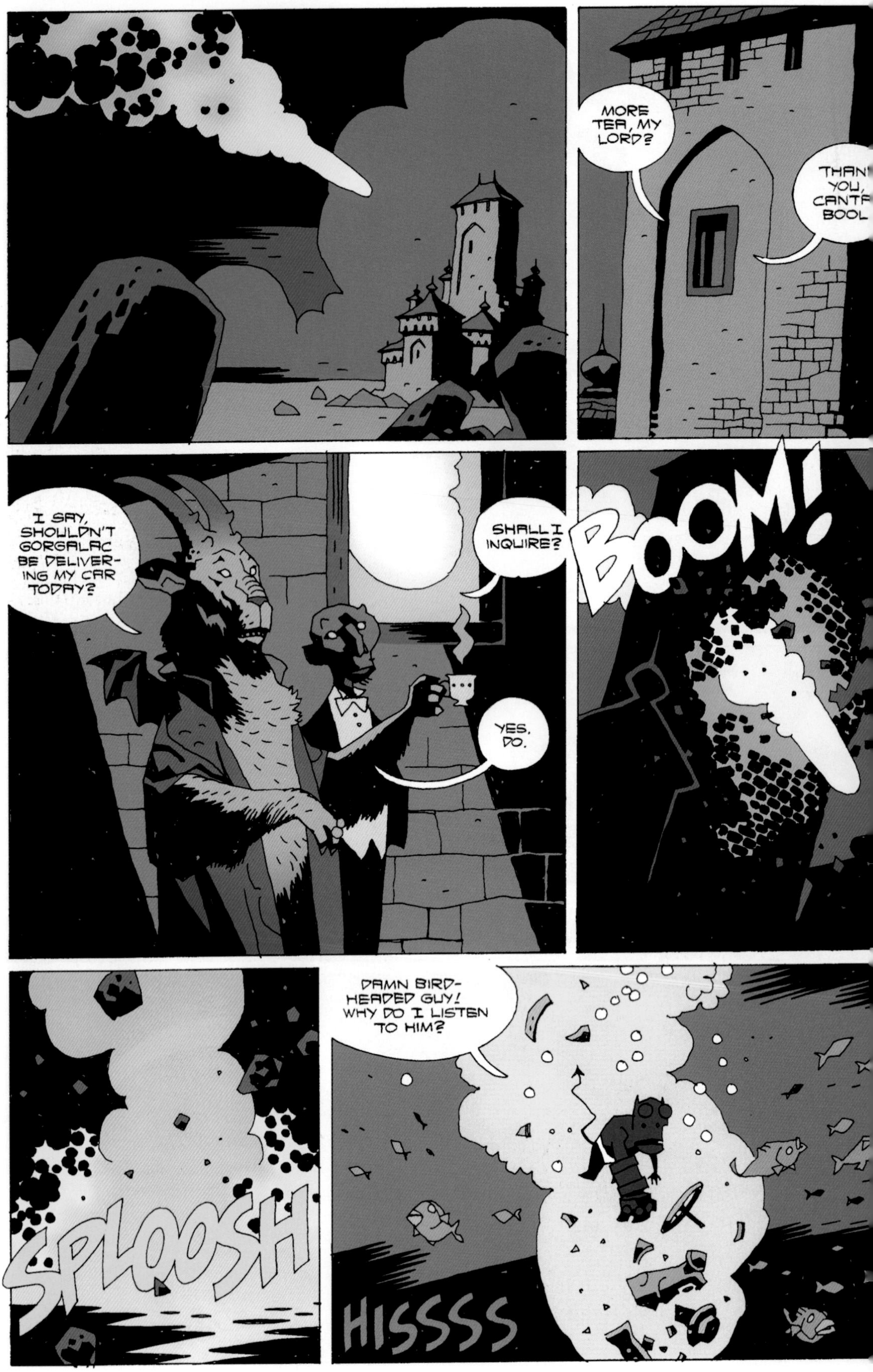
MORE TEA, MY LORD?
THAN YOU, CANTF BOOL
I SAY, SHOULDN'T GORGALAC BE DELIVERING MY CAR TODAY?
SHALL I INQUIRE?
YES, DO.
BOOM!
SPLOOSH
DAMN BIRD-HEADED GUY! WHY DO I LISTEN TO HIM?
HISSSS

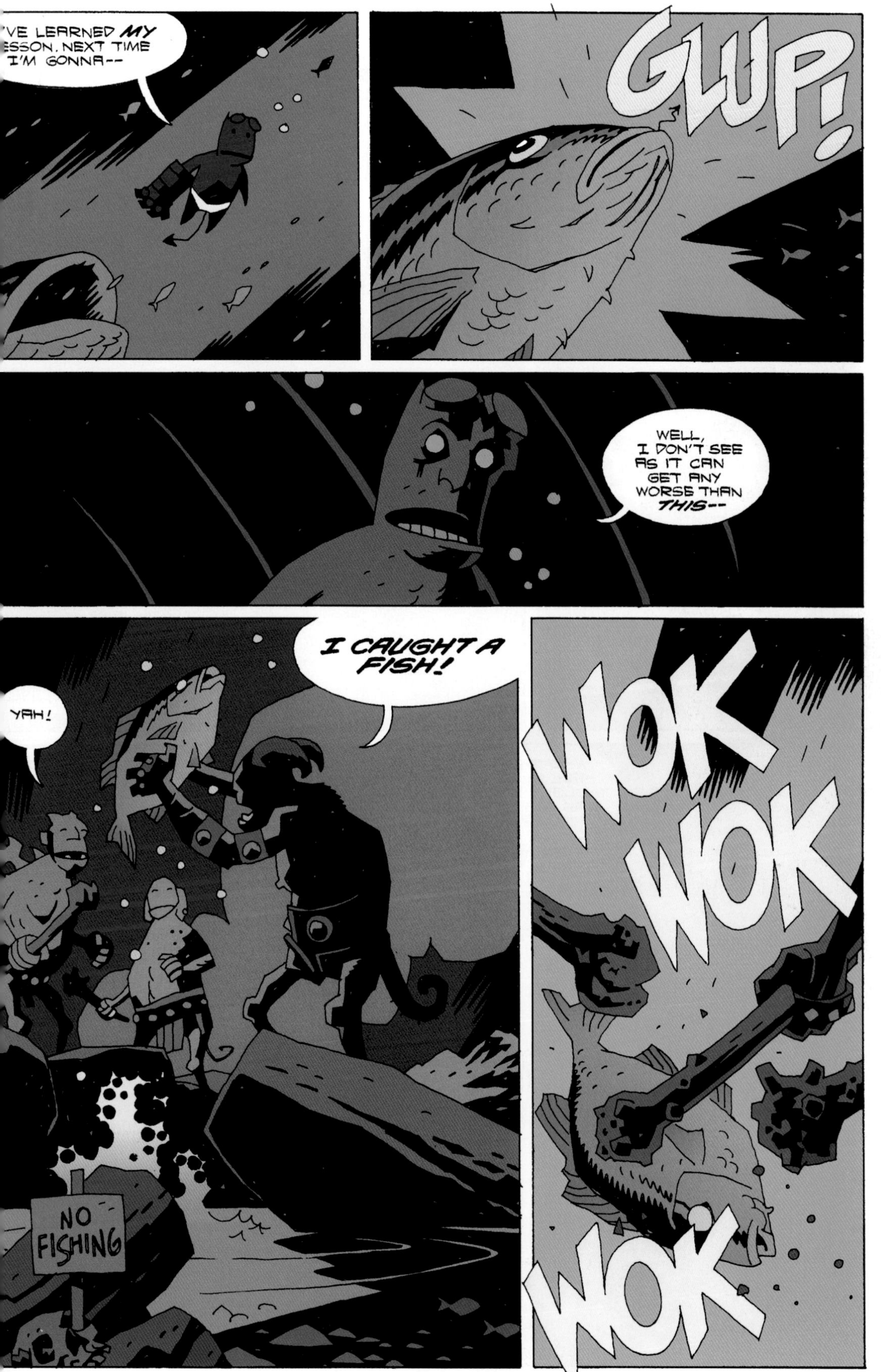
'VE LEARNED MY
ESSON. NEXT TIME
I'M GONNA--
GLUP!
WELL, I DON'T SEE AS IT CAN GET ANY WORSE THAN THIS--
YAH!
I CAUGHT A FISH!
NO FISHING
WOK
WOK
WOK

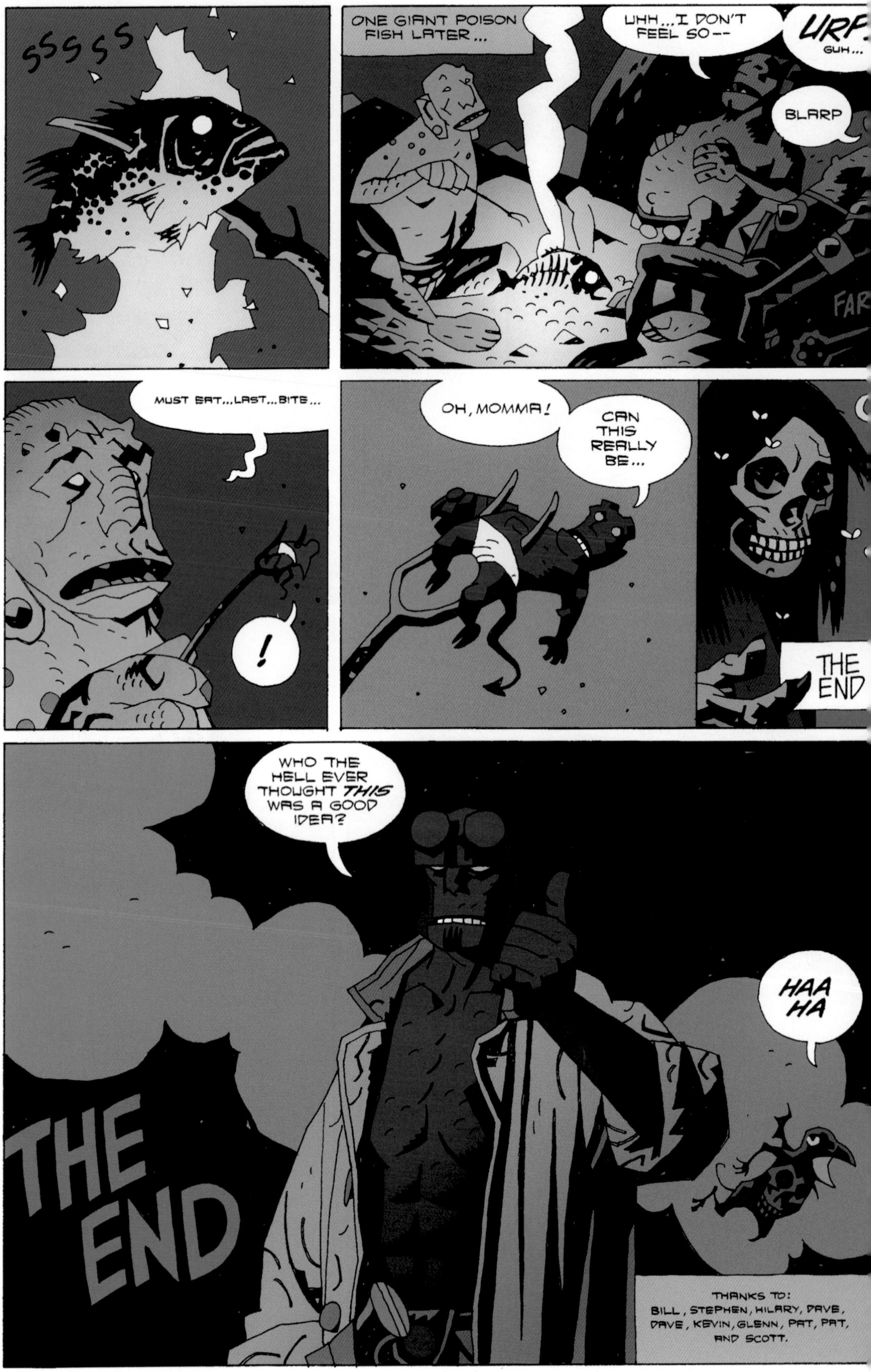
SSSSS
ONE GIANT POISON FISH LATER...
UHH... I DON'T FEEL SO--
URF
GUH...
BLARP
MUST EAT... LAST... BITE...
!
OH, MOMMA!
CAN THIS REALLY BE...
THE END
WHO THE HELL EVER THOUGHT THIS WAS A GOOD IDEA?
HAA HA
THE END
THANKS TO:
BILL, STEPHEN, HILARY, DAVE, DAVE, KEVIN, GLENN, PAT, PAT, AND SCOTT.

HELLBOY JUNIOR™
sketchbook

Since most of the work in this book was done over four years ago, not all of the cartoonists involved were able to locate their sketchbook material from back then. The pencil sketches on these first few pages are from Bill Wray's new story, which was created especially for this collection. The painting on the following page was a recent commissioned piece.

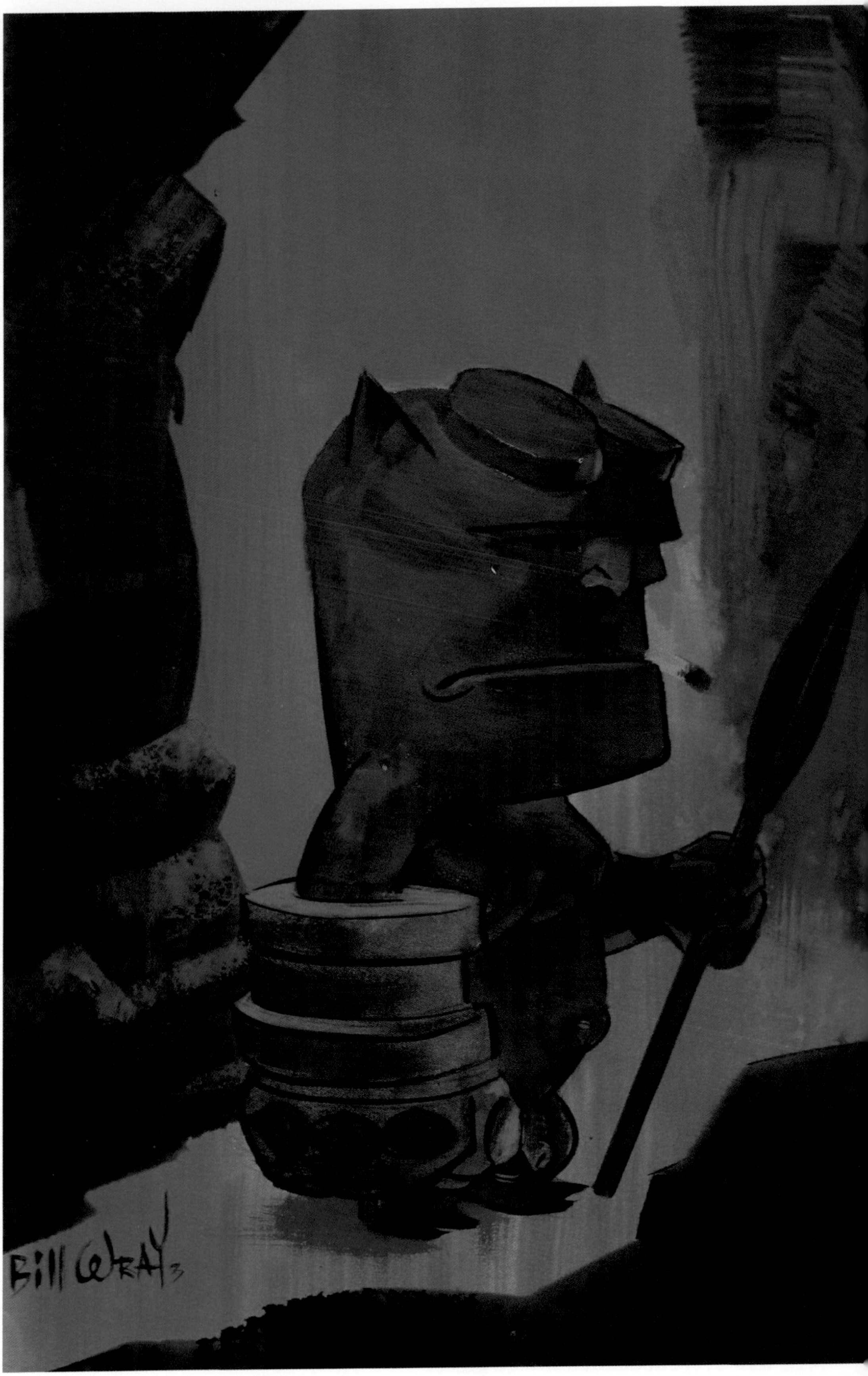
BILL WRAY

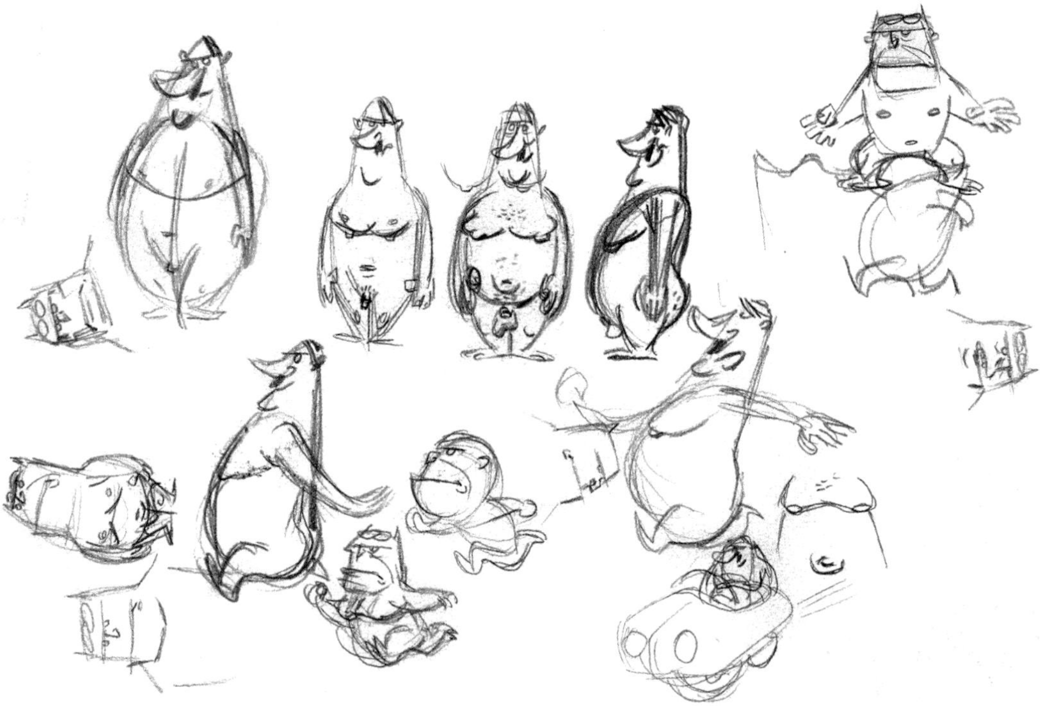

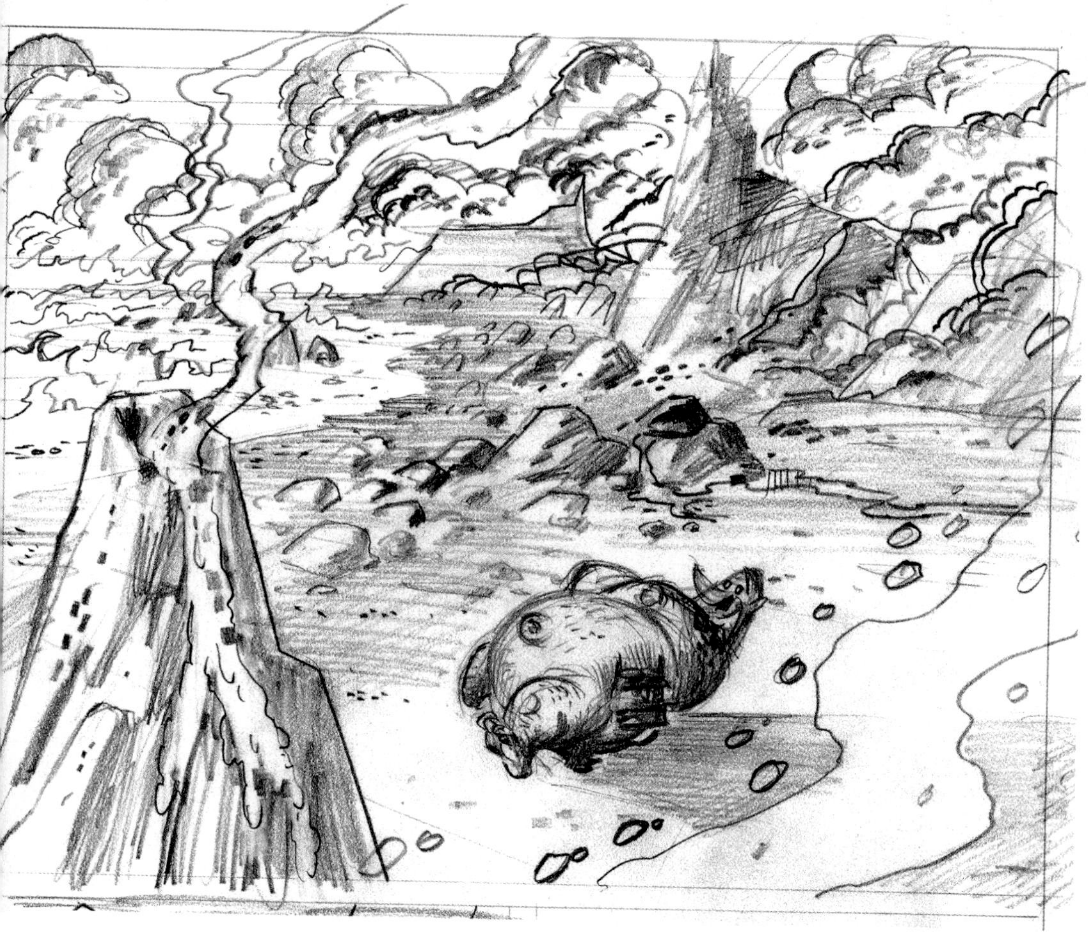

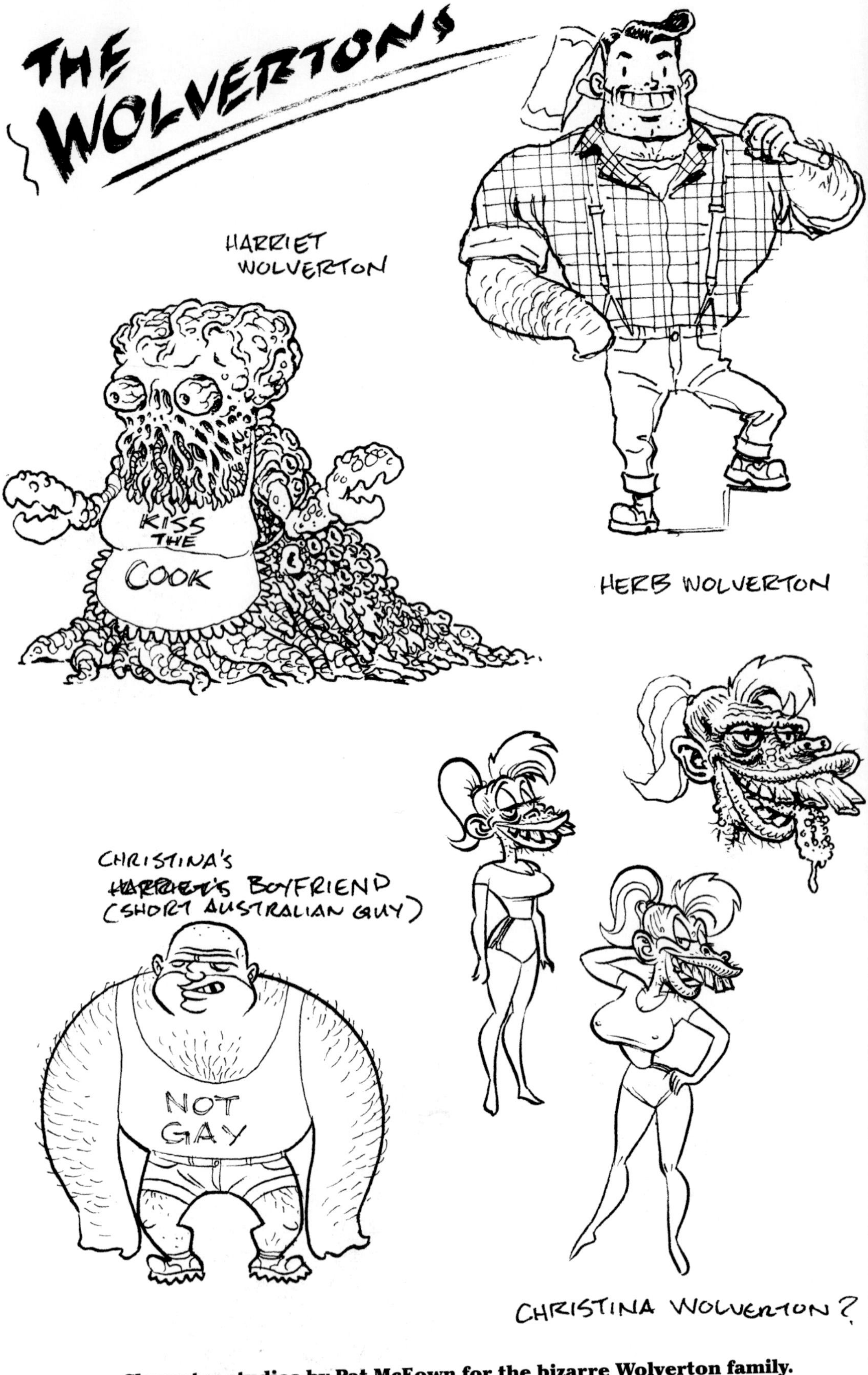
THE WOLVERTONS
HARRIET WOLVERTON
KISS THE COOK
HERB WOLVERTON
CHRISTINA'S ~~HARRIET'S~~ BOYFRIEND (SHORT AUSTRALIAN GUY)
NOT GAY
CHRISTINA WOLVERTON ?

Character studies by Pat McEown for the bizarre Wolverton family.

BRAD WOLVERTON

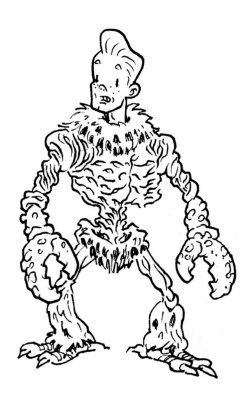

BRAD'S GIRLFRIEND
(LI'L ESKIMO GIRL)
BLIND

CHRISTINA WOLVERTON

CHRISTINA'S
BOYFRIEND

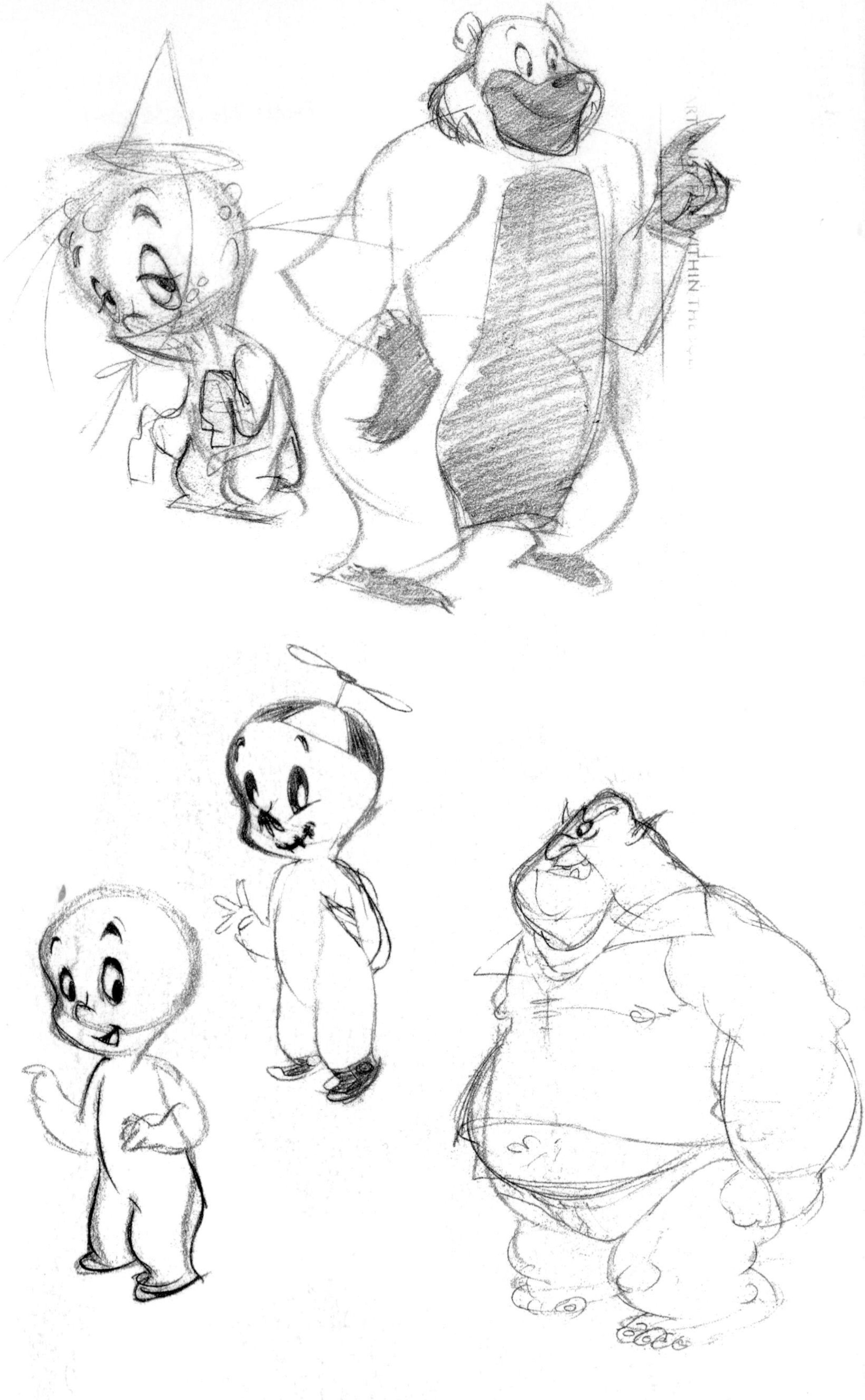

Stephen DeStefano's character studies for "Wheezy the Sick Little Witch."